И откуда он взялся на нашем дворе —
Где матери в окнах, а дети — в игре,
Где старушки в киваюшем серебре
Держат память в три поколенья?
Во дворе, где знают по именам —
Кто убит, кто жив, кто уехал;
И кого зовёт из чьего окна
Надтреснутая Пьеха!
Мимо стука костяшек за стёртым столом
И дизельного автомобиля —
Он проходит, неся на плече рулон
С чуть заметным запахом пыли.
Может, он на этом ковре живёт —
И, найдя подходящее место,
По-хозяйски велит: — Расстелись, ковёр! —
Предварив заклятьем уместным.
И ковёр развернется со всем, что на нём:
С этажеркой и клавесином,
И с продавленным креслом,
И лампой с огнём,
И с играющим в кубики сыном.
А быть может, ковёр обучен летать —
И тогда, завершая прогулку,
Он шарахнется вверх, не оставя следа,
Из пустынного переулка.
И блаженно расправит упругий квадрат,
С южным ветром знакомый коротко.
А хозяин будет курить до утра,
Наблюдая мерцанье города.
А потом потеряется в синеве,
Обронив невнятное слово.
Чудак-человек,
Чужак-человек —
Чего и ждать от такого? 1985

Лукавый старец, здесь ты не солгал:
Остановить высокое мгновенье
Нам не позволит вечное сомненье —
А может, выше будет перевал?
Ведь наш зенит ещё не наступил,
И дымный запах будущей победы
Тревожит нас, и мы стремимся следом,
По-иному исполненные сил.
Не истинная наша высота
Неузнаваема, пока мгновенье длится:
Наполеон Аркольского моста
Прекраснее, чем над Аустерлицем.
И кто посмеет, будто птицу влёт,
Стоп-кадром сбить пернатую минуту?
Но счастью мы и сами, в свой черёд,
Безудержны в стремлениях и смутах.
Всегда на шаг за завтрашней чертой,
Во всех свершеньях наперёд повинны!
И если время скажет нам „постой" —
Пройдём насквозь, плечом его раздвинув.
1985

Сядь, закури.
Мы вдвоём, но так ненадолго.
Мы ничего не успеем: этот сон не имеет конца.
Нам уже не понять,
Что за книги стоят на полках,
Что за крыша над головой, что за лошади у крыльца.
Нас уже ждут, пора — и времени нету,
Чтоб говорить о годах, проведённых врозь.
Наше с тобой „вдвоём" — на одну сигарету,
На молчаливый миг —
Глаза в глаза и насквозь.
Знаю: мы что-то везём туда, где нас ожидают,
Что-то важнее нас и наших потерь.
Что ж, мы готовы в путь,
Но докурим, пока седлают,
И намертво сцепим руки, пока отворяют дверь.
1985. ШИЗО

Песенка
Быть бы мне цыганкой,
А тебе — ясным пламенем,
Я б тебе напела
Разлуку и встречу.
Быть бы мне речкой,
А тебе — бурьяном —
Я б к тебе сходила б
Каждый вечер.
Быть бы мне рекою,
А тебе — горьким морем —
Я б твою горечь
По капле разлила.
Быть бы нищим семьям
В королевской ссоре —
А к тебе босая

Стану клюкву брати,
Людям считати,
Забуду кручину —
Как и нет на свете.
За горелым лесом —
Нехожено место:
Запою ль, заплачу —
Никто не ответит.

Ох не буду строго,
Обойду сторонкою,
Чтоб ночью не сн...
Суженому завтра
Дальняя дорога,
А вернётся, нет —
На то Божья ми...
1985, ПКТ

Детям тюремщицы Аким...

И круг, очерченный белым,
Смыкался намертво с ней.
[зачёркнуто] Дело было в России.
В Мордовии, чтоб точнее.
Стране, вошедшей в Россию
Полтысячи лет назад
Она за эту заслугу
Орден теперь имеет.
Об этом здесь регулярно
По радио говорят.
И песни поют — про реки
С лирическими берёзами.
Поверим на слух: с этапа
Не очень-то разглядишь.
Зато здесь растут заборы
И вышки торчат занозами,
И путанка под ветрами
Звучит, как сухой камыш.
Ещё тут водятся звери:
Псы служебной породы.
Без них ни этап, ни лагерь,
И ни одна тюрьма.
Испытанная охрана
Всех времён и народов:
Про них уж никто не скажет,
Что лопают задарма.
А небо над этим краем
Утверждено добротно —
Оно не сдвинется с места,
Хоть годы в него смотри.
А если оно замерзло —
Так это закон природы.

Приводится в исполненье
В положенном декабре.
Шёл снег — четвёртые сутки,
И в карцере мёрзли бабы,
Совсем ещё молодые —
Старшей — двадцать один.
— Начальница, — говорили, —
Налей кипятку хотя бы,
Позволь хотя бы рейтузы,
Ведь на полу сидим!
А им отвечали: — Суки,
Ещё чего захотели!
Да я бы вам, дармоедкам,
Ни пить ни жрать не дала!
А может, ещё вам выдать
Валенки да постели?
Да я б вас вовсе держала,
Свиней, в чем мать родила!
...Ну что ж, они заслужили
Ещё не такие речи.
Небось не станет начальство
Зазря сюда присылать.
Зима — так пускай помёрзнут,
Ведь не топить им печи!
На то и ШИЗО: не будут
Режим нарушать опять.
Они не голые — выдали
Казённые балахоны.
За многие им осталось —
Дело уже к концу...
Они уже обессилели,
Лежат, несмотря на холод,
И сбрасывали не мыли
Беганут по лицу!
А впрочем, никто не умер.
Вышли, как отсидели.
И нечего выть над ними:
Калеки — да не с войны!
Кто через десять суток,
Кто — через две недели.
А заступились — некого,
Кроме себя, винить.
Пускай отбывают сроки
Законного наказанья,
Да лечатся на свободе,
А тут и без них возня!

Найдётся, кому постр...
Заводы, цеха и дома...
Найдётся — кому ...
Ещё не такие ...
— А в истории ...
1985 ПКТ

Девчонку?
Что же ты,
Что же —
Даже и не ждёшь!
... А в общем-то, что ...

Где же ты,
Где же ты была!
— Мамочка, мне здесь холодно,
Заверни в пелёнку,
Мне всё это снится...

И станет будить и нечем
Тоненький голосок!
— Ты меня слышишь,
Ты меня слышишь!
Помнить тебе снилось...

А что режим не сможет,
Они пока еще не знают,
Да если только подумают,
На их это дело: знать!
Потом, конечно, с сожалением,
Начнут не враз, а ...
В надежде ... через ...

Так разве страшно
Создатель,
Чтоб подо тем ...
Не хватает на всех
Отпущенной на смерть
1985

Пора выходить рубильник!
Мне ...
Что нежно на нас ...
Ещё, кроме вечной ночи?
Какой ты ещё назначишь
Своим городам завет ...
В невыключенный свет.

Поплывет по глазницам снова
Небо — чёрное и голубое —
Бесконечно знакомым зовом.
1985

Прямой?
Ну как?
Становишься ли — в бессмертье?
1985

...ю осещенной, услышав
козлов,
...ада, что поздно пришли,
...долгую вахту озябнув,
...к любая дворняжка Земли
...одились к нам добрые
люди
...окольчик у наших дверей
...е обязательно будет
...рого из январей?

...е не вернется.
...ки понимаешь!
...многих дней
...чем

GREY IS THE
COLOR OF HOPE

IRINA RATUSHINSKAYA

GREY IS THE COLOR OF HOPE

Translated by Alyona Kojevnikov

ALFRED A. KNOPF   NEW YORK   1988

THIS IS A BORZOI BOOK
PUBLISHED BY ALFRED A. KNOPF, INC.

Library of Congress Cataloging-in-Publication Data
Ratushinskaĩa, Irina.
Grey is the color of hope.
Translated from Russian.
1. Ratushinskaĩa, Irina—Biography—Imprisonment—
Russian S.F.S.R.—Mordovskaĩa A.S.S.R.
2. Women prisoners—Soviet Union—Biography.
3. Poets, Russian—20th century—Biography.
4. Political prisoners—Soviet Union—Biography.
I. Title.
PG3485.5.A875Z466   1988   891.71'44 [B]   88-45322
ISBN 0-394-57140-1

Manufactured in the United States of America
First American Edition

AUTHOR'S NOTE

Readers may wonder, quite justifiably, how much of this book is truth, and how much is fiction? The answer is that there is no fiction at all; I do not have enough imagination for it.

The only liberty I have permitted myself is to change some names: not the names of my fellow prisoners in the Small Zone, nor the names of our tormentors, but the names of those who sympathized with us and helped us secretly. The reason is obvious: to protect them from reprisals. Therefore, I have changed the names of almost all the criminal prisoners, the warders and some of the officers. In a number of instances I have also altered the sequence of events, to prevent the KGB from working out how, despite all their efforts, we managed to maintain contact with the world outside the camp. In making these small changes I have taken great care not to distort, in any way, the true picture of our camp existence. It remains for me to offer my sincere apologies to the many thousands of victims of Soviet women's camps for omitting so many other events from this book due to limitations of space. And finally, to offer my deepest gratitude to those people, who, although not mentioned in this book, helped me to survive everything, regain my freedom, and therefore—to write my testimony.

I.R.

MAP OF SMALL ZONE

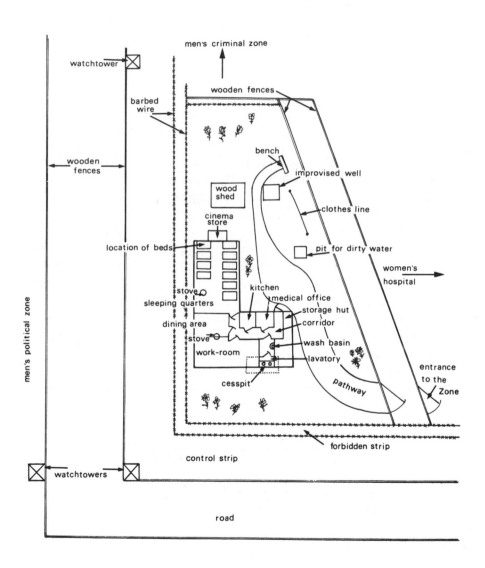

GREY IS THE
COLOR OF HOPE

1

So here I am, riding along in a black Volga. They said that they are taking me home. For good. A "clean" release. They have even returned my passport without any entry about my criminal record. And to cap it all, they even offered generously to drive me home—in a KGB car. What can all this mean? I sit in the car, trying to gather my wits. They are watching me, so I must not show any sign of confusion, any emotion at all. The reflexes evolved during four years of imprisonment function automatically—never trust them! Never drop your guard!

The KGB man sitting beside me makes small talk. Of course, he knows exactly what is going on, whether I am really being released or whether this is just another exercise in psychological pressure. As yet, I am not privy to his knowledge. I will not know for another half hour. There are plenty of reasons for my doubts; after all, did they not tell me, three months ago, when I was taken away from the Mordovian labor camp, that I was going home? Yet instead of home, I was brought under guard to the KGB prison in Kiev. "So, you've come to be released, Irina Borisovna?"[1] they said to me upon arrival. "But you still have three years of camp and five of exile to serve. Now, if you were to write a clemency plea, who knows what might happen . . . ?"

I remember how furious I felt at that moment—not with

1. The patronymic, literally "daughter of Boris," is used as a courteous form of address.

them, but with myself. For two whole days I had travelled on a special transport believing that I was going home. Home to Igor, home to Mama, home to our dog, Ladushka . . .

What a gullible fool! Just as well I did not let them see at the time that I believed them: gave no start of surprise, maintained a stony face and a steady voice—the Stanislavsky method of acting par excellence. So their psychological gambit did not pay off. They got no pleas for clemency out of me. Nor will this latest trick, if it is a trick, gain them anything. But maybe, just maybe, this time it is for real. After all, is it likely that they would try the same deception twice? On the other hand, they do so many idiotic things.

Don't think about it! Look, instead, at the falling leaves outside—yellow, red—it's October. My fifth October as a prisoner—can it be the last? Don't think! Listen to what the KGB man is saying . . . What on earth is he on about? About radical changes in the education system. Fine. Respond in top form: discuss language study, physics, math. And indeed, some changes would not come amiss, the existing system is useless. But what direction should those changes take? Ah, there's the rub!

We move on to the weather: green grass, blue skies. A black Volga. But where is the prison grey to which I have become so accustomed? Here it is, right beside me—my prison uniform. Strange that they did not take it away as they usually do before releasing a prisoner . . . Stop thinking about that!

Let's talk about literature. Don't you think Bulgakov is a wonderful writer? Yes, he did live in Kiev, his house is on the Andreyevsky Incline. Lovely place, Kiev, by any standards. No, I can't say I like Boroday's contemporary sculpture: a big statue is not necessarily a beautiful one. You don't care for it either? What an amazing likeness in tastes—and between whom! We laugh a little.

The car window is open a crack and, oh, the smells, the heady smells. Forbidden smells, free ones: that one, now, that's freshly cut grass. And this one—almost like mushrooms, or maybe it's just damp earth? Here's a familiar one—gasoline. Pull yourself together! Remember, you're travelling under guard, even if it is for the last time. I wonder what the driver is thinking about?

As if on cue, he joins in the conversation. We discuss Gorbachev's anti-alcohol campaign and the clandestine moonshine industry which flourishes alongside it:

Moonshine liquor, moonshine liquor,
We'll just have to make you quicker!

The driver introduces a historical note: this is not a new ditty, he tells us, it dates back to Khrushchev's time. History repeats itself . . . We laugh again. Isn't this trip fun? And what's that building over there? Oh, that's a new one, Irina Borisovna, it was built when you were no longer here. Brief silence. We pass a young couple, arms entwined around each other, but too quickly to see their faces.

The driver makes no unnecessary detours: here is our street, Vernadsky Prospekt. Just a few blocks from home now . . . Anyone can stop their hands from shaking if they try . . . Well, almost anyone. Heartbeat and pulse are harder to control, but controlled they must be—I'm as thin as a rail, you can see the tremor of the smallest vein in my neck. The best thing to do at such a time is to start playing Tchaikovsky's First Piano Concerto in your head; that makes everything inside slow down. There, that's better. Now everything is as it should be. Well, comrades, what next?

They open the door for me.

"Here, Irina Borisovna, let me help you with that bag . . . On which floor is your flat?"

Good heavens, on which floor is it? I can remember the address and telephone number—I have given them to so many people at so many times. But the floor? A blank . . .

"The fifth," I say suddenly, the words floating up out of my subconscious. And the fifth it is. Our door, the doorbell, Ladushka barking inside. What if there is nobody home? I don't have a key. Still, maybe KGB men always carry something that will open any door.

"Who's there?" That is Mama's voice. She is really Igor's mother, but I have called her Mama ever since they arrested me. From the time I sat in the courtroom and heard her frantic cry in the corridor: "Let me in! My daughter is in there!"

Of course, they did not let her in. They did not let anybody in. But from that moment, I became a daughter to her, and she became a mother to me.

"Who's there?"

What should I say? "Ira"? Or should I call out a warning: "House search!" After all, I still do not know for sure why they have brought me here.

"Ira."

Our hallway, with familiar clay dishes decorating the walls. The smell of home. Ladushka jumps around, barking. Either she has forgotten me—four years is a long time—or the strange man is upsetting her.

Mama stands there, frozen in shock.

"For good?" she manages finally.

"For good," I tell her.

Only now does she let herself burst into tears. My nieces peer out of their room: slim, and so much older than I remember . . . They were such tiny creatures when I was taken away, the youngest had not even started to talk. They are silent now, too, watching me with big, round eyes. In any case, there is enough confusion around without their adding to it.

Mama keeps crying and hugging me, I mutter something in response. This is just the moment for my escort to depart if I am really going to be left here. On the other hand, how is he to take me if not? The driver did not come up with us, and a KGB escort always consists of at least two. Moreover, it would be rather beneath his dignity to drag me out of the house by force, he is a KGB general, no less. Well, let events take their own course.

"Thank you for the lift," I say in the manner of a social hostess. "Would you like a cup of coffee?"

He responds in the same vein. "Thank you, no. I don't want to be in your way."

He really leaves. I hope that a few transgressions will be forgiven him, come Judgment Day, for declining that cup of coffee. There follows a confused telephone conversation with Igor. He's leaving work straight away and rushing home, right across town. And I sit in something soft, nursing the receiver against my cheek, even though it is now silent. Now I can let myself go. Mama is fussing around in the kitchen, I ought to go and offer to help. What a silly thought—help. How can I possibly help when I have forgotten even simple household tasks, cannot even remember where everything is kept? Still, I ought to go there, be beside her. Instead, I wander over to the mirror. Well, Madam, how do you like what you see? Mirrors are not permitted in prison. In the last three months I have only seen my reflection once, in an open mirror door of one of the prison offices. A thin, close-cropped urchin looks back at me now, with very dark eyes.

What of it, that I offered a KGB man a cup of coffee? I am the victor, not he! Igor will be here any moment, then a horde of friends, and I shall be able to look them in the eye without flinching; everything is in order, there has been nothing in these four years of which I need to feel ashamed.

I will tell them everything, I think, not knowing yet how difficult that is, to tell everything: how you want to leave out all that was so terrible, and dwell only on the funny moments. Even now, as I sit down to write this book, a small voice whispers at the back of my mind: leave it, forget about it, enough is enough! But I will remember. I know what must be done.

2

For seven months now, I have been living like a queen: doors are flung open before me wherever I go—into cells, interrogation rooms, the courtroom . . . Other hands close these doors behind me, too. Not that I do much walking these days, just the odd stretch now and then along some corridor. Still, I maintain the correct regal bearing. Mostly I am driven from place to place. An impressive number of people are employed in "serving" me: just to get a pencil sharpened I summon a junior officer of the guard. Should the Queen desire to have a fresh pair of socks issued out of her personal effects, any number of minions must spring into action, including the prison governor (he has to sign all paperwork, and Her Majesty's demand for socks must, of course, be duly recorded). The prison in which I am being held is called the Isolation-Interrogative Prison of the KGB, but during World War II, under German occupation, it was used by the Gestapo. Here, for the very first time in my life, I have a room all to myself. It is even furnished with a steel cot, a small night table, and a slop bucket which serves as a lavatory. All the Queen's papers, in view of their importance to the state, are regularly scrutinized by "competent persons." For this very reason, my first collection of poems written in prison is not committed to paper, but has been memorized painstakingly, word for word. In principle, heads are also subject to scrutiny in this place, but the principle has not been enforced in my case because of my very decisive "veto." This privilege was not easily won, and gives me the right to walk proudly. Make the best of it, gentlemen; such is my royal will.

Today I am leaving my Kiev residence for one in Mordovia. Today is the start of my journey to labor camp; a van will deliver me to the station in an hour's time. All my papers, I have been told, will be sent on separately, "so that you won't have to cart them around yourself." The papers in question are my sentence, my appeal against it, my statement at my trial, my notes concerning the official record of the trial, and poems by Tyutchev, Pushkin, Shevchenko, Lermontov and Zhukovsky, copied out of books from the prison library. Oh, well, I would probably not get a chance to read them during transportation to the camp. I feel a slightly feverish exhilaration, as always before a journey. Of course, I know full well that this will be no ordinary trip: guard dogs, yelling guards armed with machine guns, the stuffiness and oppression of *Stolypin*[1] railway cars, the stench of transit prisons ... Nevertheless, my spirits are high; these first seven months have not passed too badly. They did not get so much as a word out of me under interrogation, I did not make a single plea to my captors, all they got out of me was the statement I made at my trial and a flat refusal to take any part in the proceedings. Quite an acceptable beginning for a political prisoner. Now comes the next step—transportation to the camp. My services to the Motherland have received the highest accolade: seven years of strict regime camps to be followed by five years of internal exile.

The sentence came as a twenty-ninth-birthday present. But I got another present on that day: Igor was summoned as a witness to my trial. From the doorway, he called out to me: "Hold steady, darling, I love you!" And then, turning to the judges, he told them exactly what he thought of them and their proceedings. Among

---

1. Carriages for transportation of prisoners, introduced by Pyotr Stolypin, Russia's Minister of Internal Affairs, 1906–11. Each carriage is divided into nine cubic meter compartments, which were shared by an average of four prisoners in Tsarist times and twelve in Soviet times. Records exist of compartments holding twenty-nine people (cf. Jacques Rossi, *The Gulag Handbook*, London, 1987, and Alexander Dolgun, *An American in the Gulag*, New York, 1976).

other things, he threw at them that I am a member of International PEN (news to me!) and then, just before they managed to hustle him out, one last look at me. Tell me, dear comrade judges, has anyone ever looked at you like that? Or at you, my warder-escort? Or at you, Prison Governor Petrunya? No, of course they haven't. And that is why you cannot understand how I can face the journey to the camp with a smile.

They issue me rations for the journey: half a loaf of black bread and some herring. From my former reading of *samizdat* ,[2] I know that this means twenty-four hours of travel before the first transit stop. Eating the herring is inadvisable, because it makes you terribly thirsty, and there will be nothing to drink. Thank you, Alexander Solzhenitsyn, for your priceless counsels! Who can say whether Igor and I would have had the presence of mind to burn all letters and addresses while the KGB hammered on our doors, had we not read your works? Or would I have been able to summon sufficient control not to bat an eyelid when they stripped me naked in prison? Without you, would I have grasped that cardinal principle for all prisoners of conscience: "Never believe them, never fear them, never ask them for anything"? Thanks to you, even such trivia as the business with the herring is known to me in advance. A zek's[3] light body, a zek's light bundle . . . The carriage is waiting, a paddy wagon. Oh, well. It's April. The journey lies before me. The van is brought right up to the railway carriage, so you step straight from one into the other. A guard dog barks frenziedly somewhere below: yes, I have read about all this. Here they are, the crowded *Stolypin* compartments. A welter of female bodies and faces penned up in a wire enclosure measuring three cubic meters. How many prisoners can there be in here, crammed in on two tiers? About fifteen? The next such "cage" is full of men. A clamor goes up as they see me.

"Look, here's a young one!"

"Hey, sweetheart, where are you headed for?"

"Girlie, look at me!"

---

2. *Samizdat*—clandestine publications, secretly circulated.

3. "Zek" is derived from the abbreviation z/k, *zaklyuchenny*, prisoner.

Someone proffers a sweet through the wire mesh. The guard lashes out, the sweet falls to the floor and the hand is hastily withdrawn—it lacks several fingers and is covered with tattoos. The sun sets behind the hills. We all look each other over, smiling.

"No talking!"

We continue to exchange smiles. They are zeks, and so am I. Later, when the train gets under way and the guard is replaced by a less obnoxious one, they get him to pass me another sweet, and I reciprocate with a pack of cigarettes (I knew these must be bought before the journey, whether one smokes or not). Soon, I learn my first word of "zek-speak": a "warmer." A "warmer" is the acquisition of something not officially permitted, such as our exchange of a sweet for cigarettes. The first, obvious interpretation of this word strikes me immediately—something to warm the heart. A further interpretation was to come some six months later: when you eat, you feel the cold less than when you are hungry. So a "warmer" can, quite literally, be calories . . .

I have an enclosure all to myself. According to the regulations, especially dangerous state criminals must not be allowed to mingle with other prisoners and exercise a bad influence on them. Who knows, ordinary criminals might just take it into their heads to stop stealing and robbing, and take to writing poetry. Or, worse still, start coming out in support of that traitor, Sakharov. In reality, however, what price isolation, when every compartment consists of three walls and a wire-mesh front? It is relatively easy, with a bit of dexterity, to pass notes through the wire from one enclosure to another, up and down the length of the carriage. And every word can be clearly heard.

"Hey, Number One, why are you travelling alone?"

Number One—that's me, because it is the number of my enclosure, right at one end of the carriage.

"I'm a 'political.'"

"Go on! Was it you, then, who took a shot at Andropov?"

"Why, has someone taken a shot at him?"

This is news to me. I was allowed no newspapers in the KGB prison and, anyway, this is not something that would have been mentioned in the press. I went into prison under Brezhnev, and only learned from the prosecutor's speech at my trial that we were now ruled "by Comrade Andropov himself."

"You bet they did, but missed, worse luck."

"No they didn't, he was hit in the knee." This is another enclosure joining in.

"No, I'm here because of my poems."

"How's that? Your poems against the government, were they?"

"No, independent of the government, so they took offense."

"About God, eh?"

"About God, too."

"Yeah, they wouldn't like that. Say, how about reciting some of them? Remember them, don't you?"

How could I forget? I recite the poem I dedicated to Sakharov:

Don't attempt to coerce,
If a boy flies the nest and bereaves you—
Write it off as a loss, you exemplary homeland and nurse!
You are quick to forget how to bless your own son as he leaves you,
And instead you have learned the cruel art of pronouncing a curse!

What you put in your bread—
So that no one looks elsewhere for savor,
How you loose on the trail your swift dogs and their practical art,
And poverty, jail and the nightmare asylum for ever—

Cease to harp on those strings.
We have studied and learned them by heart.

Those with wide-spreading wings,
Who from birth have been stubborn and awkward—
Don't attempt to coerce, using bribes or the menacing word—
We're not reached by such things.
We leave and go onward and onward . . .
People say that a shot in the back simply cannot be heard.

They are all quiet, listening. Heavens, what do they make of it? These are common criminals, half of them would not have so much as read a book in their lives. On the other hand, maybe they are not all like that: how varied are the people who have passed through our prisons! These listen avidly.

"No talking!"

I fall silent without demur; it is wiser to wait until the early vigilance of our guards loses its edge. This won't take long. Some ten minutes later, a voice calls out: "Number One, you write it out and pass it along to us in Number Six, okay? What's your name?"

"Ira."

"Start writing, Irinka!"

Generally speaking, writing is a bit risky. Under Soviet law it qualifies as "dissemination of slanderous documentation in poetic form." Discovery can lead to the institution of new criminal proceedings. On the other hand, I have no intention of spending the next seven years in camp cowering in silence like a frightened mouse. That would be playing right into the hands of the KGB, whose aim was to make me fear giving my poems to anyone. As for my travelling companions—well, they are human, too, criminals or not, and I am not the Almighty to sit in judgment on them. For better or for worse, they are my people, just as the young guard in his military uniform is, too. No, I shall not stoop to self-censorship.

Writing is difficult, though, because the train jerks and words jump on the paper. Better wait until the train stops. What should I write, so that they will all understand? I know—the one about the prison gnome. And something light-hearted—say, the poem about the flying cat. And the one about the old lady, who waits for the return of her son. The next halt is a long one, and I cover a double sheet of paper ripped out of an exercise book.

"Girls, pass this on to Number Six, will you?"

"How about something for us?"

"You can have this when they finish reading it. I can't write it all out ten times."

"Is it all right if we copy it out for ourselves?"

"Of course. But you could get into trouble if the guards find it."

"Zero is what they'll find."

"Another word out of any of you, and nobody will be allowed out to the toilet until tomorrow."

This last remark is from the guard. The threat is a weighty one. What are you supposed to do if they don't let you out of the pen to use the toilet? Moreover, trips to the toilet are regarded by the guards as a nuisance: one of them stands watch outside the lavatory, one plays sentry in the passageway, and a third must open every enclosure in turn and escort the prisoners to the toilet and back, one by one. So from the point of view of the guards, the fewer trips there are to the toilet the better, and toilet detail is kept to a minimum, driving the prisoners to desperation. The men occasionally cannot hold out and urinate into plastic bags, if there are any around, or into their boots. The women weep and wail, but hang on. However, this fair-haired youngster is clearly not one of the nasty ones, and has issued his threat simply to restore order. The women in Number Three sense this immediately: "Hey, there, my fair little soldier-boy. Why are you so cross, eh? Come here and I'll give you a kiss!"

"Behave, will you."

"But I'm not misbehaving, am I? I'll just give you one kiss, and it will make your whiskers grow like anything. Do you want fair whiskers, or ginger ones?"

"That's enough of your chattering, you hear?"

"Oh well, if you don't want us to talk, we'll sing you a song. Come on, girls, all together now:

> Valentina Tereshkova
> Stupid bloody fool
> Went to suck milk from a cow
> But got under a bull . . ."

"Watch it, girls, don't try my patience too far."

"We'll try you, all right, and get a bun in the oven. All the better, it means we'll get out come the next amnesty."

"Yes, we'll have nice little fair-haired girls out of you."

"Shut up, will you! The convoy commander will be coming through any minute now."

This appeal works, for the prisoners know that the young guard could get into trouble for talking to them. Everyone quiets down. In any case, it must be time to bed down now; they loaded us onto the train in the evening, and how much has happened since then! It would be interesting to know what the time is. This interest is purely academic: prisoners are not allowed to have watches or clocks. You are wakened when necessary and taken where necessary. How strangely reality narrows in prison. I know nothing: not where I will be tomorrow, not the direction in which I am travelling, nor what is going on there, in the outside world. I don't even know anything about Igor, whether he has been arrested or not. A month has passed since my trial, and we have not been allowed to exchange letters or see each other in that time. Where is he now? Probably getting ready to go to sleep, too—but where? On our folding couch at home, or on a plank bed in prison? Sleep, my dear one. May the Lord give you strength.

3

Morning. The train has been stationary for several hours now. I have learned that we are being taken to Moscow, and shall arrive there only in the evening, at best. It is twelve hours by ordinary passenger train from Kiev to Moscow, but carriages with prisoners are attached to freight trains, so our journey will take at least double that time. I half-doze most of the time; this way, the hours do not drag so heavily, nor do the surroundings impinge so much on one's consciousness. There is a swell of noise in the carriage, though, which cannot be ignored: "Hey, chief! Take us to the toilet."

"Toilets aren't supposed to be used during stops."

"Well, when are we going to move, then?"

"When the time comes, that's when."

An outburst of helpless swearing among the prisoners. Who can say when the train will move again? After a while, the train finally jerks into motion.

"Hey, chief!"

The "chief" does not deign to reply. This is not yesterday's young lad; the guards have changed. This new one must be an "overtimer," one of those who remains in this job of his own free will. Though what could motivate someone to take up this kind of work for a living voluntarily is beyond me. We cannot see his eyes, as he stands with his back to us. His fat cheeks, however, protrude from both sides of his head, which looks red and robust, even from the back. Does he hear the pleas of the zeks, or has he learned to switch off? A woman in the third enclosure is weeping, she has just about reached the end of her endurance.

"Chief! At least let the pregnant one go."

The chief doesn't give a damn about pregnant women; you can tell by that expressive back of his head.

How much time has passed? Half an hour? An hour?

"Hey, fellas! Start 'er rocking!"

Our seemingly deaf and mute tormentor reacts as if stung: "Who said that?"

But in the general uproar, it is quite impossible to determine the culprit. It was a young male voice, but there must be about seventy men in the carriage. In the next moment, I find out what that seditious call to "rock" means: the prisoners bodily start to rock our carriage. All together, in unison, throwing themselves first against one wall of their enclosures, then against the opposite one. The carriage is so packed that the results can be felt almost immediately. In this manner, the carriage can be tipped off the tracks, derailing the whole train.

The convoy supervisor comes running: "Who started this?"

Up yours, mate: the whole carriage keeps rocking. I'm doing my bit, too, in my solitary enclosure. We'll die and take you with us, you fat-faced swine! Obviously, this prospect does not appeal to him—two guards with keys appear on the double. One of them opens the enclosure in which the pregnant woman is locked. I see her as she passes my cage: a small, tear-stained face, a shock of hair peeping out from under a washed-out headscarf.

The tension dies down. Keys rattle, enclosure doors bang, and my travelling companions all pass by me, half a step away, to the toilet and back.

My God, how many of them are there? I ought to keep count, for did I not promise myself, as I stepped across the threshold of my first prison cell, that I would miss nothing? That I would watch and remember everything, down to the tiniest detail? For the day would come when all this information would prove vital, and not just the emotional aspect, but facts and figures. But right now I simply cannot force myself to keep a tally: grey faces, grey clothing . . . Only their eyes are different. They all look at me with unconcealed curiosity: a "political" is no mean title.

"How's it going, Irinka?"

I smile. Eyes looking into eyes. And another look on the way back. I stand right up against the wire. What terms stretch before you, lads? How many of you will survive the camps, how many will emerge crippled or deranged? Whom have you left behind, and will they live to see you? And how many of you actually have a place to call home? What will be the fate of the child the woman in the third enclosure will bear? What will his first words be, learned in the camp? It was only later that I found out that the average mortality rate for babies in the camps is one in eight. How much I still have to learn, despite all that I have read about prisons and camps. So this is what you are like, zeks of my time. Let us exchange a forbidden smile. That, too, is a "warmer."

With amazing sleight-of-hand, someone slips something into my pocket through the wire mesh. So adroitly is this done that I scarcely notice it, and the guard misses it altogether. And again. And again. A small square of paper, folded several times, falls to the floor. A note! Quickly, I cover it with my boot: like all the other zeks, I wear tarpaulin soldiers' boots. Only mine are smaller than the regulation issue; Igor somehow managed to get a pair in my size and passed them to me in prison. Whew! Looks like nobody saw the note. I drop my handkerchief, then scoop up the note as I bend to retrieve it. I have not yet acquired the dexterity of a zek. Never mind, I will learn.

When everything quiets down and the guard turns his back on us again, I start to examine my booty.

"Hello, there, Irisha! My name is Volodya. My term expires in three years' time. I am very fond of poetry. My favorite poet is Omar Khayyám. Here are some of his verses that I remember by heart, I hope you like them too."

And, on a separate bit of paper, verses out of the *Rubáiyát*, closely written in tiny script (he must have written them when the train was stationary). Almost no grammatical errors. How about that! Much can be expected during transportation to the camps, but hardly something like this. Later, these verses were to be confiscated when I was searched upon arrival at Lefortovo prison, as were the Tyutchev and Pushkin poems which I had copied out and which were "travelling separately." Instead of having them returned to me, I was given a document listing them as confiscated; the document stated that these poems were found to be slanderous, ideologically dangerous, and for this reason had been destroyed by burning. The reason for this bizarre act was not hard to guess: the Kiev KGB staff are not expected to know anything about literature, and they had simply decided that these poems had all been written by me. It had not occurred to me to note that this poem was written by Pushkin, or that one by Tyutchev, as I had known them from childhood. So, by courtesy of the ignorance of the Kiev KGB, I was arbitrarily elevated to genius rank: writing about the mountains of Georgia, the depths of the Siberian mines, about thunderstorms in early May . . . Naturally, this "creativity" only served to increase the vigilance of the KGB. That's right, my bright sparks: keep your eyes peeled and your ears open; what will be, will be. In the meantime, on to the next note.

"Irinka, our names are Vera and Lyuba. We're on our way from a juvenile offenders' zone to an adult one. We both have a year left to serve, though it's not likely we'll end up in the same zone. Write how long you've got to serve, we didn't hear when you told the others. Vera thinks you said seven years, but that can't be right, can it? Is it true that our political prisoners get sent to America in exchange for our spies that the Americans have caught? Write about your politics and pass it along to the fifth cage. All the others in here want to know, too."

"Ira, you said that there is a political camp. Is that the one where they kept Solzhenitsyn? I read his *One Day in the Life of Ivan Denisovich* when I was still free. Some of our boys say that Solzhenitsyn is a Jew, and that he has been imprisoned again. Is that true? Send your answer to the seventh, and mark it for 'The Lip'—that's what they call me."

Among the notes, I discover a caramel in my pocket. The aniline colors of its wrapper have imprinted themselves on the sweet itself in bright red and violet diamond shapes. We used to joke about these caramels in Odessa, saying that they were made of pure acetone. It melts slowly, slowly, in my mouth. I will never know whose gift this is. Maybe it was slipped to me by that young, blue-eyed man with ringworm on his shaven head, or that elderly, homely-looking woman with smiling wrinkles, or that swarthy "stripey" (a term applied to those who are on special regime,[1] and therefore almost certainly doomed). Whoever it was—my heartfelt thanks. This caramel is the best I have had in my life. I reply to the notes as clearly as possible. The notes themselves I destroy, for we shall soon be in Moscow and that means we will be searched. I keep only the verses of the *Rubáiyát:* if they find them, let them search for a zek called Omar Khayyám.

I am transported through Moscow alone, in a large truck with a canvas hood. My guards are two young men, cradling submachine guns. Naturally, they are curious to know who it is they are guarding. I tell them my story. They are incredulous: "Surely not seven years plus five?"

I open a shutter in the door to catch a glimpse of Moscow. The night wind blows my hair back from my forehead. Lights. The area is unfamiliar. After a little awkward humming and hawing, my custodians come up with an amazing offer: I'm young, so are they. Maybe I would like to have "a quickie" with whichever one of them I fancy most? There is still some way to go, and the other one will turn his back. Moreover, if I chance to become pregnant, I'll almost certainly get out of camp early, because pregnant women or women with children are usually included in the amnesties proclaimed from time to time. In fact, two amnesties are expected quite soon in connection with the forthcoming revolutionary anniversary dates.

Luckily, I have enough sense to take no offense at their generosity. When all is said and done, in their own way they honestly want to do me a good turn. As tactfully as I can, I explain that

1. There are four types of regime regulating conditions of imprisonment: ordinary, intensified, strict and special. Each entails progressive reduction in prisoners' rights to visits, correspondence, supplementary food purchases, etc. Prisoners on special regime are held in cells.

while I think they are both fine specimens of manhood, I am a married woman, and faithful to my husband.

"Religious, are you?"

"Yes, I am."

To them, this is a perfectly acceptable explanation, and the subject is closed. No—then no. They are, in fact, immeasurably more sensitive than KGB men, whose response would certainly have been: "Where's the husband who will wait for you for seven years!" How many times I heard such remarks during the seven months I spent under investigation!

My poor investigator, Lukyanenko, was at his wits' end to come up with something that would shake my composure. He never did, and finally gave up trying. After every question, without even expecting an answer, he would note down "no reply" in the protocol. But these lads—their questions I do answer, whatever they want to know. I recite poems, explain who Sakharov is. In this way we pass the journey to Lefortovo. They give me a pack of cigarettes and I take it, even though I do not smoke myself; they will be a welcome gift for others. After all, I am not alone any more. With whom will it fall to me to share skilly?[2]

At Lefortovo prison, after being searched, I get what is a treat for any zek—a shower. This is one good thing about being in transport: the prisoners have to be able to wash once a week, and I still had five days to go before my next scheduled wash. This unexpected bonus is because all incoming prisoners in Lefortovo have to be given a wash. How long will they keep me here? No use asking, of course. I have a cell to myself, thank God. Faces, shaven heads, swim before my eyes . . . I have become unaccustomed to people during seven months of solitude. KGB do not qualify as human beings, after all! But my erstwhile travelling companions are people, even though some of them may be killers and thieves. Our nation has always referred to those sentenced to hard labor as "unfortunates." And unfortunates they are, and I pity them as, no doubt, they pity me. Certainly I know about the vicious camp "laws" by which criminals live, about merciless

2. A thin swill, the staple food in the camps.

revenge, about the exploitation of the weak among them . . . Yet there is something else to them as well—and that I will never forget. I shall try to appeal to that "something else" which exists in even the most hardened criminals, and the guards, and maybe even in that one, who has just peered in through the Judas-hole in the door to check whether I am asleep or not. Oh, Lord, save my unfortunate people and have mercy upon them!

4

The next leg of my journey begins after two days of solitary confinement in Lefortovo prison. This time, to my surprise, I am pushed into an enclosure with ten other women, either through oversight or because of shortage of space. For obvious reasons, I make no protest: new faces, new encounters. Introductions are quickly made, stories swapped. Some of the women are reluctant to talk about themselves, turning the conversation to other subjects. The old lady in the corner is called Granny Tonia by everyone. She cries almost incessantly. During the journey she recounts how she, at the age of sixty-five, was sentenced to four years for making moonshine vodka.

"Come off it, Gran," scoffs Lida, who has obviously been around and seen it all. Her lipstick is a vivid slash in an unwashed face. "Nobody gets four years for hooch if they're a first offender."

"That's just it," sobs Granny Tonia, "they shouldn't." She blows her nose, not into a handkerchief, but a small white rag with fraying edges. "All my life, as long as I can remember, everyone in our village has brewed moonshine, and nobody got into any trouble over it. All you had to do was give Misha, our local policeman, a ten before a holiday and he'd turn a blind eye. But then he got drunk and drowned when he rode his motorbike into the pond, and they sent such a swine to replace him, you wouldn't believe! Where they got him from, God knows. So he turns up at my place just before the October festivities—the bastard nosed out that I live alone, don't have nobody to stand up for me . . . Well, he found everything, he did. I tried to talk my way out of it, but 'No,' he says, 'I'm going to report you.' My neighbors advised me to slip him twenty-five rubles so's he wouldn't report me, and, as it happened, I'd just sold some potatoes and had a bit of ready cash. So off I went and offered him the twenty-five. And what does he do? He takes it, that's what, and right then and there starts writing out a new report this time accusing me of trying to bribe him. Oh, I begged and I pleaded, but they still took me to court on two charges . . . While they were still holding me, even before my trial, there was an amnesty for moonshiners, but not for bribes. And the judge says to me, he says: 'For the illegal brewing, citizeness, one year, and you would have been on your way home now. But for offering a bribe—it's four years of ordinary regime camps for you.' "

Granny Tonia sobs again into her little white rag. Her house is left untended, so is her cabbage patch. How likely is it that she will survive four years in the camps? Better that she had been left to die quietly in her little village hut.

"Don't worry, Gran," everyone tries to console her, "ordinary regime isn't that strict, you'll pull through. There's good folks everywhere. You're old, nobody'll push you around. And they won't set you to sewing, either, they only put strong and healthy ones on that. Come on, now, stop snivelling."

A discussion starts about assignment to sewing detail. The worst of these is the heavy-duty work: making quilted jackets and pants, military greatcoats. The workrooms are full of floating fibers and fluff, which you inhale during the entire shift. Moreover, the cloth has usually been treated with chemicals, and contact produces skin ulcers which become progressively worse with continued handling of the material. If you go to the camp medic, you will be told that the ulcers are the result of engaging in "homosex"—that is, lesbianism.

"But I don't," protests the sufferer.

"In that case, it must be from sexual deprivation," counters the medic.

These two causes suffice to explain away any eventuality, and in both cases imply that the prisoner is at fault and shouldn't waste the medic's precious time.

Judging by what I hear, everyone's ambition seems to be to get themselves assigned to some kind of "domestic" duty—in the kitchens, as cleaners, or something similar. Prisoners given these duties are housed separately and in less crowded conditions; their chances of early conditional release are greater. All this wisdom is not a whit of use to me; political prisoners are not subject to amnesties or early releases—just as they do not indulge in lesbian practices or have anyone to tend to their needs. Nevertheless, all this makes fascinating hearing. I estimate that there are some one and a half million women in Soviet camps, and they all face similar problems.

Another of my new travelling companions, "Auntie" Lyuba, killed her husband with an ax. She talks about this quite willingly, even with a touch of bravado:

"For twelve years that no-good drunk spent every penny on booze, and would beat me up every which way. One day, along he comes, all set to lay into me again, so I grabbed the ax, showing him that he'd better keep his distance. But he paid no heed, just kept coming at me, so I bashed him one with the butt end. Dropped like a log, he did. First I thought it was just because he was drunk—I hadn't hit him all that hard. But it turned out that was enough to do him in. Well, I ran to get the doctor, and when he came he said: 'That's it, Lyubov Yakovlevna. You're a murderess!' But I don't regret it—not for a moment I don't. I spent three months in prison, and the guards only hit me once. Before, I'd get bashed around practically every day . . . And the investigator, he didn't raise a finger against me either: I told him the truth right away, that made it easy for him to wind up the case. He even sympathized with me, gave me cups of tea . . ."

Her hands are plump, short-fingered. There is a visible indentation on one of her fingers from a wedding ring. She confides that the ring had been such a tight fit, they had not been able to get it off in the prison, it had had to be sawn off. It is against regulations for prisoners to wear rings, even wedding rings. And why would she need a wedding ring now, anyway?

It is time to eat, so we pool our resources. I had laid in supplies before transportation, for while under investigation you may buy up to ten rubles' worth of foodstuffs a month. I had made a special effort, in order not to arrive in the camp empty-handed. Alas, all that was left by the time I reached my destination were several heads of garlic; everything else was given away during the journey to my pitiful, emaciated companions. At least half of them would not have had anyone to bring them anything while they were in prison, to say nothing of those who were being shifted from one camp to another after years of confinement. Grey-faced, withered, with bluish lips were some of them; others sought to brighten their pallid faces with defiant slashes of bright, cheap lipstick. My hands seemed to move of their own accord to share what I had with them, while something inside me screamed and screamed its pity for these pathetic creatures . . .

Later I was to learn that I had acted in error; after all, these women were from and for ordinary regime camps, a far cry from the strict regime camp which was my destination. In the strict regime camps one may purchase food only up to the value of five rubles per month, parcels are few and far between (you are entitled to one parcel weighing five kilos once a year, after you have completed half of your sentence) and the camp administration can deprive you of both these "privileges" at any time. And does, as a rule. So the women with whom I was to share the coming years in Barashevo were even hungrier and more emaciated than my companions on the train. Yet the Barashevo women were more human, for all that: it was something in their eyes, in the way they held themselves. When I joined them, they immediately forgave me my misguided charity during transportation, making a joke out of it; it turned out that just about all of them had done the same. When all is said and done, this was no more than a normal reaction, when you see something like that for the first time. The garlic I had brought with me to Barashevo was eaten, bit by tiny bit, over a period of two months, and every time it was produced I would cringe with shame, even though my folly had been forgotten by the others long since.

In the carriage, the fact that I am a "political" arouses much interest. I have to explain everything from scratch yet again: about human rights, about my poetry, then read that poetry—to the whole carriage. The guard is clearly interested, too, for he makes no move to stop me. Nowadays, since my arrival in the West, people frequently express surprise at my ability to recite from memory, and at the ease with which I answer questions. The reason for this, ladies and gentlemen, is that my first large audiences—a hundred people or more—were crammed into these carriages, where not everyone could see me, just hear my voice. The poetry had to be read in as straightforward a manner as possible, and the questions answered simply, without trying to be "clever," just as I do now in English, for my knowledge of English is no more sophisticated than the "ordinary" Russian of my fellow prisoners. There may be the odd few in the camps who can recite the verses of Omar Khayyám, but the overwhelming majority of camp inmates are semi-literate. Nevertheless, I recite:

> I see a household cat in my despairing,
> Who makes no noise and knows how to behave.
> Her needs are few—a scratch will start her purring,
> A scrap to eat and whispered words: "Be brave!"
> My throat escapes her claws' unlooked-for pricking,
> She never interferes if I have guests.
> The minute hand enchants her with its ticking
> And brings her consolation, even rest.
> She climbs up on my knee when sensing nightfall,
> And, childlike, noses round and falls asleep
> As on my book I see the patterned light fall,
> Those meaningless cast-iron shadows creep.
> But in the darkness, like a mouse a-chewing,
> She stirs as if in sleep she seemed to see
> A dwelling that sets off her tiny mewing,
> The house of warmth that you will build for me.

I read on: what price I and my poems if I can't get through to this audience? Too many of us have been too far "removed from the people" already. I recite whatever comes to mind: the poem about the unattainable cherry-red dress, the one about the exemplary Motherland, who executes the best of her children, the one about the flying cat. . . .

Granny Tonia weeps again. After blowing her nose, she fishes out a wrinkled apple from somewhere. "Here, daughter, you have it, you're young. I'm not going to come out of the camp alive, anyway, but you'll live. You keep writing!"

I accept the apple, my first honorarium, still warm from her hands. I'll keep writing, Granny Tonia. If I survive, I'll write. Actually, sentimentality exacts a just price, like any tendency to paint something in one color. The prison administration tries to reduce every prisoner to grey, and it would be equally wrong for me to depict the same in rosy hues. While Granny Tonia and I were succumbing to sentiment, someone stole my toothbrush out of my bag, and it would be silly for me to be surprised by that.

The train rattled on and cheery, worldly-wise Varyukha instructed me in camp know-how: "The main thing is to keep your wits about you. As soon as you get to the camp and pass through quarantine, make sure you're issued everything you're supposed to get, and have it locked in the store, otherwise someone's bound to swipe it. Then, when you put your sheets and things out to dry, stay right there: your underpants will be pretty safe unless they're a foreign make, but your sheet will disappear, you can bet your life!"

"But why the sheet?"

"Simple. Thing is, you should get three sheets, but you'll be lucky to get two. The bunks have to be made up 'white,' that means sheet on top. While you're away working, they go around checking that the sheets are clean and without wrinkles. That's what these top sheets are called, raid sheets. You don't sleep on it, just keep it for the bosses to look at. So in fact you've got the one sheet, to put on the bottom and on the top and to wash. The next set you'll get only in about two years' time. So it's no wonder they get swiped."

"But even if everyone has them stolen, that still leaves two for each one!"

"Nah, that's just in the beginning. The ones that've been in for long stretches have had several issues, they can have five or six sheets. Then the ones going away leave their sheets to others. You'll soon get the hang of it all, you're educated. If you write clemency pleas for the others, they'll give you all sorts of things as payment."

"What do you mean, write clemency pleas?"

"Appeals for clemency: addressed to Valentina Tereshkova, say, or the Government, saying things like 'I'm sorry, I realize the extent of my crime and ask to have my sentence reduced.' Everyone writes them."

"And does it help?"

"Like hell, especially if they're sent to Valentina Tereshkova. She's a prize bitch anyway, it was her that introduced the zek uniform and identity tags."

"How?"

At this point, the whole carriage hurries into emotive speech. This was the first occasion of many when I witnessed the virulent general hatred the zeks have for Valentina Tereshkova, the chairwoman of the Soviet Women's Committee. Not once in four years did I hear a good word about her. At first, I could find no obvious reason, but from the explanations which ten or twelve women, all talking at once, gave me on this occasion (and they were all from different prisons and camps, so there could have been no collusion) the following story emerged.

Formerly, the women prisoners had been allowed to wear their own clothing, both under Stalin and under Khrushchev. Khrushchev even repealed the regulation about the wearing of chest identity tags. So in Khrushchev's time, women prisoners, not close-cropped and in their own clothes, looked reasonably human. They could even buy material in the camps to sew clothes for themselves. That was until Valentina Tereshkova paid a visit to the Kharkov camp. The camp administration, bowing and scraping, had the prisoners lined up. And here our "Valya" really made her presence felt.

"What's this?" she demanded. "Some of these women are better dressed than I am!"

Some object for envy! But as a result, all the prisoners' clothes were confiscated, and a standard uniform was devised: it is not hard to imagine the creations dreamed up by the State. Identity tags to be worn on the chest became mandatory: failure to wear them ranks as a violation of camp regulations. Similarly, head-scarves have to be worn at all times, in line, at work—in fact everywhere, to be removed only at night. This is hardly beneficial to the hair and scalp, but what can one do? Then there are these ghastly boots: with typical inconsistency, women are allowed to wear light shoes in summer in the Ukraine, but not in the Russian republic. The only warm items of apparel permitted are socks and undershirts. So in winter the women must line up, teeth chattering, in short standard issue cotton skirts. It's easier for the men—they, at least, have trousers and long-johns. Still, Valentina Tereshkova's aesthetic feelings are now satisfied. She can visit the Kharkov zone without any undue apprehension (this zone, because of the scare Tereshkova put into everyone, was turned into a "show" zone and disciplinary measure upon disciplinary measure were heaped upon its hapless inmates). Still, Tereshkova can now come to this zone—and, indeed, any other in the USSR—secure in the knowledge that nobody will be better dressed than herself. All will be dressed equally badly. Long live communist legality! I must have heard this story in different places from different zeks at least thirty times.

The prisoners express their appreciation of Tereshkova in ditties, only one of which contains no obscenities. That is the one I have already cited, the others are absolutely unprintable.

"In that case, why does anyone bother addressing clemency pleas to her?"

"Because they're stupid, that's why!" retorts Varyukha. "They all keep hoping for something: an amnesty, a pardon. Mind you, sometimes one'll get released before some anniversary or other, but that will be one in a hundred thousand. I've never written any, there's enough silly idiots without me."

Yes, all this tallies with what Solzhenitsyn has written. I try to quote him as closely as I can from memory. The carriage is enthralled: what else has he written? Impossible to retell the whole *Gulag Archipelago*, of course, but I recount as much as I can. The guard (they've changed shifts again) utters a word of

caution: "Be quiet for a bit, the boss is about due to come around."
And once his senior has been through, he prompts me: "Go on,
what else is there?"

I do go on. Who needs this more than you in uniforms, be they
zek uniforms or military ones? Not all of you are lifelong thieves
and bandits. Your lives have been disfigured, but your souls are
intact. How do your souls fare, hammered by the machinery of
lies and violence from early childhood? How wonderful if they do
not succumb, but is there any chance of that? I continue to hope
that there is.

5

The transit prison in Potma is a disgusting place. Not that there are any pleasant transit prisons, I suppose. The powers that be recollect my status and isolate me in a solitary cell. It is a large, cavernous place with no bunks, just two tiers of uninterrupted wooden shelves along the walls. High above there is a small window, its glass long gone. Heating is switched off at the beginning of April, and we are now in the middle of the month. Hummocks of snow lie here and there on the floor. Oh, but I'm going to be cold in here! I did not know, then, of the cold I would have to endure in the years ahead. The cell boasts a tap—truly a touch of luxury. Unfortunately, this luxurious fixture leaks, creating a large permanent puddle on the floor: I can jump across its length, but not its breadth. The presence of the puddle means constant, chill damp. In a couple of hours, all my clothing is clammy. I sit there, teeth chattering, rhyming "sanitation" with "civilization." Then I hear tapping of another kind: someone is signalling along the heating pipe which passes through all the cells. That means I am being invited to establish contact. I was taught on the train how this is done. You place the base of an empty mug against the pipe, and press your ear to the open end. That way, you can hear everything. To say something yourself—yell into the cup, keeping the base against the pipe.

"Sixteen, sixteen, come on the pipe."

That means me.

"Speak up!"

"Write a letter to your folks, there's a chance to send it from here. Keep it by you—they'll be loading us on the train tomorrow, so you just slip it to us. No sweat. Oh, write out some of your poems for us, will you? The girls in here are asking for 'em. They won't look for poems on us, so don't worry. Me—I've had a whole exercise book of poems for years now, and nobody's so much as given it a glance. So get cracking. You got envelopes?"

"Yes, thank you."

"What's that?"

"Thanks!"

"Right y'are. See here, when you're on the pipe, talk slow, like. Otherwise it's hard to make out. That's all then. Cheers!"

To write, or not to write? Never mind the poems, but the letters. . . ? How reliable are these chance travelling companions of mine? You come across all kinds—one of them may really somehow manage to send my mail on; but another could well turn it over to the guards in the hope of some reward or concession . . . The conversation took place "on the pipe," I could not see the face of my would-be benefactor. Even if the letter were to go safely on its way, how should I address it? Our home address is out, for a start, because the KGB checks the mail. The best thing would be to direct it to some "low profile" friend or acquaintance in Kiev, and ask them to forward it to Igor. I have committed a number of such addresses to memory, so there is a choice. And I really ought to write: my trial was extraordinary even by Soviet standards, violating every possible judicial norm. I was deprived of defense counsel, and of the right to a final word. The only spectators allowed into the courtroom were KGB "extras," so the officials were free of any constraints whatsoever. To this day, I don't know why they chose the five poems cited in the indictment at the trial: if they were looking for "anti-Soviet" material, there were others that were much more suitable from a KGB point of view. Yes, I will write, and come what may. For a while, I even forget the cold as I set everything down in detail: the names of the investigating officers, the judges, the appeals panel

... What a pity I don't have a copy of my sentence—there are some truly mind-boggling passages there!

My letter is written, the envelope sealed and addressed. It contains a full account of my period under investigation, my trial, and a note asking the addressee to pass the contents on to Igor. From the moment he receives this letter, the risk passes from me to him: how should he publicize this information? If he is still free, that is . . .

As it happened, this letter was not confiscated, and did reach the addressee. Igor, who had not been arrested, learned of its arrival from mutual friends, but was unable to secure it. Nor would the person who received it give it to me after my release. Either he still has it, or he gave it to the KGB—this highly educated gentleman, who had never been tried or imprisoned. If one is to compare him with those simple, petty criminals who volunteered to post a letter for a "political" with whom they had nothing in common, it is the criminals who emerge favorably. Sadly, such occurrences are not infrequent. I withhold this person's name not because he had been in our house and broken bread at our table, nor because he has two children who bear his name; it is because a book is no place to settle personal scores. Furthermore, why single him out? There are all too many like him, alas . . .

My letter written, I set about writing out poems. The difficulty does not lie in writing out some ten to fifteen poems in tiny script, but in something quite different. During every transit stop, I "resurrect" the full index of my poems, and then burn the paper on which I write it out. At the next halt, I repeat the process. I have managed to recall twelve poems written before my arrest, and I wrote another forty-four during the period under investigation. During transportation, I started on a new poem in Lefortovo prison, and I ought to complete it here. Yet every time I start to recreate the full list of my work, there is always at least one elusive poem which tries to escape recollection, and it's never the same one. This is more annoying than a nagging tooth—sometimes half a day is wasted before everything is fully recalled. On this occasion, it takes half a night. Admittedly, there is not much else to do here. I have no bedding, my clothes are damp through, and a film of ice forms around the edge of the puddle. Not much chance of getting any sleep. Every twenty minutes or so I start jumping across the puddle to get my circulation going and to warm up a bit. The shape of the puddle is reminiscent of the Mediterranean Sea, and even the uneven concrete "shores" around it bear some resemblance to the countries which surround it. The climate, unfortunately, could not be more different . . .

Water drips monotonously from the leaky pipe. Wooden shelves, steel door, solid walls. The walls of Potma transit prison are not white. They are not even grey or institutional green. They are silver, no less. Covered from floor to ceiling with aluminum paint. At first glance, you feel quite bowled over: there you are, locked into a silver cage. Why silver? Why not gold, then? All government institutions in the Soviet Union, from schools to prisons, are usually either whitewashed, or painted a particularly bilious shade of pea-green, which is slapped on as a matter of course. Yet here we have this astonishing flight of fancy. Try as I might, I can think up no reason to explain the astonishing decor in Potma prison. I learned the answer by chance about a year and a half later: aluminum paint is supposed to repel bedbugs. The bedbugs in Potma prison don't give a damn about this theory, though; they are large, spry and well nourished. I think it would be easier to exterminate the entire prison personnel and all the prisoners than those bedbugs. Still, when I heard this explanation—silly as it is—I somehow felt a bit better. Truly, we live in a land of wonders!

The cell walls are inscribed with the usual prison graffiti.

"Tanyusha, I'll be waiting for you in the Fourteenth Zone." "We're off for a two-year stretch. Katya and Lyuba, 14.3.83." But here are a few unusual ones: "Masha—snake," and "WULTOT." What is "WULTOT," and why is Masha called a snake? This is not a customary zek insult.

Had the scribbles been something more simple or crude, I probably would not have paid much attention or remembered these two enigmatic messages. It was not until the following summer that I found out what they meant. There are about a hundred "zek-speak" acronyms which are totally incomprehensible to an outsider. And so it emerged that nobody was saying a word to Masha's detriment, let alone calling her a snake: on the contrary, she was being referred to as "My One Bright Star."[1] As for "WULTOT"—that is a real cry from the heart: "Wake Up, Lenin, They're Overstepping Themselves!" It must have been thought up by some naïve soul who had been taught at school that Lenin was "the most humane of all humans," who would not, consequently, dream of overstepping himself.

The widely used abbreviations of zek slang do not always form pronounceable words. If it ever falls to you, my reader (though God forbid!), to see your name written on a prison wall and followed by the letters LYMTL, that will simply mean "Love You More Than Life." These letters are no harder to remember than KGB.

---

1. *"Zvezdochka Moya Edinstvennaya Yasnaya"*: the first letters of these words make up the Russian word for snake—*zmeya.*

6

Finally, my last search before entry into the camp zone. All my "civvies" are confiscated with the exception of tights and a woolen kerchief. The junior official carrying out the search turns out to be quite a nice woman. Her name is Lyuba. She points out to me that the kerchief, strictly speaking, ought to be confiscated because it is checkered and not plain. However, she will let it through so that I can unravel it and knit myself some socks. Colored socks are not forbidden, so nobody will take them away from me. She issues my zek wardrobe—two chintz dresses. I am allowed to keep my jacket and boots because they conform to regulation design. After a moment's hesitation, Lyuba returns the track-suit pants she had confiscated five minutes earlier: "Here, keep them, just don't let anyone see you've got them." She smiles at me, flashing a formidable array of metal crowns. "Well, let's go then, all the others are waiting for you, won't eat till you show up."

Her speech is a strange mixture of the formal "you" and familiar "thou" forms of address. The reason for this, I learn later, is that the "politicals" are known to be high sticklers, and take exception to camp personnel addressing them in the familiar form. Still, human nature is human nature, and even in the camp, ordinary conversations take place from time to time between prisoners and personnel: in such cases, if the conversation is an amicable one, the "thou" form may pass unchallenged. For the present, I make a mental note of Lyuba's strange grammar and follow her to a gate set in a high fence. So here it is, the political zone, a camp within a camp. Whom shall I meet there?

Cursing under her breath, Lyuba wrestles with a bunch of keys and a huge padlock. The gate shudders, then finally gives with a screech of hinges. Barbed wire. A path leading to a small wooden structure which bears no resemblance to an "institutional" building. Rather, it is reminiscent of a dilapidated little summer holiday cabin. Nothing unofficial, though, about the watchtower on the other side of the barbed wire and the submachine gun in the hands of the guard manning it. A few birch trees grow around the little hut, a few blades of grass poke up here and there. That's all. I shall spend the next six years and five months on this small patch, surrounded by barbed wire.

A thin grey-haired woman comes down the path toward me. There is something instantly winning about her, from the first glance and forever. How could they have put her on trial and looked her in the face? How did that make them feel?

"Hello, there. Let me take your things."

We look at each other, almost without smiling. Then that "almost" melts, melts, melts . . . and disappears. It's a tough test, the first scrutiny of a zek.

She carries my meager bundle to the little house, even though she is twice my age. This is how guests are welcomed here, and today I am a guest. Lyuba does not accompany us, but goes back out. There are no guards around—now that is a feeling to be experienced! Guards are out there, beyond the barbed wire, but here there is just us—in our own home. With conscientious concentration, I close the door of my new home behind me: I've lost the habit of closing doors . . .

The first person I see is a dark-haired, intense, painfully thin young woman: this is Tanya Osipova. She has just come off a four-month hunger strike.

Next is petite, smiling Raya Rudenko. You can see faces like hers in any Ukrainian village. Your hands simply itch to wind a traditional scarf, ends tucked in, around her head to complete the picture.

Then there is Natasha Lazareva, wafer-thin and almost transparent, an unruly shock of hair falling over her forehead.

The one who came to greet me—the woman with the amazing face—is Tatyana Mikhailovna Velikanova. I had heard about all of them on Western radio broadcasts, and now here I am, among them. My name means nothing to them—this is not their first year behind barbed wire, nor was I mentioned all that much on the radio. The length of my sentence tells them immediately that I was tried in the Ukraine. I confirm their conclusion and outline the details of my case. This is useful information, but, even without that, they will have my measure before too long. We will be together for many years, and in that time, get to know all that there is to know about one another—maybe even too much. In the meantime, I tell them as much as I can about what is new "out there," even though my latest news is already seven months old. They, in turn, acquaint me with the history of our Small Zone: from now on, this is my heritage, too.

I am introduced to a very important personage—the Zone's cat, Nyurka; she is a fully fledged member of the family, has lived here longer than most, and shares our rations. In principle, prisoners are not allowed to keep cats or pets of any kind. Unfortunately the camp rats, blissfully unaware of this prohibition, had decided to make our Small Zone their headquarters, and became so rapacious and fearless that they drove not just the prisoners but also the guards to distraction. Just try rummaging through a prisoner's locker if there is a huge rat sitting inside! All very well if it only just leaps out and makes a run for it to the accompaniment of your startled yells, but what if it bites you? For this reason, when the women in our Zone obtained a kitten from the criminal zone, the guards pretended not to notice. Nyurka quickly grew into a large cat, sober of mien and the scourge of all rats, let alone mice. She brought the rodent population to book very quickly, and her progeny was always much sought after by camp personnel: excellent heredity plus Nyurka's training produced superb ratters. I shake Nyurka's polite paw with due deference. Her eyes are bright yellow and traditionally enigmatic. We try to determine Nyurka's pedigree, even though a greater mixture would be hard to find. "Mordovian Sentinel," suggests Natasha, and "Mordovian Sentinel" she is henceforth.

More discussion, laughter, a happy confusion of words and thoughts . . .

And I really do feel happy: this is my home. They are all impossibly thin, my new friends, dressed in a motley collection of rags and tatters, yet how they hold themselves! They have all known each other for a long time, but invariably observe the courteous "you" form in speech. Living in close quarters makes it essential to maintain some degree of psychological distance, and one way to achieve this is to use the formal rather than the familiar form of address. Scrupulous observance of norms of courtesy prevents the flaring up of irritation over trifles, inhibits the tendency to pry, helps to avoid that multitude of faux pas that make life in the criminal camps such hell.

"Prison is less to be feared than people," said elderly "Auntie" Vera to me during transportation.

Here, in our Zone, the inmates are not to be feared, though, simply because they are human beings in the full sense of the word. We may be crammed into a small house, we may be dressed in rags, they can carry out searches and lightning raids in our quarters, but we retain our human dignity. We will not get down on all fours to them, try though they may to make us. We will not carry out demeaning or senseless commands, because we have not surrendered our freedom. Yes, we are behind barbed wire, they have stripped us of everything they could, they have torn us away from our friends and families, but unless we acknowledge this as their right, we remain free. For this reason, we study every camp rule very carefully. We have to get up at six o'clock in the morning? Well, why not? Work? Certainly, unless we are ill or on hunger strike. We do not object to work: making protective gloves for workers is a clean and worthwhile task. Meet the output quotas? That will depend on what condition we are in, and that, in turn, depends on how you treat us: if we have the strength, you'll get your quotas in full; if not—blame yourselves . . . wear zek clothing? There is no alternative, short of going naked. But if you expect us to clear the no-man's-land strip—forget it! We will have no part in the building or maintenance of camps and prisons, either directly or indirectly. Prison upkeep is your job, not ours. You forbid us to give things to each other? That is none of your business, screws and KGB scum; we shall give or lend each other whatever we will, the last thread off our backs, if need be, without your sanction. As for springing to attention at the entry of any member of the camp management—well, we don't acknowledge your authority, nor do we have the slightest interest in your penal pecking order—we don't belong to your ranks. Furthermore, elementary good manners decree that it is men who should rise to their feet when a woman enters the room, not vice versa. You have different standards of behavior? Yes, we've noticed that, it would be hard not to. But we'll stick to our own, with or without your consent. Of course, we know that we shall be penalized for this. However, we shall retain our sense of human dignity, and not turn into trained circus animals.

When a dog is trained to jump over a stick, the stick is raised a little higher every time. When a dog licks a hand, persons like you command it to lick your boot . . . But we are not dogs, and we will not jump at your command. Remember that. Exert yourselves to address us formally, or we will not respond, even if you shout until your lungs burst; we will simply not hear you. Stop pestering us to attend your political sessions, your lectures and similar propaganda; we shall walk out of the room without listening.

The result? Young Officer Shishokin had to admit, crestfallen: "It's easier to deal with two hundred ordinary criminals than with you in the Small Zone."

Yet why should that be so? We are invariably polite—to you, and among ourselves. There are no fights or thefts in our Small Zone, no escape attempts. We do our work conscientiously, all the gloves we turn out are without defects . . . In other words, we live like decent human beings and give our guards no headaches.

"It's because," admits Shishokin candidly, "when we are in the criminal zone, we feel the power of our position."

How true, how very true. *This* is what they value above all else—power. Let the inmates of the criminal zone brawl, swear, rape, sabotage working tools and machinery on the sly, sink to the lowest depths of depravity. Nevertheless he, Shishokin, is their master, and when he enters a room, they will stand to attention. As for us, we don't care about his good will, even though he has the power to deprive us of the right to use the camp kiosk for a month, or to have us thrown into the punishment isolation cell, the so-called SHIZO.[1] Our attitude gives Shishokin an inferiority complex—and not just him. Still, there is nothing we can do about that. We are not psychiatrists, and the chances are that he has been suffering from this complex for some time. Why else would someone become, quite voluntarily, a prison keeper unless he felt the need to bolster up his confidence at the expense of people who have been stripped of their rights? Well, you'll get no chance to boost your ego in dealings with us. Why, none of you even dare to look us straight in the eye.

I absorbed these basic tenets of Zone life as my due heritage, and they suited me down to the ground. In fact, I had observed these norms even earlier, in the frightening solitude of the KGB investigation prison, partly through instinct and partly through common sense.

Just because I am imprisoned it does not mean that I shall let anyone deny me the freedom to behave like a normal human being. High-sounding words? Yet they are worthless unless backed up by deeds. Had we in the Small Zone valued our skins above all else, we would not have ended up as political prisoners; we would have stayed put in whatever place decreed by our residence permits, licked boots as ordered, and called ourselves "free" . . . But now I am no longer alone, I am amongst my own kind. What luck!

The Zone does, however, pose a problem I have not encountered before: the wearing of a cloth identity tag on my chest. I had seen such tags en route to the camp, but on others. What are they? At first glance, something that hardly seems worth a fuss. A black cloth triangle, inscribed with your surname, initials and work brigade number. But what brigade? As far as I know, I am not a

---

1. Derived from *shtrafnoy izolyator*—literally, punishment isolator.

member of any brigades or organizations (International PEN Club aside). Joining organizations and brigades is something free people do voluntarily, and nobody here has asked my consent; merely, the camp administration assigns all prisoners to brigades, each of which has a number ... The identity tag must be sewn on to one's clothing and be worn at all times. The official reason is that the tags make it easier to determine who is who. What utter nonsense! There are only five of us in the Small Zone. At times, both in the past and in the future, the population of the Small Zone exceeded ten people—but not by much ... And anyway, everyone in Barashevo (our camp took its name from the nearest settlement) could recognize us at a glance from any angle. We do not make up a work brigade, nor do we need these ridiculous fictions. Therefore, why should we wear identity tags? Ah—it's regulations, is it? Now, what should I do? Should I sew on the tag, or not?

7

The question of wearing the identity tag or not is raised by the others on my second day in the Small Zone. As a measure of precaution, we go outside to talk. The house is bugged, so any conversations not intended for the ears of the authorities take place out in the yard. If anything confidential must be said inside, it is written down on a piece of paper which is later burned. But at present the weather is holding out, the discussion is likely to be a long one, so we spread our jackets on the ground and sit outside. Nobody tries to influence my decision either way: I am simply warned that as tomorrow is Monday, the supervisor of our fictional work brigade, Senior Lieutenant Podust, will be coming around to order me to don the identity tag. Therefore, it is best that I give the matter some thought now, and determine my course of action in order to avoid regrets later. I can see that the inmates of the Small Zone have rejected identity tags as a senseless and humiliating demand. But we are not a real brigade, and I am in no way bound to observe this Zone tradition: it is purely a matter for my own conscience. Not one of my new friends would expect me to emulate her behavior—we are free individuals, after all. The voice of my conscience has already given me a clear response, but nobody is pressing me for an instant declaration of intent.

Tatyana Mikhailovna explains that I, like everyone else on strict regime, am entitled to three meetings a year with relatives.

One is a "long" meeting, lasting from one to three days at the discretion of the camp authorities. Two other meetings, at least six months apart, last two hours. These "short" meetings take place across a table (you cannot even exchange a kiss) and a representative of the camp administration sits between you, with the power to terminate the meeting immediately should the conversation touch upon any forbidden subject. The long meeting could be granted virtually straight away. What a blissful thought: alone with Igor in the small meeting room, if only for twenty-four hours. And, oh, how I need such a meeting: there is a full collection of new poems in my head, I must get them out of here . . . And the Zone needs it, too, for it is past time for more information to go to the outside world. After all, so much has happened since the last lot: things like Tatyana Osipova's four-month hunger strike, just about everyone has been in the SHIZO, there was a strike . . . But Tatyana Mikhailovna makes no mention of these events; the time has not yet come to discuss such matters with me. She stresses that the administration can deprive me of any or all these meetings for "violation of camp regulations." As yet, I have a clean record and, should Igor arrive today, the camp authorities would be obliged by law to let us meet. Still, that is an impossibility, there is no way he could get here in under a week. First, he must receive my letter, informing him of my whereabouts, then the journey itself would take time . . .

But the question of the identity tag must be resolved tomorrow, and if I refuse to wear it, that will be construed as a violation. And that could mean a cancelled meeting. Before my time, the inmates of the Small Zone did not have to wear identity tags for some time; everyone realized the absurdity of it. Then the authorities began a gradual tightening up of the screws. Last autumn, Lieutenant Podust was assigned to the Zone, and she has a real fixation about identity tags. Indeed, the more ridiculous the regulation, the more it is to her taste. So, for the past six months she has been waging war with the Zone: cancelling meetings with relatives, depriving the women of use of the camp kiosk, threatening confinement to SHIZO . . . Therefore, my possible meeting with Igor is under a very real threat. Nor are the subsequent ones likely to be granted, either; the authorities are bound to find plenty of reasons to cancel them in the course of a year. The choice facing me is clear cut: either I wear the tag and have a meeting with Igor—possibly the only one for the next seven years—or I refuse, and take the consequences. In any case, the outlook for the future is bleak—SHIZO is SHIZO. What SHIZO is really like I have yet to experience, but I already know that it means cold, hunger, filth and inaction. SHIZO is total deprivation. Yet at present I am not particularly worried about the future: the meeting with Igor is another matter . . .

My dearest love, will you find it in your heart to forgive me for placing our possible meeting under threat? You know that I cannot do otherwise, that I dare not jump even once over this prison rod at their command. What would you do in my place? Did we not once promise each other that in the case of arrest we would not let them use either of us as a tool to blackmail the other? So I say firmly: "No, I won't wear the identity tag."

Oh, how hard it is, at times, to do what one must! And, paradoxically, how easy it is, too: would I have been happier if I had donned the identity tag, pleased Podust, had a meeting and retained access to the kiosk, and then, burning with shame, watched Tatyana Mikhailovna going off for a spell in SHIZO because she wears no identity tag, and I do? . . . Beyond a shadow of a doubt, that tag would have been a burning coal against my breast.

Tanya Osipova and Tatyana Mikhailovna beam delightedly at my words. "That's the spirit," approves Tanya, while Tatyana Mikhailovna makes certain: "Irochka, are you sure you have thought everything through carefully?"

My dears, I have, and Igor will understand, no matter what happens. So let's all rot in the SHIZO together, if need be. That's what camp is for—a test of strength. Nyurka the cat prowls over and settles herself in Tanya Osipova's lap. Nyurka doesn't wear an identity tag either. She purrs contentedly and rolls over on to her back. The spring sun is making itself felt.

Raya Rudenko is poking around in the ground, sowing seeds: flowers (which the law permits) and vegetables (which it doesn't).

We urban dwellers are not entrusted with such a vital task; it will be our job to water the crop later. Right now, Raya asks Natasha Lazareva and me to make some small wooden stakes to which future clumps of flowers will be tied. She needs several dozen of them. None of us are allowed to have tools of any kind apart from those essential for our sewing work. So there is neither a knife nor a hatchet to hand. Still, there is a hammer in the sewing room. What relation it has to sewing God knows, but one should never question one's luck. We dig around in the ground and find some longish, sharp pieces of flint—the soil around here is very stony. There are several boards in the woodshed, and we split them into pieces using a bit of flint as a wedge. Our success rate at producing suitable stakes is not high, but the unsuitable pieces can be used for kindling later. We laugh helplessly—talk about Stone Age technology!

Natasha is from Leningrad. She is serving a sentence for producing a *samizdat* journal, *Maria*, which was devoted to feminist issues. The problems raised in this journal, such as the double workload of Soviet women—eight hours at work followed by five to six hours queuing for food, the horrors of communal kitchens, doing the entire family wash in a hand basin—were to appear in the official Soviet press also, but much later, in 1986. In 1982, when Natasha was arrested, talking about such matters was classed as "anti-Soviet agitation and propaganda."

Natasha has tormented eyes and a merry mouth. We exchange jokes as we sit there, skinning our hands against the rough boards. Tomorrow, Natasha is being hospitalized: the camp food has wrought havoc with her intestines. Alas, she was not to be given any treatment after admission into the infirmary, but discharged for socializing with the maintenance staff. Right up to the beginning of 1984 the camp authorities accused her of malingering, and had her confined, time and again, to SHIZO. It took a number of our collective hunger strikes to finally secure medical treatment for her in 1984. She was diagnosed as suffering from neglected ulcerative colitis, an ailment impossible to cure in camp conditions ... But for the moment, we are all enjoying a peaceful, happy day. One of the few that is left to us.

The evening meal is brought around. That means it must be five o'clock. The meal consists of very salty water in which bits of fish—scales, guts and all—and a couple of small potatoes float dismally. Raya sets to work: carefully, she removes the scraps of fish and cleans them (better late than never). The pathetic handful of edible fish is chopped up together with the potatoes, a bit of garlic is added for flavor and the whole is topped with a frugal dash of sunflower seed oil; by law, we are supposed to get 15 grams of this oil per head daily. As for butter—well, we can forget about that for years to come. Presto, Small Zone Salad is served. A light meal, by any standards.

"A real lady never eats heavy food after six o'clock," we decide, amid laughter. As there is nothing else, there is not much left to do but laugh.

Tanya Osipova switches on our ancient black and white television set. It is constantly breaking down. We patch it up, it works for a few days, then another valve goes. At one stage, the camp management decided to connect this set to a master switch in the guardroom, and thus control what we could or could not watch. But Tanya Osipova and I quickly learned how to jumpstart it by crossing a couple of wires, and the guards pretended not to notice. Not everyone, after all, was like Lieutenant Podust and, truth to tell, they did not really care whether we watched television or not, so long as it was switched off after lights out. As far as the administration was concerned, steps had been taken to control our viewing, and that was all that was necessary for their report to tell to their overlords.

Today, however, nobody tries to interfere and we watch a play by Rostand: good old *Cyrano de Bergerac*. Tanya sheds tears as Cyrano dies. That's our Tanya; she'll cry over a book or a film, and then stick out four days, alone and unsupported in a solitary punishment cell, refusing food and water to get our confiscated Bible back. It worked, too. The administration caved in and our Bible was returned: they knew that the fifth day of a "dry" hunger strike—that is, when no fluids at all are ingested—is tantamount to a death warrant, and they did not want to risk the undesirable publicity that would ensue once the outside world got to hear that a political prisoner died because of a confiscated Bible. Admittedly, on that particular occasion, Tanya did get some quite unexpected support: there were prisoners from the criminal zone in neighboring cells, and they all conducted a twenty-four-hour hunger strike of solidarity. In fact, they intended to strike for a longer period, but Tanya herself dissuaded them—it is easier for the administration to implement reprisals against ordinary criminals than against the "politicals"; their situations would have been too disparate.

Tatyana Mikhailovna and I wander outside to look at the night sky. Nyurka follows us. They say that cats do not distinguish colors, and I wonder whether red Betelgeuse and yellow Capella look the same to her. We discuss the likelihood of this, then the talk veers to the human biological field, to Tatyana Mikhailovna's inexplicable aversion to cartoon films, to those we have left behind "out there" . . . It's harder for them than for us, right now. We have spent a quiet, pleasant day, whereas they will be tearing themselves apart with worry about us. By the time you write a letter, by the time it passes through censorship and reaches its destination, everything could have changed radically. They could be thinking that we are as well as can be expected, and in the meantime, we would all have been consigned to SHIZO. As a matter of fact, the censors will not let any mention of SHIZO go through; "Nothing about punishments" is the standing order. Absolute shrinking violets, our KGB: they are ready to torment us from morning till night, but they are too shy to let the world know about it. And we have to maintain silence, too, or our letters will be confiscated. But we'll get the better of you yet, boys—we shall do our utmost to spread the word about everything that goes on here. You can deprive us of our meetings with our loved ones, confiscate our correspondence, but the information will still go out and reach its target. How shall we manage that? Ah, these are our zek secrets. I would gladly share them with all decent, honest people, but—who knows?—this book may fall into KGB hands . . . As they say, the less you know, the sounder you sleep.

8

The next morning, Raya Rudenko sets about getting me clothed, for the two chintz dresses issued to me are nowhere near adequate. Although it's April, the frosts will be with us until June; quite a while to walk around shivering. Clothing is always a problem for the politicals: our Zone is appended to the hospital, and that has no clothing allocation—who needs clothes in hospital? Therefore we are not eligible for standard zek-issue apparel. It's one thing for the authorities to dress two to three thousand prisoners, but clothing five women appears to pose insuperable problems. So we get whatever is left over in the store, and that is invariably short of something. The disadvantage of this state of affairs is that while your own things are confiscated, there is no regulation issue to replace them. Yet there are advantages, too, in that you can't walk around half-naked, so the administration will occasionally turn a blind eye to the wearing of non-regulation clothing. You can run up something for yourself out of miscellaneous bits and pieces (including scraps of mattress ticking) and there's not much anyone can do about it. As the camp authorities have nothing to offer instead, they must accept our improvisations, willy-nilly. Of course, we make the most of our pitiful opportunities, because anything is an improvement, both in appearance and comfort, on regulation issue. The result is that we even appear to be better dressed than the ordinary women prisoners.

About eighteen months before my arrival, the women in our Zone were unexpectedly issued railway-type coveralls made out of heavy drill, with metal buttons embossed with crossed rifles. Heaven knows whose uniforms they had been originally. The ever-economical Raya (she is our "housekeeper") saved one of these coveralls for the proverbial rainy day when someone left the Zone to go into exile. The coverall is so large I can wrap it around myself twice, but that makes a choice of style possible—there's more than enough material here to work with. Why should style be a matter for concern in this place? After all, who is there to look at us? If it comes to that, I won't even be able to see myself, because the largest mirror in the Zone is no bigger than a dessert plate. Yet a woman is a woman wherever she may be, and I start designing my future skirt—should it have four gores, or six?—in all seriousness. Well, perhaps not quite in all seriousness, because I can't help laughing at myself. Nevertheless . . .

With great enthusiasm, I undertake to alter a similar coverall for Raya. I had done a little sewing before my arrest (I could hardly afford to buy anything decent on my tiny income) and now I can't wait to take up needle and thread again. Sewing materials were a problem in the KGB prison; occasionally they would let you have a needle for fifteen minutes and a piece of thread about one and a half meters long, but at other times you could get neither. Should you wear holes in your socks (and you do, because they take away your shoelaces), you must hand them in for mending by the service personnel of the prison. Judging by the results, you may as well simply throw the socks away, because the clear aim of the service personnel is to discourage any such requests. So it came about that in prison, I went around with gaping holes all over me. But here in the camp I can get what I need, because needles are allowed and there are even electric sewing machines in our workroom. Just as well our allotted work is sewing.

Seeing my enthusiasm, Raya drags me off to the "projection hut." Once upon a time they used to show films in the Zone— one a week—so a small hut was constructed to store projection and other necessary equipment. Then the film showings were abandoned, the equipment was taken away, and the hut was used to store old padded jackets and *babushki's*[1] rags. Why *babushki's*? Because there had been women in our Zone who had spent twenty to thirty years—some even longer—in other camps. They belonged to the so-called True Orthodox Christians, those who refused to join the official Russian Orthodox Church after the death of Patriarch Tikhon, or to recognize the Patriarch whom the Bolsheviks put in his place. These Christians—faithful to the memory of their driven Patriarch and their crucified Church— became a catacomb church, just like the church of the early Christians. They lived their daily lives in the world (who would have ceded them a monastery?) but under a number of self-imposed restrictions: they refused to work in any Soviet institution and to so much as handle Soviet documents or Soviet money, as something emanating from Satan. They would work privately for people of good will, who paid them in kind, with food and clothing which they did not need themselves. From the point of view of the Soviet government the True Orthodox were, naturally, malicious violators of internal passport regulations, parasites, and, worst of all, unregistered religious believers.[2] It follows that they received sentence after sentence. In the camps they refused to work, which meant spending more time in the internal camp prison than out of it. Nobody but the KGB knows how many True Orthodox Christians perished in the camps. Yet some survived, and our *babushki* were from their number. That is how they were referred to in the Zone—*babushki*—because by that time most of them were very old and ill. The other zeks and the guards called them nuns. Later, by association, we came to be known as nuns, too: "Where are you coming from?"

"From 'Three,'[3] political zone."

"Oh, you're one of the nuns, then . . ."

These gentle, steadfast and humble women obviously made a powerful impression on everyone who encountered them. And

1. *Babushka* (pl. *babushki*) is the Russian word for "grandmother."
2. Under Soviet law, all religious communities must receive state permission (registration) to exist legally.
3. The Barashevo zone was Number Three.

understandably so. An ordinary female zek will shower you with
a string of curses for the most trivial reason, but these women
would react quite differently: "May the Lord forgive you, my
son."

Even upon release, they would refuse to accept the document attesting to the completion of their sentence. Off they
would go, without a single scrap of paper, heading for a new
and certain arrest and sentence. From their point of view, this
was perfectly normal: were they not suffering for God? In their
eyes, it is we who act unnaturally: we submit to Satan and his
minions—the Soviet government—in order to escape persecution. And Satan, they know, will never give up of his own
accord—he will merely exploit any sign of weakness to his
greater gain, penetrate ever deeper into your soul. That was and
is the reasoning of the True Orthodox. Some of them are still
alive, living in internal exile. Yet the exile sentences of some of
our *babushki* had expired, and they did not return to the Zone;
so Satan was defeated, after all, forced into retreat. Others of
them are still to be found in some of the camps, with calm,
serene faces, ever ready to lay down their lives for the Lord: to
what greater honor can one aspire?

How many of them are there, International Red Cross? No
answer. They don't know, and how could they? How many of them
are there, Amnesty International? Silence. They do not know,
either. How many of them are there, official Soviet Patriarch of All
Russia, Pimen? He, too, is silent. Maybe he really does not know:
the True Orthodox are outside his jurisdiction, so why worry about
them? How many of them are there, the KGB of the Union of Soviet
Socialist Republics? Silence. They *do* know, but won't tell.

About eight True Orthodox passed through our Zone, the last
being Granny Manya and Granny Shura. From our Zone, they
went on to serve out their terms of internal exile. Granny Manya,
according to the stories I heard, was meek and gentle. She found
joy in the smallest things, such as the sight of a tiny beetle on a
leaf: Look, she would say, how wondrous are the works of the
Lord. How detailed, how perfect. How beautiful are all God's
creatures.

Granny Shura was made of sterner stuff, and given to uttering "denunciations" from time to time. She would march out and upbraid the inhabitants of the Zone for succumbing regularly to temptation: watching television, smoking, forgetting to pray— iniquity! Her denunciations, however, were never motivated by spite, but by her sense of duty, and occurred not more than once every two to three months. She herself explained it thus:

"The Lord will ask me: 'Did you sin?' And I will reply, saying: 'Not a great deal, Lord.' 'What about the people around you? Did they sin?' So I will have to say: 'Yes, they did.' 'And what did you do about it?' He will ask. 'Why did you not point out the error of their ways?' So that's what I'm doing, it's my duty. Forgive me, for His sake."

In the Zone the *babushki*, with endless patience, repaired everything for everyone; any heavier work was physically beyond them. The camp authorities tried to avoid placing them into the camp prison, because they were so frail it would have taken very little to kill them. But other inmates were not spared the camp prison and the *babushki*, their hearts wrung by compassion, did all they could to help as much as possible. In punishment cells you are stripped to your underwear and given a special smock: its low neckline rivals the most daring ballgown, and it has very wide, three-quarter-length sleeves to ensure that the wearer will freeze. That's what these cells are for—officially known as SHIZO, punishment isolation cells. Extreme cold is regarded as a necessary feature of the corrective process, but it never yielded the required results with the women in our Zone. The *babushki*— experienced zeks one and all—did everything possible to beat the cold. They sewed underwear out of flannel footcloths (long strips to be wound around one's feet) which were issued for winter, and, whenever possible, quilted them on the inside with cotton wool. Instead of brassieres, they made something akin to shortened vests. Everything was multilayered for maximum warmth. All these garments were made out of a multitude of scraps of cloth, for large pieces of material were not obtainable in the camp. So we inherited a box full of what we called the "*babushki*'s trousseau." Looking at the shirts they had made, I found them to be a veritable patchwork of all shades and textures: here a scrap of cotton, here something knitted, there a small woolen insert—all painstakingly gathered and cobbled together into a garment. The underwear they produced would hardly have merited that name elsewhere—at first glance, one was hard put to determine which part of the body it was supposed to cover. Everything was much worn, much washed, carefully darned again and again. In some cases, there were patches on patches, darns on darns. And all done with such care, such love for one's neighbor, as if for oneself! Not only were the *babushki* willing to sacrifice the shirts off their backs for others, they tried to prolong the life of every bit of clothing *ad infinitum*.

And for some reason, as I looked upon this "inheritance," my throat constricted painfully and, for the first time since I became a zek, I felt tears in my eyes. My dear ones, how many times did you don these rags and head for the SHIZO? How much human warmth is stored up in these beggar-like witnesses to the ingenuity of our *babushki*? What twentieth-century museum has such artifacts to display? There are concentration camps that have become memorial shrines—Auschwitz, Treblinka—but each tattered garment in that box had had a longer life than the period those camps existed. Those terrible camps were closed and became museums. And our Zone existed even then, and the "bustiers" wrought by the *babushki* lay in their box, awaiting the next spell in SHIZO.

The SHIZO was waiting for us, too. It did not have to wait long. By the end of the next winter, however, the camp authorities suddenly took exception to non-regulation underwear. Women's regulation underclothing consists of one item—a sacklike shift with shoulder straps, made out of the same material as the bedsheets. Everything else was ordered to be confiscated and burned, or—who knows?—the prisoners may not be cold enough. And that would be a serious impediment to the re-education process. So the handiwork of the *babushki* was duly confiscated and burned. Just as well none of the *babushki* will ever know—they were all gone from our camp by that time. Those who are still alive probably continue to rejoice in the thought that their creations made us feel a little bit warmer. And let them continue to think so.

The trousseau left by the *babushki* was reduced to ashes; no one else will ever look upon it and feel the sting of tears in their eyes. Our Zone is closed now, too, but I fear that it will be a long, long time before it becomes a memorial to times gone by.

9

Our Zone was now in its last days of peace. We all sensed this, and it gave an added edge to the pleasure of spending mild May evenings digging around in the not yet forbidden vegetable patch, tanning surreptitiously in a spot behind the hut which was not visible from the guard tower, writing letters (a whole two letters a month) which, at that time, were still reaching their destinations instead of being confiscated as a matter of course. My two-day meeting with Igor had been permitted despite my refusal to wear the identity tag. Although he was searched and checked, Igor managed to smuggle a considerable amount of information out of the Zone: a diary of recent events and my first collection of prison poetry. The feeling that I had acquitted myself well in the KGB prison and in my first weeks in camp made me feel as though I were walking on air.

Yet the storm clouds were gathering and Lieutenant Podust buzzed around us like an angry wasp, seeking out any excuse to make trouble: "Why are there clothes drying in the workroom?"

"Because it has rained for the past three days. Where else can we dry them when we can't hang them up outside?"

"I don't care where you dry them, but you can't do it inside. Don't wash at all, then, but don't you go breaking regulations."

"But the camp regulations stipulate that prisoners must be clean and tidy at all times," objects our "lawyer," Tanya Osipova.

"You, Osipova, and you, Velikanova—get ready for PKT.[1] You're a bad influence on the others."

PKT amounts to a prison within the camp. Our humane laws allow confinement of prisoners to PKT for a period of up to six months at a time. Food in PKT is issued in accordance with the so-called limited norm—in other words, it means constant malnutrition. Letters are reduced to one every two months, any meetings with relatives are suspended for the duration of confinement to PKT (and, for that matter, SHIZO). If you are consigned to PKT for six months, your annual meeting with relatives moves a further six months into an uncertain future. As is to be expected, filth and cold are an integral part of life in PKT. The cell is the same as SHIZO, the only difference being that in PKT you get to wear your own zek clothes—the ones you are allowed to keep, that is, after a dozen checks to ensure that you have not managed to slip on something warm under your blouse. In short, a cheerful outlook . . .

Podust redoubles her efforts: "Lazareva! Have you got socks in your bed again?"

Striding into the Zone, she heads purposefully for Natasha's bed, turning it inside out to search for those wretched socks. She knows, the bitch, that Natasha is particularly sensitive to the cold, is running a constant temperature and therefore sleeps in woolen socks (our blankets being what you could call symbolic), which she keeps in her bed with her nightdress, separately from her other things. Storage space is at a premium anyway, because every small bedside locker must be shared by two prisoners. These lockers have two shelves and one drawer, and everything must be crammed into them—letters, toothpowder, clothes and the like. At first, after the *babushki* left the Zone to go into exile, there was one locker for every prisoner and the "surplus" lockers were removed only a year later. Even so, it was a tight squeeze. Try to picture it for yourself, my readers: go through your cupboards and wardrobes and pick out what you would consider to be the barest essentials to serve you for the next seven years. Don't forget to include your maximum allowance of five books, letters,

1. Abbreviation of *Pomeshcheniye Kamernogo Tipa.*

photographs of your nearest and dearest (whom you won't see for years to come), stamps, envelopes, those treacherous underclothes, a couple of towels . . . Hold it! You're overdoing it a bit, aren't you? Forget about the address book—that will be confiscated during your very first search. Better just sit down and memorize the most important address. Put that toothpaste back, too, it's against regulations. You can take a box of toothpowder, though. And why are you packing those red socks? Do you want to find yourself on report for them, the way Lagle Parek, later to join us in the Small Zone, did in 1985, and forfeit a meeting with a relative? Better not risk it. You're taking a track suit? What on earth for? To do exercises? Well, of course, doing exercises is not forbidden by the regulations, but there is no time set aside for them, and it's better not to keep the track suit in your locker: it will be confiscated. Stow it away somewhere safe. Oh, and keep the amount of underwear down to a minimum; the regulations are that you wear one set, and have one change only. You could try secreting a few more things, but the chances are they will be found and confiscated.

Now take a look: see how much stuff you have gathered? Virtually impossible to pick it all up at once, isn't it? And now, try to fit it all into a locker with an actual storage space of thirty by thirty by seventy centimeters. It must be stowed tidily, too, so Podust will have no cause for complaint. You can be sure that a year later your storage space will be halved. You can always try keeping your things in the store, but bear in mind that it is kept locked and the duty officer, who has the keys, might not show up in the Zone from one week's end to the next. Furthermore, you can always be stopped and searched as you leave the store, just to check what it is you're taking out and that it's not too much. In the meantime, the rats inside the locked store will have unimpeded access to your property, and it will be a while before you solve that problem by making a hole in the bottom of the door so that Nyurka can squeeze through and restore order. The windows of the store are firmly sealed off with sheet iron, so you can forget about breaching them . . . In such circumstances you, too, will have problems finding room for a pair of socks.

Still, Podust may not choose you as her victim; her choice is emaciated, highly strung Natasha Lazareva—an ideal candidate from Podust's perverted viewpoint. While under investigation after her second arrest (always much harder than the first), Natasha faltered. She signed a statement of repentance, took part in a television program, but was still sentenced to four years—admittedly with no exile term to follow. The KGB decided that she would be their informer in our Zone. But all their carefully laid plans foundered. At first Natasha agreed to wear an identity tag (later she tore it off and threw it into the stove), but she flatly refused to inform on those with whom she shared skilly. Moreover, she was unsubmissive by nature and ever sensitive to any hint of injustice, especially here, in the camp, where the difference between the human and the inhuman is so painfully manifest. What was she to do? She told us everything, and we never reproached her with the past, even though there were certain sanctimonious souls "out there" who declared that they could not possibly "forgive her betrayal." Christ preached forgiveness, but the moral code of the "builders of communism" preaches just the opposite—intolerance and irreconcilability. Not exactly a multitude of options.

Of course, the KGB builders of communism were hardly motivated by Christian feelings toward Natasha; on the contrary, they were infuriated by her refusal to cooperate just when they thought they had her on the spot. So let's scare her a bit more, they decided, let's make her life such a misery, she won't know which way to turn. That's why Podust made Natasha the focus of her attention, ignoring the rest of us for the time being.

At first, Podust did not harass me. Even though the length of my sentence spoke for itself, I looked so much younger than my years that she obviously thought she would be able to sway me at any time with little or no effort. She caught me alone once and tried fishing for information about the subjects discussed in the Zone, even though there was nothing in my previous record to encourage such an approach. Although I refused, then and there, to tell her anything and added a pithy indictment of her attempts to weasel information out of me, she did not start to persecute me immediately. That was to come after our first hunger strikes. For the present, she was concentrating on Natasha, with the occasional jab at Tanya or Tatyana Mikhailovna.

Podust's reasoning was patently obvious. Tatyana Mikhailovna Velikanova was a member of the Initiative Group for the Defense of Human Rights, an active human rights campaigner since 1968, a woman whose name was known worldwide and therefore, in Podust's opinion, a socially undesirable element. The KGB and Podust shared a belief in the theory that it is environment that determines consciousness, so they could never understand how someone could evolve independent views. Because of this, they were always searching for "bad influences." Outside the camps, the standard scapegoats are foreign radio stations—where else could a Soviet citizen pick up ideas about human dignity or rights? But the only broadcasts to be heard inside the Zone are from Moscow Radio, so what could possibly be the source of treacherous ideas? Why, of course, it must be Velikanova leading the rest of us astray! She is older than the rest of us "second generation" dissidents, and it is quite clear that we acknowledge her authority in our debates and discussions. Tanya Osipova is rated as a youngster—she is only thirty-four. Nevertheless, how much she managed to accomplish before they locked her up in 1980! Her indictment, for instance, reflects her defense of the rights of fifteen nationalities in the USSR, let alone her defense of universal human rights. She played an active part in the production of the famous clandestine *Chronicle of Current Events*, was a member of the unofficial Helsinki Monitoring Group, and always exhibited the same "unhealthy" interest in scrutinizing Soviet laws as Velikanova. That was considered far more dangerous than my poetry or, indeed, the poetry of Mykola Rudenko, which led to the imprisonment of his wife Raya. That, however, was also considered an outrage, so they gave Rudenko, poet and Helsinki Monitor, seven years plus five. Then, to add insult to injury, Mykola's wife, instead of showing proper feeling and denouncing and renouncing him, travelled up to see him at every possible opportunity and, what's more, smuggled out his poetry by some unknown means instead of doing the right thing and handing it over to the KGB. She concealed his work, she disseminated it, she memorized every word; indeed, Raya knew Mykola's work better than he did himself. What she did was, perhaps, the greatest stroke of luck ever for Ukrainian literature, but it earned her a sentence of five plus five: camps, then internal exile.

These were the kind of people gathered in our Small Zone. The KGB was in no doubt that we needed to be ruled with an iron hand. One can understand why Lieutenant Podust, with military directness, told us: "It's not my job to prove to you that you are wrong. I don't have the education or the words for that. My job is much easier: to make your life here so miserable you'll never want to come back."

And she tried to do just that, to the very limits of her ability and opportunities, with an incredible pettiness to be found only in a bored woman endowed with extensive powers. We called her the "blonde fiend"—for some reason, she always evoked Fascist images. So we were not particularly surprised to learn, after we had managed to establish a clandestine correspondence with the men's zone, that there she was universally known as "Ilse Koch": and this by a hundred men, totally deprived of female society and despite the fact that she was young, very good looking, blonde and invariably well dressed. Yet she reminded them, too, of that very Ilse Koch who, nostrils flaring with pleasure, personally tortured and killed prisoners in Ravensbrück concentration camp . . .

Even my Igor, who had scarcely any contact with the men's zone, mentally dubbed her "Ilse Koch" the very first time he met her. True, it was not a very fortuitous meeting:

"What is it you people want?" she snarled at him as soon as they met. "I don't make those women lick my boots as though they were common criminals, do I?" I am certain, however, that her sweetest and most unfulfillable dream would have been of the Small Zone collectively licking her boots . . .

10

Reveille is at 6:00 a.m. That means the warders will be along to count us (just in case someone has escaped overnight) and, at the same time, make sure that nobody is still in bed. The ordinary zeks are lined up for the morning count, irrespective of the weather, and remain in line until all two or three thousand have been leisurely counted. Occasionally they have to stand in line for thirty minutes to an hour before the count even starts. Moreover, they can be searched during the count. I remember from one of my stretches in SHIZO how the neighboring cell was occupied by one Yulia N. who had refused to lift up her blouse in the line-up when overseer Kravchenko took it into her head that Yulia might have put on a civilian-type sweater under the blouse. It was, after all, a very cold November with severe frosts. Maybe Yulia had provided herself with some illegal warmth. When this "incorrigible criminal" refused to undo her blouse, she was immediately given nine days in punishment cell, and stripped by force, anyway.

Having a line-up in our Small Zone is senseless, because we can be counted on the fingers of one hand; moreover, it is a moot point whether we would agree to such a thing. Every refusal on our part to fulfill some asinine official demand is perceived by the administration as a personal humiliation, so they're a bit more circumspect in their dealings with us. There are, after all, plenty of other reasons to harass us: our refusal to wear identity tags alone provides great scope for repressive measures.

So the morning starts with the concession of no line-up. The warders stamp through (why has nobody ever taught them to wipe their boots before coming in from outside?) and leave. They will return at about 8:00 a.m. with our breakfast. This usually consists of wheat or oat porridge, or what purports to be pearl barley but which we call "pansies" because for some reason it turns blue when it cools. Actually, "pansies" is its prison nickname. In the army, where the soldiers loathe this pearl barley every bit as much as we do, it is commonly referred to as "shrapnel." Oats are nicknamed "Oh-Ho-Ho" and wheat porridge is "speckled hen." Breakfast is important, for it determines whether we shall remain hungry until dinner, or not. You would not think it possible to ruin a dish consisting of only three ingredients—the main one being water, then grain, then salt— would you? It is possible, though, if you use an inordinate amount of salt. Just throw it in without stinting, and in no time at all you will have us bloated like so many balloons through fluid retention; Raya Rudenko, who has a kidney ailment, will collapse altogether. The swelling of the body is easily explained—it is the physiological reaction to the introduction of too much salt into a semi-starved organism.

Later, in the autumn, when food portions were drastically reduced and we were starving rather than half-starving, even the exclusion of salt did not stop our bodies from swelling. It happened to each one of us with varying degrees of severity. Our camp medical officer, Vera Alexandrovna, described this condition delicately as "protein-deficiency distension." The swelling came as no surprise to us: it has been known since time immemorial that starving bodies swell up. As for protein deficiency, how on earth could we remedy that? The regulations stipulate that each zek should have 50 grams raw weight of meat daily (33 grams when cooked) and 75 grams raw weight of fish. However, raw products are never issued to us, and it is categorically forbidden that we should cook for ourselves. Cooking is done by the hospital service staff, and our portions are brought to us. This means that our rations pass through two barriers of theft: one part is stolen by the guards, and another by the hospital kitchen help.

The remainder comes to us cooked, in portions considerably smaller than the statutory 33 grams of cooked meat and 45 grams of cooked fish per head. We were never able to establish the exact extent of the shortfall because prisoners do not have scales or other measuring equipment. Anyway, that was the total amount of our protein . . .

We could, however, determine that overabundant use of salt with our tastebuds. Testing food for salt was one of the tasks of whoever happened to be "Cinderella," a duty each one of us undertook on a weekly rotation basis. Cinderella's main job was to wage war with the kitchen by refusing to accept food which was unfit for consumption. Too much salt in the porridge? Back it goes. We'll sit around hungry and write letters of complaint to the Procuracy, despite the fact that nobody there bothers to read them. Occasionally, the results of such complaints border on the surreal: you write a complaint, say, that light summer shoes have not been issued despite standing regulations, and the reply you receive states: "Sentence found to be just, and is not subject to appeal." But although our complaints are not heeded as such, a tally is kept of their number. The Procuracy has its records to keep. And so: "What's this, comrades? Forty complaints from Corrective Colony Number Three in one month? A bit over the top, isn't it? Aren't you conducting re-education work among your prisoners?"

How, one might ask, can our camp officials do anything of the kind? If they increase repressive measures against us, we'll swamp the Procuracy with a torrent of protests. On top of that, we might go on hunger strike. Of course, punishment for hunger strikes is severe, but the camp commander won't escape entirely un-scathed, either: a hunger strike means an emergency situation in the camp, which, in turn, means that our administrators will get reprimands instead of bonuses. So on a number of occasions our administration preferred to back down: "All right, damn you, have your food without salt!"

The need to conduct incessant, enervating battles for the most trivial rights is the main feature of daily life in the camp. What was the sum of our victories? Skilly without maggots in it; issue of the correct bread ration for the Zone (Cinderella demands a receipt to ensure there is no shortfall); 15 grams of sunflower oil per head; the right to wear shoes instead of boots in summer (no mean achievement—try wearing tarpaulin boots when the temperature hits 35°C! Women in other Mordovian camps still have to do this); the right to send and receive registered letters. All these concessions were the result of our Zone's stubborn, united determination to fight for every trifle.

Yet every defeat suffered by us in this endless warfare meant permanent loss. For instance, in the spring of 1986 we lost the above-mentioned 15 grams of sunflower oil. With brazen effrontery, the adminstration informed us that henceforth our allocation of oil was being mixed into our food (try to check that!) so oil would no longer be issued separately. Naturally, we all knew what we ought to do in this situation: had we not won the "salt war" by returning absolutely everything cooked in the kitchen for three whole weeks? We were reduced to skin and bones, but held out to the end, even though Camp Commander Porshin declared: "If I get a directive to serve you pineapple—why, I'll do so! But as you're supposed to get twenty-five grams of salt per head, I'll see to it personally that that amount goes into your food."

Although Porshin received no orders to serve us pineapple, he had to back down over the salt, too. The row we kicked up reached the Central Administration of Corrective Labor Institutions. They sent a group to check us out (and we looked really choice by that time) and it was decided that the best thing to do was to ease up on us and hush up the whole incident.

But we lost out over the oil: nobody in the Zone at that time had the strength to go on an indefinite hunger strike. If a hunger strike is to be effective, everyone must take part in it, but if half the Zone refuses food while the other half eats, the adminstration's reaction is predictable: "So what are you going on about? Your friends are eating without complaint, aren't they?"

In such a situation, you simply cannot carry your point. We conferred among ourselves and came to the conclusion that we were not up to a hunger strike right then. So we had to swallow the "innovation" and lose our oil rations. Luckily, the overall food situation that spring was not too drastic, or who can say what the ultimate price of that weakness might have been? But, oh, how infuriating was the realization that we were in no condition to conduct a hunger strike then, and that afterwards would be too late. Still, it is better to act sensibly rather than take on something we might not be able to carry through. Camp life had already taught us that.

But now we are still in the summer of 1983, and Raya comes in with our porridge—it's edible today—brews tea for everyone, and we sit around the table planning that day's activities. Theoretically, we should be at our sewing machines from 7:00 a.m. until 4:00 p.m., making industrial gloves. The daily quota is seventy pairs per prisoner. A dray delivers them to us, already cut and ready for sewing. The dray is pulled by a friendly, tired-looking mare called Starlet. Poor thing, she always has gashes here and there on her body from barbed wire, of which there is an abundance all over Barashevo, so the hapless Starlet invariably injures herself as the dray maneuvers through its tangles. We have to unload the dray, drag the packages of gloves into the workroom of our little house, sew up the gloves, turn them right side out, pack them into lots of twenty pairs and load them onto the dray when it comes again. This job could have been a real curse were it not for three things.

First, it is physically impossible for the administration to check when we are working and when we aren't. Neither the warders nor the officers are in the Zone all the time. They come in to do the daily head-count, to conduct searches, to bring our food, or simply to check on what we are doing and whether we are still alive. It is absolutely impossible for them to take us by surprise because there is a path from the Zone gate to the house, and the gate is clearly visible from our windows. So we can always see who is coming and make an educated guess about their business. Furthermore, the gate makes a great deal of noise when it's opened. There are not enough sewing machines for everyone, so we work in two to three shifts. That makes checking even harder: the second shift works until 1:00 a.m. So the administration decided to take the line of least resistance, so long as the work was all completed and submitted on time. That means we can pretty much choose our own working hours.

Secondly, the supervisor in charge of production, Vasili Petrovich, is a very decent person. His job is to ensure that the two political zones—the men's and the women's—meet the set production targets, and he knows that in dealing with politicals, it is better to tread softly. It is highly unlikely that he would have acted harshly in any case, because there was no nastiness in him, either outwardly or inwardly. Instead of pressuring us, he prefers to adapt to existing circumstances. Natasha Lazareva, for instance, simply cannot meet the daily quota—all right, then. Let her do as much as she can. Vasili Petrovich will simply juggle things so that some invalid in the men's zone, who doesn't have to turn out a full quota, can make up Natasha's shortfall and earn himself a little extra to spend in the camp kiosk. The important thing is that the overall production quota will be met and, thanks to Vasili Petrovich, everyone will be satisfied—the administration (whose bonus payments depend on the plan being fulfilled) and the zeks, who, if necessary, will go out of their way to help Vasili Petrovich. He would come into our Zone from time to time, fair lashes blinking rapidly, with an appeal: "Girls, they've taken fifteen from the men's zone to Saransk, and we're coming up to the end of the quarter. The annual production plan is standard, nobody's going to change it. If you could do me three thousand gloves by the end of the month, I'll organize a break for you later."

So we would do the gloves, and he would be as good as his word about a break. After all, the whole production process is bedeviled by delays of various kinds: there's no electricity, or the gloves to be sewn up have not been delivered, or the sewing machines keep breaking down. All the sewing machines are ancient models which have been written off elsewhere and, you might say, function only thanks to the power of Vasili Petrovich's prayers. The administration knows perfectly well that Vasili Petrovich plays the liberal in his dealings with us. This causes some grumbling, but nobody does anything about it, knowing full well that in the general maelstrom of delays and inefficiency, only

Vasili Petrovich can get the work done and meet the production targets. Therefore when he holds off delivering work to us for a week, and we laze around without so much as setting a stitch, nobody says a word. Vasili Petrovich is the only one who can persuade us to salvage the plan by working flat out when things look bad, so the administration tolerates him as he is: kind-hearted, wily, and a great hand at getting things done, the only member of the Barashevo camp personnel who really works.

Thirdly, we do our work conscientiously: if we are on strike, then we are on strike, and even Vasili Petrovich can't sway us (in any case, he was always philosophical about our strikes—politicals are politicals, what can you do?), but when we work, we really work. We turn out first-class gloves as a point of honor, we do not sabotage the equipment, and see nothing demeaning in our job: the gloves produced by us are used by workers on building sites and not by our persecutors. What use would a KGB officer or some Party boss have for protective industrial gloves? We sew as many gloves as we can—but Vasili Petrovich is always pleased with us and will affirm that we have sewn up everything he gave us; he knows our limits and never tries to load us beyond our capacity. In any case, just let anyone try to take Natasha Lazareva or someone else to task about how many gloves she has made on a given day—they would be hard put to establish how many each of us made in a month. We supply Vasili Petrovich with figures (for accountancy and payment purposes), but we have our own system to determine how much production to credit to whom. And should we see that someone is being targeted for victimization, who can stop us from putting her down as having made more gloves and ourselves as less? No, the camp authorities prefer not to poke their noses into our work; they know that they will only make fools of themselves and place the production plan under threat. In this instance, it is they who are dependent on us, and not vice versa.

So, in fact, our work is not a burden; we sew as much as we can when we feel like it. There are, of course, times when you might spend twelve hours a day at the machine (when Vasili Petrovich has put out a distress signal), but that is voluntary, and a challenge. Yet on a day when you feel ill or out of sorts, you may not go anywhere near a sewing machine. When you're up to it, you'll catch up, if not—the others will help you; we're all in this together, after all. However, sitting over our breakfast we discuss our own Zone problems rather than production matters. For instance, what should we plant in our vegetable patch? We are not supposed to grow vegetables or fruit, so we do it under the guise of flowers and shrubs. I send requests to my husband along the following lines: "Dearest, please send me seeds to grow asters, gladioli, onions and cucumbers." The words "onions" and "cucumbers" are the English words written in Cyrillic letters. As the names of these vegetables are quite different in Russian, how can our censors guess what these mysterious "onions" and "cucumbers" really are? Later, all the seeds we had were confiscated (apart from the ones we managed to hide) and receipt of seeds by mail was forbidden. But while the "golden days" lasted, we used to get seeds stuck to strips of adhesive tape by registered mail. There was, however, little we could do about the vagaries of the Mordovian climate . . . In one of my letters home (by a stroke of luck we managed to get our entire correspondence out of the USSR when we left), I wrote: "Thank you for the seeds, they're exactly what we need. Fortunately we didn't have time to plant them, because the weather has gone from bad to worse: frosts, rains, hailstorms, and then the whole cycle over again. June 26, 1983."

Today, Raya heard the weather forecast on Mordovian radio, and they said there would be a ground frost tonight. That means that this evening we shall have to rig up some ingenious wooden supports (using stools, among other things) and then drape blankets and pieces of plastic over them to save our seedlings from destruction. We shall also refrain from planting anything new for the time being. Tatyana Mikhailovna gets to work sewing bits of plastic bags together, all the ones we can find, to make an insulating sheet. Tanya and I go to water our crop, drawing buckets of water from an improvised well. There is a leaky pipe under our Zone, so we dug a hole, lined its sides with pieces of wood and, as a result, had a well of ice-cold water. The administration looked askance at this well at first, but finally let it be. Just at that time, the hospital water supply broke down, and our Zone would have been without water for a whole week had it not been for that well. Rather than make emergency arrangements to keep us supplied with water, the administration decided to let us make do with our well. So we had a constant supply of fresh water for our vegetable patch. Natasha busies herself by the hole into which we dump scraps—she's making a cover for it. Nothing goes to waste in our Zone. Say the soup is inedible, and the duty Cinderella has missed her opportunity to send it back to the kitchen. What do we do with it? We tip it into our refuse pit, as we do the dish-washing water. We have no sanitation, so all used water is carried out in buckets: soapy water from the washing of clothes goes into one pit, everything else into the scraps pit, including cut grass and peelings of vegetables from our patch. The local soil is very sandy, but the soil in our Zone has been "enriched" for decades. Poor Podust once even admitted to us that her husband had pointed out nastily that the cucumbers she had grown were wizened dwarfs by comparison with the ones the politicals had in their vegetable patch. Maybe it was this that made Podust regard our little vegetable garden with such dislike?

11

The day progresses: Raya is busy with some household task or other in the house, Tanya is reading the journal *Literary Questions* and I poke fun by asking insidiously whether there is, anywhere in the world, a journal called *Literary Answers*? And, if there are no answers, what is the use of questions? Natasha puffs and pants over our burnt-out iron; she has taken it to pieces and is now trying to reconnect its blackened wiring. Tatyana Mikhailovna and I go off to cut firewood. We were allowed to drag some logs from an old fence into the Zone, and they will be our firewood for the autumn. Even now we can get some very cold days. The stoves in our Zone are as ancient as can be, missing a lot of bricks, but better than nothing. Just an hour ago Tanya accidentally converted the stove in our dining area into a fireplace by taking a swipe at a fly with our home-made swatter. The blow dislodged two bricks which were miraculously holding the stove door in place. Now the front of the stove is a gaping hole, and we can't stop laughing about it, because the fly got away. Sawing firewood is a long and boring job. The logs are very thick—they probably kept that fence standing ever since the Mordovian Dubrovlag[1] was founded. Tatyana Mikhailovna and I are both city-dwellers, but we manage to get the hang of how to saw and

1. From the early 1940s, a network of strict regime camps in Mordovia for especially dangerous habitual criminals and persons sentenced for especially dangerous crimes against the state. The administrative headquarters are in Potma.

our work moves on apace, enlivened by conversation. What do we talk about? Anything and everything, as usual. Tatyana Mikhailovna will be leaving the Zone in the autumn to serve her term of exile, and we are both conscious of how little time we have left to enjoy each other's company.

The following poem is the only one I wrote for Tatyana Mikhailovna while she was with us, and even later I dedicated fewer poems to her than I should have. Yet she was the most important person in the Zone to me: the closest friend, the wisest counselor and an example of that incredible patience toward the failings of others that should be a hallmark of life in the camps. She was also a walking encyclopedia of the human rights movement and its traditions. How many times, after she had gone, I was to recall with gratitude her enormous achievement in establishing the honorable practices of dignity and care for others in the Zone.

> A clumsy saw,
> Plenty of sawdust.
> Pre-autumn work.
> Let's live till exile!
> Soon, soon you'll be joining the convoy,
> Soon you'll be putting on a warm sweater,
> And freedom will be treading on your heels,
> Half with cursing
> Half with searches and spying.
> We'll saw through the year nineteen eighty-three
> —with salt to eat, but without bread—
> Right down to the last crunching bits,
> Until at last it gives at the seams.
> And they won't find out.
> Outside the gate, outside the perimeter—
> With every note higher,
> Our quiet angel will have flown away.
> Fate will see to our tasks—
> Just let's survive!
> Well, until we meet somewhere.
> Here's Zeks' luck—
> Smile!
> Bon voyage.
> I've no strength to say farewell.

Raya calls us in to eat. She has added some chopped mint leaves and dillweed to the skilly which was brought around from the kitchen and done something else which makes it possible to eat without gagging. She has also made a salad of finely chopped young nettles and wild chives with a dash of oil. Raya had nettle seeds sent from the Ukraine, because there were no nettles growing in the Zone. Even now we have only a few clumps of them, and it is not every day that we can treat ourselves to a few carefully clipped young nettle leaves. Wild chives we cultivate under the guise of grass, which they resemble closely, and snip off bits now and again with scissors, just as we do with the nettles. Smiling mischievously, Raya rounds off our meal by bringing out an aluminum dish in which—glory be!—there is a small handful of wild strawberries. We have a couple of wild strawberry beds hidden on all sides by tall flowers. This handful is our first harvest. With great concentration and care, Tatyana Mikhailovna divides the tiny wild strawberries into five equal portions: a whole four berries for each one of us! We call this process of dividing food by its slang prison term, *deriban*, and Tatyana Mikhailovna is our "deribanner" or "divider-up." After she left, I became the deribanner because I have a good eye for measurement, and later, when I was under constant pressure and spending more time in SHIZO and PKT than in the Zone, the job passed to Lagle Parek.

But the deribanner's job goes beyond mere division—she must now preside over the allocation of portions: "Natasha! Look at that bird!"

According to the rules of the game, Natasha turns away to face the window "to look at the bird."

"Who gets this lot?"

"Raya."

"And this one?"

"Ira."

"This one?"

"Well, I'll have to think whether Osipova deserves to get anything at all . . ."

We laugh, the distribution goes on, and the four tiny wild

strawberries make each of us feel that she is present at a splendid feast. Nobody but the warders has come into the Zone today, Podust is on leave, and the rest of the camp officers couldn't care less about us. It has become noticeably colder, but we try to cheer ourselves up with the thought that this will kill off the mosquitoes. Mordovian mosquitoes are ravenous beasts, to say nothing of Mordovian midges. Tanya swears that they can bite through the sole of a boot with a single snap and says she envies Nyurka: the insects don't bite her, and she is impervious to the cold. Oh, the advantages of fur!

"Her meetings aren't limited, either," chips in Natasha as we contemplate the advantages of feline existence.

"That's right—Antoshka's been prowling around under the windows again."

Antoshka is a real mafioso of the feline world. He is a vagrant tom who usually hangs around the infirmary. Judging by his appearance, he sleeps on the coal heap near the boiler room, because his naturally white coat is barely discernible under a layer of coal dust. We feed him occasional scraps because he is, after all, Nyurka's official beau and allows no other tom anywhere near our Zone. When this disheveled, disreputable scalawag starts making up to our neat, spotless Nyurka on the woodpile, we fall about laughing at the odd couple they make. Even now, Nyurka paces gracefully out of the house and heads in the direction of the woodpile.

As for me, I sit down to work. On the table, I lay out all my letters from home, as well as an unfinished one of my own. However, correspondence is not what I am about. In minute letters, I write out my latest poems on four-centimeter-wide strips of cigarette paper. This is one of our ways of getting information out of the Zone. These strips of cigarette paper are then tightly rolled into a small tube (less than the thickness of your little finger), sealed and made moisture-proof by a method of our own devising, and handed on when a suitable opportunity presents itself. I mention this procedure because it is one already known to the KGB. One such "capsule" was intercepted and Novikov, one of the camp officers, showed it to me in triumph, hinting at the possibility of an additional sentence. But in the summer of 1983 this method was still unknown to the KGB.

I become so engrossed in my work that I do not hear the stamp of boots, nor do I get a chance to conceal my handiwork before duty officer Kiselyova looms in the doorway. Desperately, I seize the only chance I have and slide the tiny strips with my poems under the jumble of letters on the table. Kiselyova (devil take her for arriving at such an inopportune moment!) hovers beside me: "Writing a letter, are you?"

Without warning, she grabs my unfinished letter, exposing my poor defenseless strips of poetry for all to see. The only hope I have is to focus her full attention on the letter.

"Give it back this minute! You're not the censor to read my mail."

Thank God she takes the bait, and jerks away her hand without releasing the letter.

"Maybe this is not a letter after all? I've got to check."

"You can see for yourself that the opening words are 'Greetings to you all, my loved ones,' so it's clearly a letter."

"Not necessarily," maintains Kiselyova, while all the time the wheels are going round in that thick head of hers; it's true that she has no right to act as a censor, yet how can she tell whether this is a letter or not without reading it? Some problem I've set her.

At this moment Tatyana Mikhailovna comes into the room and, sizing up the situation in a flash, enters the debate: "Never mind prying into other people's letters. You should be ashamed of yourself. Don't you have enough family matters of your own to think about without poking your nose into other people's?"

"I don't care about her family affairs," blusters Kiselyova, but she is on the retreat. "It's my job to check whether this is a letter or something else."

"There are plenty of officers to do that. You can tell from the opening words that it's a letter, and that's enough. No reason for you to take on other people's responsibilities."

Kiselyova is obviously not keen to get involved in a row. She did not come into the room with any specific aim in mind and, though she is loath to admit it, only seized on my letter out of curiosity to see what these politicals write to their husbands. She thrusts back the letter and waddles away.

Oh, the tongue-lashing I got from Tatyana Mikhailovna! Never mind that all ended well—but my carelessness! I'd come within a breath of being caught, of giving away our method to the KGB. That would have led to searches, intensification of surveillance, and then what would our chances be of getting any information out of the camp? Couldn't I have asked somebody to stand watch? There was nothing I could say to justify myself, so I stood there meekly under the thunderbolts of her strictures. Of course, the postmortem was conducted outside, away from the concealed microphones in the house. Finally, Tatyana Mikhailovna relented; after all, I had not lost my head and did manage to deflect Kiselyova's attention elsewhere. But the reprimands Tatyana Mikhailovna rained down on my head that day were to serve me in good stead, for they put an end to any remnants I had of pre-arrest lackadaisical trust in chance. Never again were our secret labors placed under threat of exposure by the KGB through carelessness on my part; I was never caught. Yet there were plenty of people besides me to be caught in our complex information network, so we had both successes and failures. However, by one means or another, everything became known "outside" sooner or later. Understandably, this infuriated the KGB, but they were forced to admit that they were powerless to stop us.

The incident with Kiselyova means that I cannot do any more writing today. In an hour or so that slow brain of hers might work out that everything was not as it seemed, and she'll be back with reinforcements. Thank God we squeaked through, and it's wiser to wait a while for everything to quiet down. We go off to sew gloves.

Natasha sits astride a special trestle for "turning." The trestle has a pintle at one end, and the sewn gloves are turned right side out on this pintle. Natasha likes turning, but hates sewing. So we usually give her a hand with sewing, and she "turns" for us. Nyurka sits there too, amber eyes glowing as she watches Natasha's flying hands.

Tanya has propped a list of French words beside her machine

and memorizes them by chanting in rhythm with her work: sewing itself requires no mental effort unless the machine starts to play up. Once you've sewn your first thousand gloves, all the movements the operation requires become reflex actions, executed with unerring precision. Beginners usually start off by sewing over a finger in the most painful spot—the nail.

My injured finger has already healed, so I pick up the tempo with ease. The sewing machines make as much racket as machine guns, so we usually plug our ears when we sit down to long sewing sessions. I don't memorize foreign words as I work, but write poetry. After arriving at the final version of five or six lines, I jot them down on a bit of paper which is concealed under a pile of unsewn gloves. When the poem is complete I commit it to memory and burn the paper after showing it to the others. They share my pleasure, and there's little chance that a small piece of paper will be found in a busy workroom piled high with pieces of cloth. The main thing is not to write too much down in one go— that way the warder on duty will spot nothing as she patrols the perimeter half a step away from the workroom window. The warders are used to seeing us keeping tally sheets of how much has been done in the past hour or calculating the number of hours necessary to finish the entire load delivered by the dray. The "perimeter" is a special path running right around our Zone for the benefit of patrolling officers. In principle, they should patrol the Zone once every hour, and the path enables them to survey it and peer into our windows without actually entering the Zone itself. The path has barbed-wire fencing on both sides and is off-limits to us. In effect, it marks the boundary between "our" territory and "theirs."

The sewing session does not last for long, because Raya comes rushing in, wet from head to foot: "It's hailing!"

Good heavens! Because of our ear plugs and the noise of the sewing machines, we have not heard the thunder outside. We race out to save our plants, but to no avail. Enormous hailstones pelt down like nuts out of a torn bag, the wind whips the blankets from our hands. We do manage to cover part of the vegetable patch, but while we are busy saving the wild strawberries and phlox, our precious clumps of nettles are battered beyond recovery. It will be two years before we manage to acquire some more for cultivation. We return to the house, soaked to the skin. After a few moments' hesitation, Raya decides to organize an unscheduled tea break.

The issue of tea leaves to zeks is strictly limited to 1 gram per head daily. It cost us quite a lot of effort to ensure that we continued to receive this ration in the form of dry leaves, because the administration had attempted to institute a system whereby the tea would be brewed in the kitchen and then brought to us. It's not hard to imagine what minute quantities of tea would have been used for our brew. Theoretically, tea can be purchased from the camp kiosk, but not in excess of 50 grams per month. However, this does not really affect us, because most of the time we are not allowed to use the camp kiosk "so that we'll never want to come back here again." Coffee is forbidden to zeks altogether. Through necessity, we recycle every brew of tea three times. We brew it fresh in the morning, then the same leaves are boiled up again in a saucepan to have with dinner (we call this brew "seconder") and finally in the evening. Third time round, of course, any resemblance between the result and tea is more in the imagination than in fact, so occasionally we add wild strawberry leaves to it, or leaves from wild raspberry canes which grow within reaching distance behind the perimeter barbed wire—in this case we call the result "fruit tea."

This is why Raya has to fight a brief battle with herself before making an unscheduled brew: she's the Cinderella this week, and has to spin out the tea ration for that period. Yet we are all frozen and shivering after our rescue operation, so what the hell! Let's treat ourselves. Our old electric kettle wheezes asthmatically on the table; elongated reflections of our faces stare back at us. Soon we'll have no kettle at all, and our long faces will not be due to distorting reflections. But we will keep on laughing, come what may; even on the darkest days, let the KGB listen and wonder about the laughter floating over their concealed microphones, the laughter of the Small Zone. The kettle bubbles, Nyurka purrs contentedly: she likes it when we're all gathered together. It's dark outside, only the boundaries are illuminated and projector beams sweep back and forth. June frost creeps slowly but inexorably across Mordovia. Before going to bed, I add a few lines to my letter to Igor: "My dearest, my love! I feel as though you are right beside me, so close. What do I care about what will happen tomorrow when now I feel you so near, and I am so happy that it makes my head spin! My kisses to you. May the Lord keep you. Your 'I.' "

12

Podust returns from leave and launches an immediate offensive. Why, she demands, do we call her "Lidia Nikolayevna" and not "Citizen Superior"? Because, we explain, she is not our superior. However, if she does not like being addressed by her name and patronymic, we can call her simply by her surname. Why are we not wearing headscarves? We remind her that none have been issued to us, nor has half of our zek uniform.

"You could have got some if you tried!" she retorts unabashed.

Yet where on earth could we have got headscarves? It's not as though we can go out to a shop. Perhaps we should have cut up our bedsheets? And anyway, why should we "try to get" anything? If the authorities want us to wear some item of clothing, let them provide us with it first, and then ask questions. But it's quite clear that this carping on Podust's part is only the beginning. Why aren't we at our sewing machines during the designated hours? That's rich! We produce the quota, so what else does she want? Actually, Podust is not interested in production quotas, she just wants our work to be as onerous as possible. Hearing our comments on this subject, Vasili Petrovich silently clutches his head in both hands; he knows perfectly well that if we're pushed too far, a strike is bound to follow. And what will happen to his production plan then?

Threats have become the keynote of our "superior's" relations with us: "It's time you found what a proper strict regime is like.

Just look at you—drinking out of enamel mugs, you've got a saucepan and a hotplate . . . And it's time to cut back on underwear, too—you're only entitled to two sets."

And then, back to an old grievance: if we don't put on identity tags, we can start getting ready for SHIZO. Of course, we have no intention of wearing them, and we know quite well that Podust is only looking for a pretext. After all, Natasha wore the identity tag at first, and that didn't stop her being sent to SHIZO on other charges.

We receive a visit from the operational sector head of the Central Administration, Gorkushov. He, too, starts off with threats of SHIZO: how cold it is, how generally terrible, how even the healthiest person can emerge a physical wreck from confinement in there. Unerringly, Gorkushov strikes at the most vulnerable spot of a woman's heart: "How do you expect to bear children after spending time in SHIZO?"

Now, more than four years later, having spent a total of 120 days and nights in SHIZO, I can confirm that Gorkushov knew what he was talking about. Even now, despite continuing treatment by Western doctors, I do not know whether I will ever be able to bear a child. Yet those same camp officials who threatened to cripple us then, will now look you straight in the eye and maintain (as they do, they do!) that we were not mistreated, that "implementation of punishment" is in no way detrimental to health, and that conditions in SHIZO are quite normal, albeit a little boring. So even as we rotted in their cells, we could not exonerate them by thinking that "they know not what they do." They knew, all right—better than anyone.

The next objection concerns our vegetable patch: it's against regulations. In fact, the only reason why the camp administration had been ignoring it was because they were unable to provide us with the legally stipulated ration of 200 grams of vegetables and 400 grams of potatoes every twenty-four hours. It had not been available either in the past or present. But being deprived of something in the camps does not mean getting something else instead. There was nothing to stop the authorities from destroying our vegetable patch and not supplying the regulation rations. That will teach us. That will have us howling with hunger!

It's quite obvious that all this harassment is not random, but a planned psychological offensive. Why? Because a political prisoner can only be broken by fear. Therefore—keep him in a constant state of anxiety, keep him on tenterhooks as to what will happen to him tomorrow, what will happen in half an hour. Once he's driven to the wall, he may agree to compromises with the KGB. Maybe. Then again, maybe not.

We have two new arrivals in the Zone: Jadvyga Bieliauskiene and Tatyana Vladimirova. Jadvyga is Lithuanian, a woman of my mother's age. This is her second sentence; she received the first one while still a schoolgirl, when Soviet troops "liberated" Lithuania and a wave of arrests swept across the country. Not only those who actually resisted the "liberation" (even morally) were arrested, but also those who could, in principle, offer resistance. It so happened that Jadvyga took part in a marksmanship competition at school, and although she came second to last, her participation was viewed with suspicion: why should she learn to shoot anyway? For the sport? Come off it! So Jadvyga was promptly sentenced to twenty-five years, no more, no less. I have often wondered what happened to the boy or girl who came first in that competition. By the reasoning of those days, his or her sentence should have been even harsher. But the Criminal Code of the time stipulated twenty-five years as the maximum term of imprisonment. Anything beyond that rated immediate execution by firing squad.

Our Jadvyga, however, only served eight years of that sentence, enduring beatings in prison, the privations of Siberia, contracting tuberculosis . . . When she was released, she was put on a course of treatment by antibiotics, which resulted in an ailment of the liver. By the time she arrived in our camp, she had had her gallbladder removed.

Dear Lord, we thought, how and with what are we going to feed her? She needs a special diet, but how can that be obtained? The synthetic fat used to "grease" our skilly would mow down someone even in robust health. Raya needs a specialized diet, too, and only gets by thanks to the vegetables from our patch . . . We ask Jadvyga how many years she has left to serve. Quite a stretch, as it turns out: four of camps, three of exile. And what was her crime? Well, it turned out that the eight years she'd served prior to the release following Stalin's death did not turn Jadvyga into a keen "builder of communism." She became a believer in God! A conscientious Catholic, she helped "treacherous" Lithuanian Catholic priests give religious instruction to children and young people. They even organized an amateur theater, held group readings . . . Then veteran KGB boss Andropov came to power, and a new period of arrests and repressions began, extending to the Baltic states as well. As a result, here is Pani[1] Jadvyga in our Zone. She is tall, thin, straight as a ramrod. She speaks Russian, but finds it difficult at first, pausing frequently to find the right word. She is not the first Lithuanian to have been in this Zone, but was preceded by Nijole Sadunaite,[2] who has completed her sentence and left. Jadvyga has a charming smile and hands that are equal to any task. Her main concern is for those sixteen- and seventeen-year-old students who were pressured into giving evidence against her by the KGB. She describes how some of them wept openly in the courtroom and asked her to forgive them. How are they now, she frets, how have they coped with such a traumatic experience? Will these children (she invariably refers to them as "children") withstand the Soviet "meat-grinder" or will they lose all that their young faith gave them? Her prayers are all for them: may the Lord forgive them their youthful weakness, help them to overcome. She is also constantly worried about her son; he is a student, will her arrest have repercussions for him in any way?

Jadvyga immediately becomes one of the team: she's got a green thumb, she quickly fashions elbow-patches for all of us, to prevent wearing holes in our sleeves as we work at the sewing machines, she sews beautifully herself and is not afraid of any work. Her faith is the cornerstone of her existence, but she sets no

1. A courtesy title, similar to "Madam."
2. A "secret" nun, as Catholic religious orders are forbidden in the USSR. She gave religious instruction to children and participated in the *samizdat* journal *Chronicle of the Lithuanian Catholic Church.*

store by denominational differences; there are many confessions, but God is one, after all, and it is to Him that we shall all come in the end. He who does not believe now will find faith later, in God's good time. Jadvyga is a woman of iron character, yet at the same time she takes such care of us that at times we feel almost ashamed; when all is said and done, she is old enough to be a mother to most of us.

Pleasant as it is to be able to write good things about good people, it must not be forgotten that we did not choose our fellow prisoners, and it was in the hands of the KGB to decide who else to send into the Zone. I find myself unable to write in as much detail about some of my fellow prisoners as I do about those I came to love and respect. We all had our failings, but with several it was more than just failings. But I cannot lift my hand to relate uncharitable details about living people who, although they may have found themselves in the ranks of political prisoners by chance, were nonetheless women who had to suffer prisons and camps. Some things I shall omit altogether, nor will I describe each and every one of our internal differences. I cannot pretend that such differences never occurred; of course they did, even though the majority of us always tried to keep the atmosphere in the Zone peaceful and cheerful. But our proud assertion that "we are human" was subjected to many tests and trials when the number of inmates in our cramped quarters rose from five to eleven. When cosmonauts are sent into space for six months at a time, they are selected for psychological compatibility, whereas in our Zone, the shortest term was Natasha's—four years! Moreover, when cosmonauts are in space, nobody can burst in on them and subject them to continuous hounding. They have constant contact with Earth, they can speak to their families, and nobody will terminate their conversations because they have uttered a "suspiciously unsuitable" word. They have adequate food and clothing, and are lauded as heroes for being away for half a year.

While I was in the Zone, I happened to read cosmonaut Lebedev's diaries in the journal *Science and Life*. He notes that the cosmonauts, too, had their moments of friction, not through innate bad temperedness, but because of fatigue and lack of space.

Yet despite everything, we retained our unity and stood by our principles. We were no angels. We were simply humans, with human dignity. I have no intention of drawing a glossy picture: we had our conflicts and I shall not omit mention of those which were serious enough to threaten our principles of conduct, to the vast satisfaction of the KGB.

Tatyana Vladimirova amazed us at once—she was such an obvious product of the criminal camps. Her very first question to us was: "How much does Teofedrin cost around here?" That simple question speaks volumes about life in the criminal camps. Theoretically, prisoners are not supposed to have any money in their possession at all; any purchases they make in the camp kiosk (when they're allowed to use it) do not involve money changing hands. Goods are acquired on the basis of how much credit the prisoner has according to the camp bookkeepers. So why the question about "how much"? The fact is that black marketeering and bribery are rife in the ordinary criminal camps. There are experienced criminals in these camps, not just people who have fallen foul of the law more or less by chance. The real criminals maintain their underworld contacts outside and have pals who are up to every possible trick. During transportation to the camp I heard many admiring accounts of such ingenious tricks as 100-ruble notes being concealed in cartridges of ball-point pens. A criminal will use his money to bribe the guards, his work squad supervisor, the security personnel. So there is a lot of money around in the ordinary criminal camps, and, as money is available, it is used in dealings between prisoners. The Teofedrin about which Vladimirova inquired is a pharmaceutical drug which has a narcotic side effect if several pills are swallowed at once. So the prisoners dope up on them. This form of drug abuse is very common in the camps. How do they get these pills? Simple. If, say, an imprisoned thief has some cash, she will go along to the camp infirmary and buy pills from the doctor in charge or the nurse. Even if she does not take the pills herself, there are always plenty of willing customers to take them off her hands. The price for a dose of Teofedrin varies from camp to camp, so Vladimirova's question would have been quite understandable in a criminal zone. But in a political zone? What, we wondered, is she proposing to do? Take the stuff herself, or sell it to us? Well, well. Let's wait and see what happens next.

Developments came quickly. First, Vladimirova spun us an incredible tale about what brought her to our Zone. She claimed that in 1981 she managed to force her way past the militiamen on guard outside the British Embassy in Moscow, where she immediately asked for political asylum. The British diplomats, with typical courtesy and correctness, granted her request on the spot. But that's not all. While in the British Embassy, Vladimirova went on, she broadcast a devastating attack on the Soviet government over the BBC (we enjoyed this bit particularly, because our new "acquisition" did not seem to know the difference between ordinary words and swear words, unself-consciously peppering every utterance with the latter, at the top of her voice). After that, according to her story, she was kidnapped from the British Embassy, right under the nose of the consul, by a detachment of KGB men who stormed the building in order to get her out. They, of course, put her into psychiatric detention for six months, and when the doctors pronounced her sane, sentenced her to six years and sent her to our Zone. Vladimirova only had part of her sentence documents with her, and none of the pages in her possession contained even a hint of these stirring events. She herself was, she told us, a veteran enemy of the Soviet regime, had been imprisoned many times, and had dedicated her entire life to the struggle for human rights. Not only that, but this doughty warrior claimed to have built up a whole organization "out there" which had bought weapons from the Japanese (of course, this was a secret between Japan and her organization), and these arms would be used to storm the Kremlin, kill everyone in it, seize power and proclaim Sakharov dictator.

The looks on the faces of our genuine human rights activists were really something to see when Vladimirova boldly included Sakharov in her scenario. A studiously serious query, however, elicited the admission that Sakharov himself is not yet aware of the role mapped out for him.

"But he'll be with us, just like Lenin was with the Bolsheviks!" she assured us confidently.

This last gem was almost too much for us. It was all we could do not to collapse on the grass in helpless fits of laughter. On the whole, though, the situation might be far from funny. Of course we realized at once that Vladimirova's "legend" was nothing but lies. The thrilling adventures she related were supposed to have occurred before my arrest, and if there had been even a grain of truth in it I would have known if so much as 1 percent of her story was true. Vladimirova had lots of other stories, too. For instance, she claimed that in 1980 she had organized a two-thousand-strong demonstration in Red Square. These demonstrators entered the Kremlin, went straight into the Reception Office of the Presidium of the Supreme Soviet (which, as it happens, is not in the Kremlin—we, of all people, had cause to know that!) and forced the authorities to accede to their demands.

A two-thousand-strong demonstration? Dream on. One and all, they would have been picked up long before they got there, for it would have been impossible to stop word about any attempt at such a demonstration from reaching the KGB.

Then there was Vladimirova's assertion that she studied at the Moscow Institute of International Affairs for three years. No matter how low our opinion of this Institute might be, it was patently obvious that Vladimirova would never have been allowed to try for the entrance exam, let alone gain admission to study.

So what should we make of all this? Had I encountered Vladimirova in a transit prison, I would not have been surprised by anything she said, apart, maybe, from the singular ineptitude of her lies. Common criminals often like to claim that they're "politicals" because they think that casts them in a heroic light. There is even a joke about this in their own circles:

A rabbit, a wolf and a fox are sitting in a prison cell. The rabbit—for evasion of military service, the fox—for theft, the wolf—for rustling horned cattle. Suddenly, the door flies open and a rooster is flung into the cell.

"I'm a political!" he cries immediately.

The others gaze at him in amazement and awe: "That's really something!" they murmur respectfully, "we're just common criminals, but you . . . Tell us, what did you do?"

The rooster assumes a heroic stance: "I pecked a Pioneer[3] in the ass!"

But all jokes aside, wild romantic liars like this don't become politicals. After all, our women's political zone, reserved for "especially dangerous state criminals," is the only one of its kind in the country. There are other women political prisoners scattered throughout other camps, but you don't find yourself in the Barashevo Small Zone just for possessing an over-vivid imagination. The KGB are not all fools by far, so what could be their reason for sending someone so transparently false into our Zone? Why do it?

Gradually, things start becoming a little clearer. Vladimirova announces that camp or no camp, she will continue her struggle. She even has a plan prepared: firstly, we must establish contact with the men's political zone—it's not far, after all, just across the road. All we have to do is cross our no-man's-land in full view of two guards armed with submachine guns, climb over the fence, cross the road, climb another fence and pass through another no-man's-land under the eyes of its guards; as for negotiating the barbed-wire obstacles—well, that's child's play. This exercise is to be undertaken in winter, across snow, but we will camouflage ourselves by wrapping bedsheets around our bodies (while leaving numerous tracks across the virgin snow). Our next step is to surprise our "colleagues" in the men's zone by turning up in their barracks in the dead of night. The fact that their zone is not our small one, and that they have informers galore, is irrelevant. What does our inventive heroine expect? That we would be foolish enough to fall for such suicidal nonsense? Vladimirova tries to put us to shame: "Well, if you don't have the guts, I'll do it alone. I'm not afraid to risk my life for our cause." At this point, I suppose, we ought to have taken pity at the possible termination of her forty-seven-year-old life and said: "Come, come, Tatyana. There's no need for all this effort and danger, no need to disturb guards or informers during the night. We already have a well-

3. A youth organization similar to Scouts and Guides, but with a sound Communist ideological basis. The next step after the Pioneers is the *Komsomol*, the Communist Youth League.

established correspondence with the men's zone." And, just to set her mind at rest, told her all the details.

Alas, we of the Small Zone turned out to be a hard-hearted lot, sadly deficient in openness and trust; we did not tell her about the correspondence, nor did we show any desire to take part in her schemes. "Well, it's your business," we shrugged dismissively, and went off to ponder what on earth all this meant. An attempt to organize a frame-up? But surely the KGB can't think we would swallow such ridiculous bait. Maybe she's just a common criminal whose brain has been affected by drug abuse? But in that case, why put her in with us? Perhaps she has been given a very long sentence on criminal charges and has agreed to act as the KGB's stool pigeon in our Zone in exchange for a reduction of her term? This is the kind of prisoner from whose ranks the KGB recruits stool pigeons, but we're in camp, not an investigation prison . . .

Vladimirova changed tactics. She sought out opportunities to tell each one of us, eye to eye, that Jadvyga, with whom she had been brought from the Potma transit prison, is a "black soul" who hates Russians and who, "like all the Baltic scum," is always out to make trouble. We all remonstrated with her individually, and some days later, when we gathered away from the microphones and Vladimirova, we discovered that she had been trying to set us all one against the other by "confiding" to each one all the unpleasant things others were allegedly saying about her behind her back. There were six of us in the Zone apart from Vladimirova, which means she had to make about thirty such attempts to cause discord. The best proof of her failure is that we got together to discuss the matter. Nevertheless (and you must give us credit for patience), even then we did not hurry to voice the obvious verdict. We decided to wait and see, but not to trust a word of hers in the meantime, to refrain from any confidential discussions, to break off any attempts on her part at intrigue, and to do our best to give no cause for conflict.

13

Conflict, however, proved inevitable. When Vladimirova's attempts to make trouble met rebuff after rebuff, she realized that she was not trusted. She then tried to assume a commanding tone, an effective ploy in the criminal camps, but that failed, too: we are equals, and all our decisions are taken together. If someone concedes to another's authority, that is a personal matter; but if there are differences of opinion on questions which concern everyone, we try to reach a decision which is acceptable to all (with the possible exception of a certain one of our number), so there is nothing to be gained in trying to order anyone around.

Vladimirova's trials were exacerbated and brought to the bursting point by a trivial misunderstanding, which arose because we had no trash can in the house. All biodegradable scraps went into the compost pit which I have mentioned, and refuse such as broken glass, tin cans and the like was gathered once a week and taken to the camp dump outside the Zone. We kept anything that would burn to feed our stoves, and that included any used scraps of paper such as drafts of letters or of complaints to the Procuracy, the endless drafts of my poems, old envelopes . . .

Not having grasped our established habits and practices, Vladimirova decided that these bits of paper which we were constantly burning contained secrets not only from the KGB but from her. Aha! After reaching this conclusion it was easy for her to imagine that we did practically nothing else from morning till night. It seemed to her that every time she came into the dining area there would be curled bits of paper smoldering in the fireplace with the rest of us sitting around looking innocent and talking about something innocuous.

Vladimirova erupted quite unexpectedly, when we were sitting at our machines and working. We were not even talking much among ourselves because it meant having to shout over the clatter of the machines. Suddenly, Vladimirova leapt up from her machine, screaming that she could no longer bear to remain in this vile Zone, and added a number of ripe epithets at a volume which drowned out the noise of the sewing machines. She then shot out of the workroom and raced in the direction of the nearest guard tower. You cannot, in fact, come right up to the tower because it is on the other side of the perimeter. In cases of emergency (say, if someone is taken ill and needs urgent medical attention) all you can do is get as close as possible to the tower and shout at the top of your lungs to attract the attention of the sentry. If he understands what you want (he might not, because most of the sentries are from the Central Asian republics and know hardly any Russian) and decides that the matter is sufficiently important, he will phone his superiors and they will send someone along. Vladimirova, however, was not calling for a doctor, she was demanding the head of the camp's "operational" unit. It is these "ideological" units that carry out censorship of mail, conduct surveillance, arrange bugging of prisoners' quarters and recruit informers. Not surprisingly, the head of the Barashevo unit, Shlepanov, came almost immediately: that must have been the first time he had ever been called to the Small Zone.

Part of their conversation was no secret. Vladimirova was shouting so loudly we could hear every word, whether we wanted to or not: "I've had enough of this Zone," she yelled, adding an absolutely unprintable description of it. "I want out. I've checked out the kind of people you've got here!" (An even less printable description of us.) "It's them and their leader Sakharov who drag decent Soviet citizens into their filthy plots, and then drink their blood!" (String of curses.) "I can see through them. I'll go on the television and radio and expose the lot of them. Just get me out of here!"

We did not hear what Shlepanov replied (he kept his voice down) but Vladimirova's request was not granted, much to our regret. The trap had snapped shut: offering to take part in a provocation is one thing, but getting out of camp is another. Shlepanov went off, and Vladimirova remained in the Small Zone, boycotted by everyone. She had thought that the KGB would release her the moment she volunteered to smear us on television, but alas . . . The only outlet for her fury and frustration was to turn on us.

As we went about our business, she darted from one to the other, screaming every obscenity she could think of, red-faced, shaking, eyes popping out of her head, tears streaming down her cheeks, spittle flying. Maybe she really is mad? Is she just indulging in a fit of hysterics, or is this insanity? Luckily, although she waved her arms around, she did not actually try to strike anyone. The most she allowed herself was to slam the doors in the house so hard that bits of plaster would flake off the walls. We did not respond in any way, but simply ignored her ravings.

Of course, this was easier said than done. Can you imagine sitting at the table and composing a tender letter to someone you love, with Vladimirova beside you, yelling curses at your bent head and bedewing your letter with spittle? Getting up and going away solves nothing, she will follow. The only thing to do is keep writing and take some comfort from the knowledge that at least the others are getting a rest from her. Eventually she will run out of invective—in an hour and a half, at the most.

After a week of incessant hysterics, Vladimirova was taken away to the camp hospital. We breathed a sigh of relief and hoped that she was gone for good. Maybe the KGB had decided to take her up on her offer to denounce us on television and would consider her task in our Zone accomplished? Regrettably, the KGB had its own reasons and plans, and Vladimirova remained with us. When she worked herself into a total frenzy (she had asthma and occasional trouble breathing), they would take her away to the infirmary for a while, treat her, then send her right back. Our peace was completely shattered, but without a doubt, the unhappiest person in the Zone was Vladimirova. What hell there must have been in her miserable, stunted little soul when it dawned on her that getting out of here isn't easy, that she has no say in her own fate, when she felt what it is like to be totally isolated amid a group of people with whom you have to share living quarters whether you like it or not. She did not even have anyone outside the camp, for the tales she told during her first days in the Zone of having a general for a father and a captain for a son were figments of her imagination. She received no mail, no parcels, and nobody ever came to visit her. There did not seem to be a single person who cared for her in the whole world. Even Vasili Petrovich, usually the soul of kindness, became infuriated when she produced three hundred defective pairs of gloves (adhering to the mores of the criminal camps, Vladimirova made no attempt to adopt our tradition of turning out only first-rate work). Nor did the fact that she was never punished bring her much joy. Vasili Petrovich did not risk deducting the cost of the ruined gloves from her earnings; the warders—to whom she was invariably rude—quickly realized that the administration would take no punitive measures against her, and neither forced her to get up in the mornings nor to go to bed at 10:00 p.m. She could do much as she wanted, but she still remained a prisoner. The warders, fed up with her aggressive rudeness, would say to us: "How do you stand her? They'd have made mincemeat out of her by now in the criminal zone."

That, of course, is true: either someone would have cut her throat, or she would have been driven to suicide by the massed efforts of her fellow prisoners. This is not as far-fetched as it may sound—just imagine, a whole large zone turned against one person who has nowhere to hide. Such behavior was totally unacceptable from our point of view. This caused us a lot of inconvenience, but was in keeping with our views on correct human behavior. Vladimirova had chosen her own punishment, so it was up to her to bear it. Our aim was to ignore her tantrums and try to carry on as though she were not there. Obviously, we had to take measures to conceal matters she should not know about. However, as we were allowed to work in three shifts, it was impossible for her to watch us all twenty-four hours a day.

14

The new wave of arrests under Andropov was beginning to sweep across the whole country, and that meant additions to our number. We were joined by Galya Barats. She and her husband Vasili were both from Trans-Carpathia, and so, in fact, were born on Austro-Hungarian territory. Later, this became part of the Ukraine and they, perforce, Ukrainian citizens of the USSR. Both had been members of the Communist Party, lived in Moscow in recent years, had a car, and, generally speaking, were doing quite well for themselves. That is, until they found faith in God. Moreover, they became members of the most persecuted group—the Pentecostals. They handed in their Party membership tickets (imagine the scandal!) and even wrote an open letter to Western Communists to the effect that they no longer wanted to participate in the building of communism or bear any responsibility for it. Western Communists do. So, suggested Galya and Vasili, let's change places: you come here and take our Moscow flat, and we will replace you in the West, away from the USSR. That letter alone would have been enough to put them behind barbed wire, but they went even further by attending prayer meetings and contacting foreign journalists. Both were arrested in the spring of 1983—first Vasili, then Galya. They were not tried in Moscow, but in Rostov-on-Don, to minimize publicity. Galya was sentenced to six years' strict regime camps to be followed by three years' internal exile.

She was a tall, sturdily built woman with a lot of grey in her hair. The sports suit in which she arrived was confiscated immediately, and then it was discovered that not one of the regulation issue dresses would fit her. Apart from these dresses, there is nothing else to choose from. But this circumstance in no way upset or worried the camp officials, or even led them to return Galya's own clothes. No, their solution was simply to walk away and leave her standing there in her underpants and bra. We had just hastily assembled at least some covering for her out of our own stuff when Podust appeared in the doorway: "Put the identity tag on your chest at once!"

"Where! Pin it to my bra? You could at least let me have some clothes first, and then demand that I pin things on them."

"That's no concern of mine. You just make sure you wear that tag."

Galya responded with a biblical quote: "Ye are bought with a price; be not ye the servants of men."[1]

"So you won't wear it?"

"No."

"In that case, you'll have only yourself to blame."

Luckily, we had some clothes put by "for those still to come," so we managed to dress Galya from our own resources. I took this opportunity to learn from Pani Jadvyga how to set sleeves and finish buttonholes with that professional touch.

Barely had Galya settled in, when Edita Abrutiene arrived in the Zone. Edita and her husband Vytas, both Lithuanians, were not, strictly speaking, human rights activists. They simply wanted to emigrate. But why should Lithuanians be allowed to leave the USSR? Their application was turned down. Instead of accepting their fate meekly, Edita and Vytas continued to insist, petition, act. As a result, Vytas was sentenced to three years' camps on charges of "slandering the Soviet state and social system" (Article 190–1 of the RSFSR Criminal Code). Edita, left with a small son to provide for, made a precarious living by doing casual work and some buying and selling on the black market. At

1. I Corinthians 7:23.

the same time, she continued her efforts to obtain permission to emigrate. Three weeks after Vytas returned home upon completion of his sentence, Edita was arrested and sentenced to four years' strict regime camps plus two years of internal exile.

When she arrived in our Zone, she was on a hunger strike which she had started in the KGB prison, demanding a review of her case. She was barely able to speak by the time she reached us, just managing to whisper out the details of her case. Later, however, we discovered that she had a very good voice. The following day she was taken away, as it is camp practice to isolate hunger strikers. She returned a week later, having called off the hunger strike. The camp authorities had promised her something or other but, naturally, failed to keep their word. They always try to convince you that they will grant your demands if you call off your hunger strike. Edita did not know yet that one should never believe anything the administration says, and later she simply did not have the strength to resume the strike. While Edita was recovering, there was no attempt to make her work; she really could barely stand. And that was still in the days when Dr. Volkova would give a week's release from work to those who had been on a lengthy hunger strike. But then we came up against a totally unexpected problem: Edita flatly refused to work at all.

"I have never worked a single day for 'them' in my life," she stated with finality.

We were honestly afraid for her: if she persisted in her determination, the camp authorities would see her into her grave with repeated spells in SHIZO and camp prison. Nothing we would be able to do could save her then—"they" would see to that. Wouldn't she have problems enough over the identity tag, which she also refused to wear? On the other hand, we reasoned, she has the right to her convictions, and it is not for us to dissuade her. But we thought and thought, and then arrived at a solution which we felt would be acceptable all around: Edita could take over from Raya as the Zone "housekeeper." After all, the housekeeper works for us, not "them." Raya had been anxious to relinquish this responsibility for some time: the joints of her hands were very painful through constant contact with water, and Dr.

Volkova had been going out of her way lately to find causes for complaint—pointing out the odd spider web, pronouncing a curtain as being less white than it should be, declaring that the sanitary conditions were not being maintained to the required standard, and so forth. An attempt by Podust to have Vladimirova replace Raya was rejected by us out of hand; we pointed out that we could hardly trust someone who is constantly threatening to poison us with our food and medications. Moreover, Vladimirova was extremely untidy, and we were always having to clean up after her. In the end we did manage to get Edita approved as our housekeeper. Paradoxically, it was Podust herself who was instrumental in this, and it put an end to her own career. This is how it happened.

On a quiet August evening we were all sitting outside the house, preparing to eat our evening meal. Vladimirova, who ate separately from us, had holed up silently inside the house. We had decided to make the most of the mild weather, so we dragged the table outside and sat down with our aluminum bowls of skilly. We had put a jar of flowers in the middle of the table, the poplar and the rowan tree (which had not yet been chopped down) rustled overhead, and the sun was in no hurry to disappear behind the fence.

This idyllic scene was like a blow to the heart for Podust when she suddenly appeared in the Zone, accompanied by a major from the Central Administration. Was this how she wanted to see the Zone? When Tanya once asked Podust exactly what it was that she wanted from us, she replied: "That you should all pull yourselves up when I come in, and that Lazareva should report: 'Supervisor, everything in the Zone is in order.' "

Needless to say, on no occasion (including this one) did we "pull ourselves up" or make any kind of report, but we did wish them both a courteous "good evening" and continued to eat without evincing the slightest interest in the reason for their presence. They had arrived just as Natasha was in the middle of telling a joke, and her rendition was like watching a one-woman theater. A grimace of pure chagrin distorted Podust's face as she and the major passed through into the house. Fine, let them socialize with Vladimirova for a while! A few minutes later, Podust poked her head out of the window and politely asked Tatyana Mikhailovna to come in for a moment. Shortly afterward, Tatyana Mikhailovna returned in silence, but plainly struggling not to give vent to fury. She was pale from the effort of containing herself. Our visitors cleared out without disturbing anyone else, but Tatyana Mikhailovna remained grimly silent. Nobody asked her anything; usually, we all told each other about any exchanges with the administration, but this was not obligatory—we did so because we wanted to. Nobody ever demanded any accounting from anyone else. We finished eating, cleared the table, and then Tatyana Mikhailovna motioned me toward our one and only path in the Zone. There were times when we would walk up and down this path for up to an hour, both to get exercise and be out of the range of the microphones in the house. It was an unwritten Zone law that nobody approached anyone using the path this way and interrupt a discussion not intended for any other ears.

As we paced the path, Tatyana Mikhailovna told me that Podust had said to her: "I am surprised, Velikanova, that you are not afraid to sit at the same table with Edita Abrutiene and use the same dishes. Don't you know that she's syphilitic? Her medical record states that she's had syphilis."

I understood at once why Tatyana Mikhailovna was so very angry—I almost went up like a bomb myself. This was not Podust's first attempt to sow discord and distrust among us. She would often drop comments like: "Osipova, don't you know that all the others detest you?" Or, in Galya's absence, say to Jadvyga: "Bieliauskiene, Barats said such-and-such about your family." When, on this particular occasion, we called Galya and repeated what the "blonde fiend" had just said, Podust's face mottled with ugly blotches and she yelled: "Don't you dare put my words to the test! I'm in charge here!"

But her vile accusation against the newly arrived Edita is just too much. Yet is it not our own fault that Podust is getting away with more and more? We are all aware that accusing dissidents of having venereal diseases is a favorite ploy of the KGB—it's such an easy way to smear someone. Of course none of us believe

Podust's disgusting fabrication, but should she be allowed to get off scot-free? We must get everyone together at once and acquaint them with our "supervisor's" latest invention. Tatyana Mikhailovna, however, hesitates: "Must we really repeat this base accusation to everyone? Isn't that just what Podust is after?"

I'm still seething with rage: "What she wants most is that we should distrust one another. That everyone should start avoiding Edita without her knowing the reason why. Nobody will believe that lie, and we'll make Podust pay."

"But Edita's new here. Won't she be terribly upset by such dirt?"

"On the contrary, she'll see from the start that the Zone is on her side."

We understand each other's point of view, we both know that something must be done, but we also realize that if we are too precipitate, we could make an unrectifiable mistake. We call Tanya over for a consultation. She weighs up the situation and gives her opinion: "Podust should be sued for this. It's slander in the full sense of the word."

So we summon everyone into the yard and Tatyana Mikhailovna explains the situation. Oh, how they all fired up! One glance at our faces was enough to show Edita that Podust's despicable scheme had failed. Nobody doubts for one moment that Podust is lying, but what are we going to do about it? We decide that from this day forth we do not acknowledge that Podust has any right to be in our Zone in whatever capacity. We write a collective letter to that effect to the Procuracy, explaining our reasons. We refuse all contact with Podust and demand her dismissal: as far as we are concerned, she no longer exists. Edita intends to sue Podust for slander, and Tatyana Mikhailovna will be a witness. Our problem is that in order to prove the slander, we need to have Edita's medical record, and nobody will give us access to it just like that.

Tanya finds a simple solution: "Let's demand that Edita take over as housekeeper. That job calls for a medical clearance, and nobody suffering from anything infectious is allowed to do it. When Edita is cleared, that will be evidence against Podust."

She's right. The medics will have no choice but to clear Edita.

The housekeeper's job is voluntary, and a prisoner's agreement to undertake it must be made in written form; under the circumstances, nobody else will agree to do the job, and there must be a housekeeper in the Zone according to regulations. Dr. Volkova will never dare to confirm Podust's lies: firstly it would involve falsification of medical records, and secondly it would indicate that she had given out confidential medical information to a third party. Who would want to appear in such an unsavory light just to save Podust from the consequences of her own stupidity?

Everything works out as planned: Edita is cleared to be housekeeper, Volkova, taking fright at the prospect of being dragged down with Podust, swears that there is no mention of syphilis in Edita's medical records, we send off our petition to the court, and Podust, entering the Zone, finds herself "invisible." Nobody even bothers to explain anything to her; our reasons are set out in our collective letter. This is the beginning of a lengthy, exhausting war: obviously, nobody in the camp administration wants to set legal proceedings in train. It's highly unlikely that Edita's new demand for a court hearing has been passed on; the camp administration's main concern is to sweep the whole matter under the rug as quickly and as quietly as possible. Various camp officials come to talk to us, singly and in numbers. Podust won't be dismissed, they tell us, so wouldn't it be better for us to "make friends"? We remain adamant: if they want to pay her a salary for doing nothing, that's their business. But she will not represent the administration in our Zone. So the camp officers are left with no option but to carry out Podust's duties in the Zone themselves; we don't even accept documents detailing our "violations" from her hands. If they want to tell us something or ask us anything, let them come and do so without her. Podust, naturally, is beside herself: she rushes around the Zone, trying to corner us individually or in groups, alternating threats with completely uncharacteristic attempts to be pleasant. She even stops hounding Natasha, and not one word do we hear from her about identity tags. But nobody unbends—enough is enough. She's had all she's going to get out of us.

Podust gives up quite soon: she hasn't the stomach to stand up to daily humiliation. It's not easy to try to draw some kind of response from people who look right through you. Her appearances in the Zone dwindle to once a week, and then become even fewer. Her game was exposed quite unintentionally by Captain Shalin, who had come into the Zone about something or other, and when Podust's name cropped up, said: "But she's already been here today."

"No, the last time we saw her was about ten days ago."

"Nonsense. I saw her take the Zone keys myself, and open the first gate. She came back half an hour later."

We're all laughing before he finishes speaking. Podust must have lurked around between the two fences that whole half hour, so that neither we nor her own colleagues could see her. She was too scared to open the second gate and come into the Zone, so she only pretended to go, but in fact stood there with nothing to do but poke the ground with her foot until she judged it safe to emerge without losing face. The truth dawns on Shalin, too. He turns quite purple in a manful attempt to stifle his own mirth, but fails and joins in our laughter.

Nevertheless, hostilities lasted from August 1983 until June 1984 before Podust was finally removed. I've heard that she now deals with juvenile offenders in the militia, setting under-age lawbreakers on to the straight and narrow. Poor kids!

15

August 1983 was a very eventful month all around. Before we began boycotting her, Podust had offered us an unexpected deal: we wear the identity tags, and the administration will let us keep our vegetable patch. If not, the vegetable patch will be levelled.

"It's up to you to decide what you prefer," she concluded her ultimatum.

Tatyana Mikhailovna even rose from her chair in indignation, but Podust pressed her attack. "Well? Do you think you have anything to gain by losing your vegetable garden?"

"Of course not!" snapped Tatyana Mikhailovna with unusual ire. "But do you think we campaign for human rights for some sort of material gain? We don't like being here."

"In that case, you should spend less time thinking about rights," retorted Podust.

We laughed a little at the time, astounded by the cynicism of the authorities—they would have been prepared to break the law (for the vegetable patch was indeed against regulations) just to get us to wear those wretched tags. Eat what you like, just agree to bend the knee.

Retribution followed our refusal. A triumphant Podust marched into our Zone at the head of a small detail of warders and women from the infirmary zone. These women carried hoes, bags and spades. As soon as we saw them, we knew it was the end of our vegetable patch. We had already decided on how we should act in such an eventuality: we would not plead, nor raise our voices, nor make any attempt at physical interference. We would simply all stand around, in total silence, watching what they did. Raya, however, must stay in the house: she would find the sight of the destruction of the vegetable garden hardest to bear. It was her work, her creation; the rest of us only helped with the digging, the carrying and the watering. But she had a real feeling for it—for every grain of soil, for every tiny carrot. So Raya remains inside, and we hear Podust's ringing voice: "Well, you women, I'm asking you for the last time: are you going to wear the tags or not?"

And then the order: "Start digging!"

They start: the vegetables are stuffed into bags, the plants are reduced to a pulp with hoes, green spray flies in all directions, the soil of the beds is turned over thoroughly to ensure that no stray root is left behind. Podust fusses around, issuing orders and instructions. Everyone else is silent. The women prisoners are obviously ill at ease, but they can hardly disobey her commands; she's a big wheel. The warders take no part, but stand there stiffly, occasionally shaking their heads. They are sorry about the wanton destruction of our vegetable patch, because they are all keen gardeners themselves and know how difficult it is to grow anything in sandy soil. They had always treated our efforts at gardening with great respect, and frequently came to Raya for advice, or for seeds which are not obtainable in Mordovia. In exchange they would secretly slip us seeds, too, for such things as carrots and turnips. They were particularly impressed by an enormous pumpkin which we had managed to grow: it was really huge, and its shoots and leaves kept pushing through into the "forbidden" perimeter zone. The warders patrolling it would carefully push this daring greenery back into our Zone, although there was nothing to stop them from trampling all over it. All they did was laugh: "That's some pumpkin you've got there. Looks like it's planning to break out. You keep an eye on it so it doesn't escape." This pumpkin was pulled up too, roots and all, and thrust into one of the bags.

Podust even had the effrontery to order Natasha to help carry the bags. Natasha is very quick-tempered, but in this instance she preserved an icy silence. The only sign of emotion was a slight quivering of her chin. The criminal prisoners exchanged gleeful looks: how about that, then? These politicals don't give a damn about Podust!

One of the warders, Sonya, even had tears in her eyes at the sight of so much unnecessary waste. She was sorry for us and for the destroyed plants: everything had been so lush, so green, and now there was nothing left. Yet, all in all, the operation did not work out the way Podust had it planned. The unvoiced condemnation of the criminal prisoners became ever more tangible with every passing moment, and finally one of the women flung her hoe to the ground in disgust: put me in SHIZO if you will, but I won't carry on with this! Podust was even denied the pleasure of seeing us suffer; we were demonstratively impassive, and just stood there burning her up with our eyes. Finally they left, leaving nothing but denuded beds. Only Vladimirova's vegetable beds (we had allotted her a separate plot) remained untouched.

Raya went away to cry in the woodshed; there's just so much one can take. We were more upset by her sorrow than by the loss of the vegetable garden. Every one of us reached the limit of her endurance at one time or another in the camps, and this was Raya's moment. After shedding her tears she emerged, red-faced and swollen-eyed, and resolutely retrieved the seeds we had hidden for future use. She then went straight to our ruined and broken garden, and began planting. Not everything, of course, only those plants which could grow before the onset of severe frosts—chives, dillweed . . . We watched her in awestruck silence. What an iron will! Then we pulled ourselves together and hastened to help. By evening, order was restored, the earth smoothed into fresh, tidy beds. We even found and planted a few surviving runners . . .

Sonya, who came around later to commiserate, could only gasp: "Well, Rudenko, you are something, and no mistake."

But of course. There'll be no bare earth in our Small Zone. It took all our efforts to console Raya, who was racked by remorse because she had forbidden us to pick any carrots the day before, wanting them to grow a little larger. Never mind about the stupid carrots, we assured her, we'll survive.

In fairness, it must be said that Vladimirova felt bad about what had happened, too. In the evening she came to us and declared that as we had given her all the seeds and seedlings for her plot, we must now take some from her, irrespective of what we think of her as a person. It's not her fault that her beds weren't touched. Silently, we acknowledge that she is right, and take what she offers. What's happened? we wonder. Has some spark of decency come to life in our "stoolie"? For can it be that there is, anywhere, even a single soul that is totally bereft of humane impulse? Time will tell.

Let us not, however, forget about our "reformers." Not for nothing did Podust herself actually participate in uprooting our plants, "setting an example" to the women she had assembled for the job by pulling up some decorative peppers with her own hands. After all, should not the "corrective instruction" directed at us show some results? How is it that we are always going on about Podust this, Podust that? Was it she who thought up the identity tags? Who, then? Whoever it was, let them see what we think of them and not pretend that they are blameless. It's easy to lay the blame later on small-fry officers. So we sent off a collective declaration:

To the Presidium of the Supreme Soviet of the USSR;
from women political prisoners in Mordovian camp
ZhKh-385/3-4 (Small Zone).

DECLARATION

We, the undersigned women prisoners in the Small Zone, have refused, and continue to refuse, to wear identity tags on our chests. On August 10 the administration advised us that unless we put on these tags, we will lose the right to purchase any foodstuffs and will forfeit all meetings with relatives until the end of our terms.

The enforced wearing of identity tags is an affront to human dignity, a fact which is universally acknowledged and which was affirmed at the Nuremberg Trials. Soviet legislation claims that "the administration of punishment is not intended to cause physical suffering or violate human dignity" (Art. 1 of the Corrective Labor Code of the RSFSR).

In connection with the above, we hereby notify the Soviet authorities that we refuse to observe those demands of the regimen which are designed to cause humiliation or are amoral in character.

We assert our natural human right to take united action, to defend one another and to defend other political prisoners.

We call upon the Soviet legislature to withdraw the wearing of chest identity tags in all Soviet labor camps: in the meantime, we in the Small Zone refuse to wear them, and are prepared to face all possible repressions.

Edita ABRUTIENE, Galina BARATS, Jadvyga BIELIAUSKIENE,
Tatyana VELIKANOVA, Natalia LAZAREVA, Tatyana OSIPOVA,
Irina RATUSHINSKAYA, Raisa RUDENKO.

August 12, 1983

Of course, nobody replied. Why should the government answer for the laws of the land? They're such shy, retiring creatures, our rulers.

In the meantime, events keep moving. I receive a letter from Igor saying that he intends to travel up for a "short" meeting— the kind that lasts from two to four hours, when you sit at opposite sides of a table. As all our mail is scrutinized by the camp censors, the administration knows of Igor's intentions before I do. I can't help wishing that he hadn't written, but turned up without any notification—that way, the camp authorities might not have time to think up some "violation" in order to deprive me of the meeting. As it is, what are the chances that it will be permitted? For the time being, however, I start to prepare: I plan what to say and how to say it, so the meeting won't be terminated yet Igor will understand everything I have to impart. I also worry about what to wear. When the maximum number of times you can hope to see your husband is three times a year, you want to look your very best. All the others play an active part in preparing me for the great moment. Pani Jadvyga digs out an ancient skirt made out of mattress ticking from the *babushki*'s rags. The skirt is heavily stained with oil, but Pani Jadvyga, with typical patience, works on these stains with bits of soap and then soaks it in bleach. The skirt emerges uniformly light grey in color. Tatyana Mikhailovna pulls out a piece of striped fabric she had put by for some special occasion. This striped material had been issued about five years ago for the sewing of new prisoners' uniforms; then the official summer uniform became blue fabric with a white diamond pattern. The remaining striped material had been hidden away to this day. I use it to make myself a Ukrainian-style blouse. As Igor's arrival draws closer, Galya sets my hair and devises a superb coiffure.

This wholehearted participation on their part is not surprising. A meeting for one of us is an event shared by the whole Zone. We prepare the lucky one as though she were a bride, cut flowers for her to take to her loved ones, escort her to the gates and wave her on her way ... If only they would grant them, these meetings! Yet my situation takes a turn for the worse. The next day I am handed an official notification cancelling the meeting. The reason? That the day before I had gone to the camp kiosk incorrectly dressed—without the regulation kerchief on my head. Despite the bitterness of disappointment, our first reaction is an involuntary burst of laughter, because on that day I had been the only inmate of the Small Zone to go to the kiosk with her head covered. Admittedly, this was not because I had been consciously observing the regulations, but because my hair was in curlers. Galya had just finished setting it when the warders arrived to take us to the kiosk, and to get there one must leave the Zone and cross the hospital compound. We normally never wore the kerchiefs, but in this instance I put one on to hide the curlers.

Still, it's all very well to laugh, but the fact of the matter is that the report used as a basis for the cancellation of the meeting is a patent lie, and the meeting has been forbidden illegally.

What is to be done? The Zone makes a unanimous decision: we go on strike. If they had wanted to, the authorities could have found any number of reasons to cancel the meeting on "legal" grounds, as it were, and been formally justified in doing so—for instance, they could have picked on my refusal to wear the identity tag. But in this instance they have been trapped by their own lie, and we are only too ready to make the most of it.

We write an immediate notification of intent to go on strike, and this brings the camp commander (Pavlov, at that time) to the Zone in next to no time. Pavlov is understandably alarmed. Tatyana Lobashkina, the warder who submitted the report against me, tries to wriggle out of the situation, but it becomes increasingly obvious that she wrote that report on someone's orders. But whose? Pavlov insists that he had nothing to do with it. So was it Podust? Or the KGB? In the end Pavlov, after uttering a few obligatory threats, suddenly rescinds the order: "Get back to work, the meeting can go ahead."

This is, in itself, proof that the meeting was cancelled on Podust's initiative. Had the order come from the KGB, Pavlov would never have dared allow himself the luxury of "sorting things out." This way, however, Pavlov is satisfied, and so are we. Pavlov can cheerfully throw our strike notification into his waste-paper basket, and nobody in the Central Administration will know anything about it.

Natasha pretends to be dismayed: "Only three days off work, and now back to those blasted gloves!"

Of course she doesn't mean a word of it. We are all extremely pleased, for a meeting rescued from cancellation is quite an achievement.

Finally Podust appears with Masha, one of the warders, and announces: "Ratushinskaya, come along to your meeting. Your husband is here." Oh, how my heart leaps! But I make no move and keep my face blank: the Zone has taken a decision "not to see or hear" Podust, and that means at any time without exception. The others keep their faces averted, but I feel the intensity of their concern for me.

"Ratushinskaya, does this mean you refuse to go and see your husband?"

I keep my mouth tightly closed.

"Silence is a sign of consent," pursues Podust.

I maintain silence: I will not "buy" a meeting at the cost of surrender, nor would any of the others. Rescue comes from a totally unexpected quarter: Masha the warder.

"Ratushinskaya," she says, "come with me. I have to search you before you can go to your husband."

My hearing is instantly restored. Strange that one could rejoice at the prospect of being searched. But in a situation like this we are all overjoyed. Podust has her responsibilities, Masha the warder has hers. All the warders hate Podust, anyway, and in this instance Masha has a golden opportunity to thumb her nose at her with no repercussions. The others rush off to pick a bunch of flowers, Masha quickly turns my clothes inside out in the infirmary, and at last I am escorted into a small room in the guardpost, where I can hear Igor's voice: "Where is she?"

He comes in: so thin, with sunken cheeks . . . How hard it is for him to be "free" and to spend days and nights worrying about me. He has brought my younger sister, Alya, with him. She turned seventeen quite recently. Hugging or kissing is strictly forbidden, and the table divides us. We have been given two hours. Masha sits between us to make sure that the conversation does not stray to any prohibited subjects. She sympathizes with us, but she has her job to do. We talk jerkily, jumping from one thing to another, trying to say everything at once. Alya doesn't say a word, just sits there staring with big, round eyes. She is completely thrown off-keel by the trip to the camp (Mordovia is covered with camps, and you can see them, one after another, from the train), and seems to have lost her tongue. And seeing me as I look now is an added shock.

Igor tries to tell me about the International PEN Club, about the success my work is enjoying abroad, but Masha interrupts him: "You can't discuss that. One more word, and I'll end the meeting."

We don't argue. By all means, let's talk about other things.

"How's our 'Leshek' getting on?" I ask.

"Well, you know what he's like as a worker. It looks as though he could get an award."

This tells me that Lech Walesa, the head of Poland's Solidarity, has been nominated for the Nobel Prize.

Resorting to such oblique language, we quickly inform each other of important events and matters—Igor about the ones "out there," I about events in the Zone, taking great care not to rouse Masha's suspicions. I only depart from these tactics in telling Igor about Vladimirova, but Masha lets it pass without demur; she's had her fill of Vladimirova, too. I describe other events with the help of carefully thought out allusions and terms. Am I getting through to him? I can tell by his eyes that he hasn't missed a thing, this brilliant man of mine.

"My dearest! My darling!"

No, I mustn't, or I'll start howling my eyes out. Silence. We clasp hands across the table, even though no physical contact is allowed. Masha appears not to notice: there are tears in her own eyes. I study his hands, hands I know so well, down to the smallest vein. They're rough and scratched now, because he's had to take a job as a metalworker in a factory. A clock stands on the table, and how mercilessly it ticks away the minutes. Surely two hours cannot have gone by already!

"Say your goodbyes," says Masha, ever so quietly.

We rise. Will she stop us from exchanging just one kiss? No, she says nothing. We clasp each other for a fleeting moment. This is no embrace, it is a spasm of pain. But it's vital to keep hold of yourself. A quick step back. We smile. My throat seizes up. We make the sign of the cross over each other. That's it. We will not see each other again for three years.

"You politicals are really something," says Masha on our way back, "never a tear out of you! All the others from the big zone bawl their eyes out after each meeting, nearly breaks your heart." She unlocks both gates and lets me back into the Zone.

The others are agog: "Well?"

In a minute, my dear friends, in a minute. I'll share all the news with you, for do we not share all our joys and sorrows? In the evening we celebrate over a cup of tea: a meeting that actually takes place is a rare event, and we mark such a special occasion with great enthusiasm. What a warm evening! August stars twinkle in the sky. What does tomorrow have in store for us?

16

What tomorrow has in store is this: "Osipova and Lazareva—to SHIZO for refusal to wear identity tags. Ten days and thirteen days!"

Naturally, the longer term is for Natasha, because she is weaker.

All things considered, this development was only to be expected. We gather the warmest of our clothing, and this is where the bustiers made by the *babushki* come into their own. What luck that by now we have unravelled the woolen shawl which kind-hearted Lyuba had allowed me to take through into the Zone: Edita has knitted "SHIZO tights" with the yarn, long enough to fit any one of us. On little Tanya, these tights look like a concertina, but that doesn't matter—she'll be all the warmer.

We take great pains to outfit Natasha and Tanya as best we can; it may be quite warm now, but August is a treacherous month in Mordovia, and how will they fare in the damp SHIZO cell? We also try to feed them as well as possible before they are taken away, for they will get hardly anything in SHIZO: the so-called hot meal is given only every second day there, and consists of a skilly which is mainly hot water. Podust mills around demanding that we hurry up, but we ignore her. Finally a warder chips in impatiently: "Women! We'll be late for the 'cuckoo' at this rate."

The cuckoo is a small locomotive that plies between camp Number Three and camp Number Two. In other words, from our camp to the neighboring one, where the SHIZO is located.

"The KGB held up a plane for two hours for me," says Tanya regally, "so your cuckoo can wait."

Those of us who remain have already agreed on our course of action: someone goes into SHIZO—we refuse to work. If someone who is ill is sent to SHIZO—we go on hunger strike. There is no doubt about it that Natasha is very ill. That means that we will conduct a hunger strike for the thirteen days that she is in SHIZO. Both Tanya and Natasha know this. We escort them to the gate, kiss them goodbye. It is August 17, 1983.

No hunger strike is a welcome event, but this one is particularly untimely because September brings the opening of the Helsinki Review conference in Madrid, which will examine the implementation of the Helsinki Agreement by the signatory states. We know that in our country, this Agreement is constantly violated. Nevertheless, Soviet diplomats at the conference will utter practiced falsehoods, their Western colleagues will nod benignly, and those who recognize the lies for what they are will be unable to prove anything. After all, those of our countrymen who are not afraid to tell the truth are hardly likely to be granted the opportunity to travel to Madrid. The implementation of the Helsinki Agreement in the USSR was checked by unofficial Helsinki Monitoring Groups, so they were the ones who should have been asked to report to the Madrid conference. But the Soviet authorities threw the members of these Groups into camps and psychiatric hospitals; they cannot get out from behind barbed wire, let alone travel to Madrid.

In short, we had decided to conduct an eight-day hunger strike, and to send our testimony to the Madrid delegates. This hunger strike was to begin on September 8, and our testimony to the Madrid conference had already been despatched along our secret channels. For this reason, there could be no turning back. We sit down and start calculating: the hunger strike we commence today will last until August 30 at least—that is, if Natasha's thirteen days in SHIZO are not extended. That means we shall have to start the eight-day Madrid hunger strike very soon after this one ends. Yet what else can we do? The Zone, however, reaches the unanimous decision that Pani Jadvyga is not to take part in this first hunger strike. She can register her protest by not working, because apart from the fact that she is the oldest inmate of the Zone, she is also an invalid, and could not possibly survive two hunger strikes in a row. Oh, the magic of those words "the Zone has decided"! Pani Jadvyga, with her iron will, would hardly have paid heed to anything else. She immediately starts fussing around us, the hunger strikers.

"Pani Jadvyga!" we protest laughing, "it's only the first day. We're not even properly hungry yet."

"None of your nonsense," she responds, unmoved, "you've got to conserve your energy from the very beginning."

Nyurka is totally bewildered. Where is her dinner? Normally we share with her anything that's fit for feline consumption out of our meals, yet here we are now, returning everything to the kitchen untouched. There's nothing in the house, either, because all of us have forfeited our "privilege" to buy anything from the camp kiosk for the whole of August. We were all taken to the kiosk, of course, but Vladimirova was the only one who was allowed to buy anything. Moreover, Vladimirova's attitude to the cat vacillates between extremes: one moment she smothers her with kisses, and the next threatens to kill her along with the rest of us. We always have to keep an eye on her to make sure that she does not do the cat any injury; with us watching, she doesn't dare.

Solemnly, we explain the hunger strike to Nyurka, and she responds with a plaintive, interrogative "Miaow?" When she finally realizes that no dinner is forthcoming, she disappears somewhere for a long time.

In the evening, I sit out on the grass, trying to ignore the onset of hunger pains. Suddenly, there is a loud, satisfied purring behind my back, and Nyurka paces up, proudly holding a large dead mouse in her teeth. This mouse she lays before me. We always made a point of praising Nyurka for a job well done, because she loved to bask in universal approval. Therefore, I react with extravagant praise: "Good girl, Nyurka. What a smart girl you are.

What a clever hunter. How would we cope with all those mice without you? And where did you get such a big one? Aren't you a heroine. Our beautiful pussycat. You're a real Pioneer. You're the best there is!"

Nyurka accepts these dithyrambs with due satisfaction, but she is clearly waiting for something else. What that something is, she proceeds to demonstrate: she has not brought the mouse along just to show off her prowess, she wants me to eat it! To the best of my ability, I explain that during a hunger strike, even mice may not be eaten. Got it? Got it. She picks up her offering and departs. Later on it emerged that she took the mouse inside and offered it to all the others in turn. Receiving polite refusals every time, she saw that a hunger strike is a serious matter, and tactfully took the mouse aside to eat it so that nobody would see. Oh, that the same could be said of Vladimirova! She, of course, is not on hunger strike, and makes no secret of her satisfaction with Tanya and Natasha's situation: "Two bitches less in the Zone."

Vladimirova makes a point of hovering around us with her food, and even brings it into the bedroom, where she chomps on carrots and sweets with as much lip-smacking as possible. At the same time she discourses, out loud, about what fools we are to be starving ourselves. We laugh about it at first, but by the third or fourth day we become very sensitive to food odors, and it is then that Vladimirova starts frying up meat and onions for herself on our hotplate.

Where, you may wonder, does the meat come from? Its issue is the first reaction of our administration to our hunger strike; and not only meat is issued, but also white bread, butter, hardboiled eggs—all undreamt-of luxuries. The naïve hope of the camp bosses was that we would not be able to resist the temptation to eat at least something. It gives us something to laugh about up our sleeve: they had been adamant in refusing to give Pani Jadvyga a proper diet, and now she'll be able to benefit from all this bounty, not just Vladimirova.

Alas. Pani Jadvyga promptly begins a fast, which excludes all meat and dairy products. We practically grind our teeth in frustration—for once dairy products are available, and all she will eat is bread and skilly. To all our pleas she responds that a fast is a religious matter, and we have no right to poke our noses into her religious convictions. What can you do with a woman like that? The warders, who are very fond of Nyurka, start feeding her after we tell them about the episode with the mouse. The days slip by, one, two, three . . .

On the third day, hunger pangs subside and you feel your physical strength waning. Usually on the third or fourth day (it varies from person to person) you experience the first "crisis" as your organism rebels. The stomach produces gastric juices, you get spells of dizziness and nausea—in a word, you feel really bad. The inexperienced take fright—if it's like this now, what will it be like on the tenth day? Yet later the condition eases, there is just the sensation that your heart is laboring, like the engine of a car taking a very steep slope. You have to move carefully, avoiding any abrupt movements. But our spirits are high, and as we gather around the table (there are only cups of water on it now) we still manage to laugh, though more quietly than usual; our voices are beginning to go. Also, there are two people fewer to laugh with us, Tanya and Natasha. How are they faring?

Vladimirova startles us with an unexpected initiative. Choosing her moment when Podust is present, she declares that she is going to take over as housekeeper: "None of them are in any shape to do any cleaning."

Podust, predictably, is all for it. We are totally opposed. You may wonder why we all attach so much importance to the matter of who is Zone housekeeper. It is because in accordance with camp regulations, the housekeeper must keep a supervisory eye on the other prisoners; for instance, it is her responsibility to order us to "stand" when some camp functionary enters the Zone, and to "dismiss" when they leave. Failure by any prisoner to respond to these commands must be reported to the camp authorities. The housekeeper is also obliged to report any breaches of camp regulations. When a representative of the administration appears, it is her task to report who is working, who is ill, any happenings in the Zone. The housekeeper has the right to go through lockers and personal possessions to ensure that everything is tidy. It is her duty to collect our food and to take charge of any medicines (this only applies to our Zone, a special regulation thought up by the camp management just for us). Clearly, all the above-mentioned duties offer a half-informer, half-supervisor enormous scope. Keeping the house clean is the last thing that interests Podust and Vladimirova, it is the other duties they are keen on. What possibilities for control over us flash through their minds! For instance, with dividing out the bread—not now, of course, as we're on hunger strike, but later. Or issuing tablets—these can be stolen, or switched for something else. Or deciding whether to sterilize injection needles, or not to bother on the premise that injections from dirty needles won't kill us. Or to go through our things—now that would be really something! As for keeping us under surveillance, well, that's a direct duty, isn't it?

Our housekeepers had not done anything of the kind, of course, but simply ignored these duties. They concentrated on cleaning the house and the sick bay, a tiny box of a room containing a bed, a trestle and a couple of chairs with white covers. Naturally, we helped Raya and Edita as much as we could: the job of a conscientious housekeeper was, I think, much more onerous than sewing gloves. Imagine the difficulties of maintaining cleanliness in a house without sewage or hot water. Just to get a bucket of hot water means an hour of fiddling around with an ancient urn that keeps breaking down. It's even a battle to get a broom to replace one that has worn down completely. All the curtains and towelling covers from the sick bay must be washed by hand in a small basin with a minimum quantity of the meager ration of household soap. The bare board floor has to be swabbed after every visit by a warder or an officer who has tramped over it with muddy boots. Outside there's clay and sand, none of the paths are asphalted, and only two or three camp officials seem to have been taught to wipe their feet. So they march in regardless—it's not their house, after all, just zek quarters, so why bother? No, the work of the Zone housekeeper is not an easy one, but very enticing for someone working against the interests of the Zone, someone like our very own stoolie.

We were determined to keep her away from this job, even if it meant prolonging our hunger strike. The camp authorities, realizing that we were in earnest, hesitated to press the matter. Instead, we received a visit from the camp doctor, Vera Alexandrovna Volkova, who "caringly" pointed out that she is responsible not only for our health, but for the sanitary conditions in the Zone entrusted to her care. As housekeeper Abrutiene is both on hunger strike and refusing to work, she, Vera Alexandrovna, is obliged, as a doctor, to release Edita from all work—even if the latter were still sewing gloves. And what about cleaning the house? She understands what a mammoth task it is, even if you only consider the number of buckets of water that must be hauled to and fro.

Ah, so suddenly you understand, do you? A blinding flash of revelation, no less. What about the times you berated Raya, claiming that the curtains were less than snow white? Where was your understanding then? Or when you couldn't be bothered washing your hands and simply left dirty finger marks all over the towels washed by Raya? How many times was Raya practically reduced to tears by having to wash what had been newly laundered towels yet again for tomorrow? No doubt about it, this unexpected kindness has blossomed in Vera Alexandrovna's heart right on cue. She tries to steer us to the conclusion that all this effort is too much for us, so the housekeeper must be—who do you think?

"Well, figure it out for yourselves, women."

Coldly, we inform Vera Alexandrovna that Edita is and will remain our housekeeper, but while she is on hunger strike, we shall all take part in the cleaning. This is our home, and it shall be as clean as it always has been. We have no intention of living in filth, so her alarums and excursions about falling sanitary standards are unnecessary.

"But how will you manage to do this while you're on hunger strike?"

"That's our business."

"Well, women, on your own heads be it. If sanitary conditions in the Zone become unsatisfactory, I'll have to report it. We'll be checking."

That means that she'll be back tomorrow, intent on finding fault: a bit of spider web here, sand on the steps there, dust behind a locker . . . It is the fifth day of the hunger strike. Pani Jadvyga is laundering all "their" camp property. She tries to do everything that there is to be done, only to ensure that we shall lie quietly and husband our strength. But it is out of the question to let her try to carry the whole load. Tatyana Mikhailovna is swabbing the steps with an old piece of sacking. Galya is dusting our dining area. I am washing the bedroom floor, making sure I get everything clean under the beds and behind the lockers. I have to stop every three to four minutes because I am short of breath. The main thing is not to sit down, on no account must I sit down! Otherwise, precious energy must be spent on getting up again. Out to the refuse pit with a bucket of dirty water, back with a clean one. Keep beating, my heart, you're the youngest one in the Zone, you can do it. Yes, like that, taking it nice and easy, pausing for breath when necessary—see? We've made it to the threshold. Good work!

Vladimirova tracks around after me, keeping up a monotonous diatribe about how she will "finish me off." As I can still lift a bucket, she limits herself to words—who knows, I might be able to fight back if she lays a hand on me. Podust enters, and Vladimirova scoots over to her. "Supervisor! I can't hold myself back any longer. I'll make a pile of corpses out of these sanctimonious prigs!"

Podust maintains a strategic silence. To raise objections would be to stifle a worthy initiative by "a prisoner who has entered on the road to reform." But to offer open encouragement would not be quite the thing, either. She is, after all, an officer, and responsible for the maintenance of order in the Zone. So she prefers to remain aloof; in any case, Vladimirova stands in no need of encouragement from anyone.

None of us took Vladimirova's ravings seriously, but after she swore an oath to bash my brains in with a hammer, I noticed with some amusement that Tatyana Mikhailovna and Pani Jadvyga were taking pains to ensure that I was never alone. When I taxed them with this, they laughed with me. Surely, I protested, they were taking caution too far.

"But she's a psychopath. She doesn't understand what's going on in her own head from one minute to the next," protests Pani Jadvyga, trying to suppress a smile. I draw them a vivid word picture of Vladimirova launching herself at me with a hammer and a battle cry, only to be thwarted by Pani Jadvyga, who hero-ically trips her up with a broom. Tatyana Mikhailovna adds a few colorful details, and we sink to the ground, laughing helplessly.

The rattle of a sewing machine brings us to our feet. What's this? Edita sewing? Indeed she is—she's making a floor cloth out of the only material available in the Zone—the gloves which are waiting to be sewn up. Bit by bit, using palm-size pieces, she fashions a cloth for washing our floors. The old one is in tatters, and where would we get a new one? Galya writes a letter to her husband: they'll be round for the mail tomorrow. Her letter will have to be cleared by several censors—one in Mordovia, one in Perm, and, in between that, by the KGB. Will this letter ever reach political prisoner Vasili Barats in his camp in Perm? Will he guess that his wife is on hunger strike? Admittedly, in her noti-fication to our camp authorities Galya used the word "fast" in-stead of "hunger strike": she explained to us that the teachings of the Pentecostal faith forbid hunger strikes, but fasts are permit-ted. Semantics aside, though, the fact remains that Galya, like the rest of us, will depend only on water and prayer to sustain her until Natasha and Tanya are back.

What a mixed bunch we are: a Catholic, a Pentecostal, several Orthodox, an unbeliever ... later we were to be joined by a Baptist. Yet we were always deeply respectful of one another's convictions. And God did not turn His face away from our small patch of Mordovian soil.

17

"Rudenko, Velikanova, Ratushinskaya—to the hospital! We have to isolate you as you're hunger-striking . . ."

These words from an officer accompanied by several warders. That means they intend to force-feed us: to do this, they handcuff you, prise your jaws apart with an iron lever which crushes your teeth, shove a tube down your throat and pour two liters of some kind of solution down it. A procedure strongly reminiscent of rape, but such is our "humane Soviet law."

I had already heard about force-feeding from Tanya Osipova: she had been subjected to it every second day of her four-month hunger strike. The object of the exercise is not to save the life of a hunger striker; even with force-feeding you will die if you refuse to eat for long enough. Force-feeding is aimed at prolonging the agony from two months to a year or eighteen months. So even if the prisoner sticks to his guns, he will still die eventually; if he doesn't, and calls off the hunger strike, it means surrender. So the procedure of force-feeding has been devised not to preserve strength, but to cause maximum suffering. Two liters of fluid pumped into a shrunken stomach causes terrible pains. On the seventh day of our hunger strike it was all we could do to force ourselves to swallow half a cup of water at a time. As soon as anything is introduced into the stomach, the quiescent pangs of hunger awaken with new intensity.

"Let them really feel it," is the motto of our captors.

For this reason, feeding takes place two to three times a week. And when they're through with you, they keep you manacled to the trestle for about an hour, so you cannot get up and vomit out what they have pumped into you.

Hunger strikers feel terribly cold even in normal temperatures, so a point is made of keeping them in temperatures below normal. Prisoners don't have warm blankets or woolen clothes. Let them freeze, that will show them. And so forth.

So that is what we are about to experience. The measure is quite clearly a punitive one: nobody dies just like that from a thirteen-day hunger strike. Of course, zeks have fewer reserves of physical energy than ordinary people. Their organism has been weakened, and to go from a state of habitual malnutrition into a hunger strike is a far cry from replacing a normal food intake with a medicinal "starvation diet."

Still, this is our first hunger strike, and we have not yet been reduced to the state when the body has no natural reserves left to draw on for as much as a day. I was only to reach this condition by the winter of 1985, and then the same thirteen days of a hunger strike were sufficient to bring me to the edge of death. Then, oh then I was to see the doctors panic, start taking my pulse, urge me to agree to be put on an intravenous drip! Only then did I see them show fear—that I would die, and they would be blamed . . . For by that time my name had, without my knowing it, become famous. But they knew, and feared the uproar that would ensue. On that occasion they did not even dare to force me, they preferred to back down. By that time they knew better than to try to force-feed someone from our Zone.

Yet this first time around, they are untroubled by apprehensions of unpleasant repercussions. We are locked into a small surgical ward and left there until the next day.

We confer about our best course of action. There is no question of calling off the hunger strike. It will be impossible to break free, because there will be a lot more of "them" than there are of us. In any case, we will be handcuffed. At the same time, it is unthinkable that we should submit meekly to their preposterous intentions. We rack our brains to devise some means of making them unwilling to try anything like this with us ever again. Let's look at the matter logically, we tell ourselves. What is it that "they" dislike most? Publicity. So let us give their actions maximum publicity, and not in a month's time when our friends and relatives get to hear about what happened, but right now! It's all quite simple, really. We are right in the center of the hospital zone to which women from three camps are brought for treatment. Then there is the resident service personnel. The hospital is full to overflowing—heaven knows how many people they've got here. The patients, moreover, have contact with the adjacent men's criminal zone. So it's a certainty that if we manage to shout out who we are and what's being done to us, at least a thousand people will know. Some of the prisoners here are due for release any day upon completion of their sentences. That means they will carry the information out of the camp in their heads. And if we have time to call out a telephone number, there will be those among them who will memorize it and phone through the information after they've left the camp. The KGB knows Igor's telephone number well enough, so it's not as though he will be placed under any additional threat. But we must start yelling as quickly and as loudly as possible before our "humanists" manage to gag us. It will be no trouble for the zeks to remember our names, because the whole Zone knows our names and our faces. The most important thing is to try to shout out all the salient details as loudly as possible before they jam a tube down your throat. What one of us may be unable to finish shouting will be picked up by the next one.

Tatyana Mikhailovna is doubtful: "I'm supposed to shout? But I don't know if I can, I've never done so! And in any case, to shout under torture . . ."

I do my best to talk her around: "You won't be shouting under torture. When they start that, you won't be able to shout. We'll do it *before* they start, when it's clear that they are going ahead. Anyway, it's not as though you'll be squealing with pain, you'll be shouting to pass on information. Pretend that you're shouting to someone in a departing train . . ."

Raya takes no part in this discussion; her condition is very bad. She experiences terrible spells of suffocation during hunger strikes. In the Zone, she would lie out on the grass to be able to breathe a little more easily, but here we are locked into a small, stuffy room, and the lack of fresh air is affecting her badly. The only window is locked and barred. We consider smashing the glass, but decide against it: they'll only split us up and lock us into tiny "box" cells, with no light and windows, and breathing will be even harder in there. We fuss over Raya without reaching any definite decision. Tatyana Mikhailovna is not against the idea we have been discussing as such, she is only afraid that she will not be able to bring herself to yell when the time comes. This is a purely psychological block: well-mannered, intelligent people are not in the habit of shouting, so she will have to force herself to perform this unaccustomed act. And is it certain that one can always force oneself to do something, even in a case of dire necessity?

It is the eighth day of our hunger strike. We do not feel too bad in the morning. We are weak, of course, but not totally drained. Our dinner is brought, and what have we here? Usually, one whiff of skilly is enough to kill any desire to eat, but they have served us a real feast, which we make no move to touch, so they have to take it all away again.

"Velikanova. The doctor is ready to see you now. She wants to examine you."

This is it. They're starting. We hear a clatter, and the sound of breaking glass . . . We learned later that our correct and reserved Tatyana Mikhailovna took out a glass door with her elbow, an incident which provided me with countless opportunities to tease her later and call her a "hooligan." Then we hear a shout. And what a shout! It is certainly true that in conditions of stress we are capable of things we had never imagined ourselves doing. I am to prove this theory myself in a few minutes' time. Raya is shuddering, and my own heart is racing—these few minutes were immeasurably worse than the moment when "they" actually laid hands on me. I strain to remember what Tatyana Mikhailovna had time to shout out. There is silence outside now, so they must have overwhelmed her.

"Ratushinskaya."

Right, my precious ones, let's be having you! I'm borne along on a swirling tide of rage such as I have never felt before: Tatyana Mikhailovna? You dared lay your filthy paws on Tatyana Mikhailovna? Oh, but I'll lead you a dance!

Six men in military uniforms. Dr. Vera Alexandrovna Volkova. And, of course, Podust. Despite the fury roiling through me, I am struck by her appearance, and will remember it forever. She is in a state of some kind of violent arousal: her eyes glitter, and her face is covered with red blotches. Her distended nostrils quiver, and she seems to be in the grip of some kind of sadistic ecstasy. I have never seen anything quite like it in my whole life, only read about it in books about Nazis, and even then I had assumed that it was a literary flight of fancy.

"Ratushinskaya," pronounces Dr. Volkova, "the regulations state that we must force-feed prisoners on the seventh day of a hunger strike. We have delayed a day as it is . . . Will you eat voluntarily?"

"I do not consent to forced feeding. I am on a hunger strike in defense of Lazareva. You are a doctor—how could you have possibly consented to her incarceration in SHIZO?"

"Ratushinskaya, we must safeguard your life."

"Does that mean that you've already taken steps to save Lazareva's life? I declare that I am capable of conducting a thirteen-day hunger strike without any need of external interference. If you examine me, you will see that for yourself. You didn't protest when you saw me washing the floor, did you?"

"Ratushinskaya, we are going to feed you."

That's Podust getting her word in. I am suddenly seized from behind. I push my elbows and wrists forward to make it harder for them to handcuff me.

"Everyone! Everyone! Remember this!"

I shout out our names, why we're hunger-striking, who's in SHIZO and for how many days, and who is being force-fed. Podust and her accomplices try to pin me down, but I'm in that state in which people can carry safes out of burning buildings or stop a moving car with their shoulder. I drag them around the room as they all cling to me and yell, yell without ceasing, repeating all the information for the second time now.

"Telephone Kiev 444–33–95! Kiev! Tell Igor everything! 444–33–95! Write it down!"

And again, and again. I feel no pain, even though they have my hands twisted behind my back, nor am I conscious of the combined weight of their bodies. I only feel the trembling in a hand which has my shoulder in a viselike grip.

This was not an easy job for the camp guards. They were not trained to handle such a situation, they were not expecting such resistance, and were still somewhat shaken by the preceding scene. They do not even realize immediately that I am not biting or kicking, but merely twisting out of their hold. Moreover, they are ashamed of what they're doing; unlike Podust, they are not in the grip of sadistic pleasure, all they want to do is stop my shouting quickly, quickly, as quickly as possible. Finally they realize that instead of pinning me down, what they need to do is make me lose my footing. So they lift me as though I were a feather, and throw me—head first against the wooden trestle. Under the circumstances, how could they gauge their strength —the strength of six large men—against my hunger-striking weight?

A red ball seems to explode loudly inside my head, and it is only from Tatyana Mikhailovna's accounts that I know what happened next.

18

I was brought, unconscious, to a windowless "box" cell in the so-called Block Twelve, that is, the psychiatric section. We were not placed here because the authorities suspected Tatyana Mikhailovna or myself of insanity. No, it was simply to ensure our complete isolation, and there are no "boxes" in the other wards. The "box" is only large enough to squeeze in two bunks and a slop bucket covered with a piece of oilcloth—our toilet. I was thrown onto one of these bunks. Some time later Tatyana Mikhailovna, still handcuffed, was brought here, too.

"Irochka, Irochka! Can you hear me?"

This frantic question pulled me back out of black nothingness. Yes, I hear you, but how can I make my eyes open? I feel as though I am in one of those dreams where you want to run, but can't make your legs move, or want to shout, and no sound emerges. Finally, the necessary muscles do their job (not at all the ones I was trying to move) and in the darkness I can just make out Tatyana Mikhailovna's face. Or, to be more precise, I see two faces overlaying each other. Why is it so dark? Has something happened to my eyes? No, it's just that the lamp is so weak, and is set back in a stone niche with a grille in front of it. There is no other source of light. Tatyana Mikhailovna uses her shoulders and elbows to prod me into awareness, because her hands are still manacled behind her back.

"Everything's all right, it's all right," I manage.

"Thank God. What on earth did they do to you?"

How should I know what they did? They threw me head-first against a trestle—it seems as though I must have struck it with the back of my head. As for what happened next—who can say? I don't even know whether they pumped the two liters of solution into me. My guess is that they didn't, because I feel nothing like Tanya Osipova's description of the aftermath of forced feeding: "It's as though your stomach is full of stones," she had said. Or maybe they took fright and pumped in just a small dose, just enough to observe the letter of the regulations? Then again, they may have done nothing else, because their aim was to inflict torture, and there's not much point in torturing someone who is unconscious. Perhaps, when the time comes for Vera Alexandrovna to think about her soul, she will tell the truth about what happened then.

Having satisfied herself that I am not only blinking my eyes but am capable of rational thought, Tatyana Mikhailovna calms down a little. I can only wonder how she can find the strength to concern herself about me after what she has just gone through herself. I try to smile at her. It seems to work. Someone comes in to remove Tatyana Mikhailovna's handcuffs. Do they take them off me, too? Or were mine removed earlier, when they saw that they had achieved more than they bargained for? No, my memory is not up to the demands I'm making on it. Tatyana Mikhailovna, realizing that none of the medical staff will be coming to check me over, carries out a simple test herself. She puts her hands over my eyes, and then turns my head toward the lamp. There is no contraction of the pupils at all. She repeats the procedure, with the same results. Concussion! That means I must lie as still as possible, and not try to read under any circumstances. Movement is reduced to a minimum anyway by the size of our cell, but after two days I begin to moan about not being able to read. Tatyana Mikhailovna heartlessly forbids anything of the kind. But at first reading was the least of my concerns.

In the meantime, I am continually plagued by nausea, and do not know how my body will react when I try to get up. In fact, the body proved reasonably obedient, even though I blundered from side to side. I lost all sense of balance at first, but this returned after a while. I was left, however, with a legacy of blinding headaches, which I suffer to this day, and they strike at the most inopportune moments. Like natural disasters, they invariably occur at the worst possible times, and in the least suitable places.

Strange as it may seem, my concussion proved to be a blessing in disguise for the whole Zone: it made our tormentors take fright. What if they had thrown me a little bit harder? What if I'd hit the trestle with my temple? Or if I had been a little weaker? That would have meant murder during a session of forced feeding. Uproar! It's not that they would have regretted my death, but just think of the unfavorable publicity: a political prisoner killed! Even without eyewitnesses, there were plenty of witnesses who heard what was happening . . . Something like this would have been impossible to conceal. And there's no guarantee that things would go better next time. Apprehension brings them to the peephole in the door every few minutes to make sure that I'm still alive. Anyway, the upshot was that they never tried anything like that with our Zone again, nor did they lay so much as a finger on the next lot of hunger strikers. And so it came about that I never had to experience personally the disgraceful ritual of forced feeding, and do not know how it feels to have some mixture concocted by jailers pumped into my stomach. Thank God for it. I prefer to suffer the headaches for the rest of my life.

But where, we wondered as we sat in our "box," is our Raya? They should have set about her when they were through with me. Maybe she is in the neighboring "box"? Tatyana Mikhailovna has not heard her voice. We are really very worried about Raya: God knows what makes up the fluid they force into you—maybe it's some kind of broth made with bones or meat? Raya is violently allergic to meat and any meat products—so much so that even a sip of broth is enough to knock her off her feet.

Later we learned that after my fracas, the six uniformed guards surrounded Raya and threatened her with physical violence unless she drank the liquid prepared for her "feed." Raya stated that she was not calling off her hunger strike, but would drink the liquid because she simply did not have the strength to offer physical resistance the way we had. So she drank it, knowing full well that otherwise they would force it down her throat. And then it started. An hour later, Raya was confronted by a triumphant Podust, who informed her that a report had been written up to the effect that Rudenko had voluntarily called off her hunger strike, having admitted that there were no grounds for a hunger strike in the first place.

"And now," commanded Podust, "you will write all that down yourself. We've already done the official document, so nobody will believe you if you say anything to the contrary."

Oh, no? And Raya promptly sat down and wrote that she had not called off her hunger strike, nor did she have any intention of doing so, but would continue as long as Lazareva was in SHIZO. She regrets, she wrote, that she succumbed to the blackmailing tactics of the doctor and the threat of violence from six large men. In future she would know better than to agree to anything "voluntary": they could mete out the same treatment to her as they had to us. It is not hard to imagine the anger of our administration. To their way of thinking, once you've conceded something, they've got you on their hook. You're theirs! A moment of weakness is interpreted as weakness forever, even if it is the weakness of a woman driven to the limits of her endurance facing threats from strong, merciless men. And if you dare to affirm your earlier stance after this—why, you are trying to rob them of what they see as their legitimate claim to your soul. And that is something they will never forgive . . .

Raya was locked up alone and given no water for more than twenty-four hours—and that on the ninth day of a hunger strike. When she called to the hospital aides on the other side of the door for water, they told her they had been strictly forbidden to give her any. Then the administration started to pressure her again: "Call off your hunger strike."

"No!"

So they took her and force-fed her through a tube inserted into her nose: this was the only such occurrence after my concussion. They did not risk forcing her again, though—she had reached snapping point. This was the penalty Raya was forced to pay for what she later referred to as her weakness, and which she considered to be a serious retreat on her part before the KGB. As for us—we only sympathized with her. Sadly, I have had occasion to encounter that breed of "burning fighters" who are always prepared to vilify anyone who has ever retreated by so much as a tiny step in the face of KGB pressure. But what is the worth of their uncompromising stance if they are as quick to condemn our own as they are to condemn our persecutors? As a rule, those who are loudest in their scorn are those who have not personally experienced even a tenth of what the objects of their denigration have had to endure. Yet those who have trodden the painful path have witnessed so much human suffering that they do not stoop to censure over trifles. When someone is at the end of his strength, lend him the support of yours, and see what wonders that can work. If he can endure no more, he will leave the struggle honestly, but help you to the best of his ability. Each bears that burden which matches his strength, and he who is not on the side of the executioners is your brother. Former zeks do not usually need to have these simple truths explained to them—but oh, how often they must be explained to those who have never had to swallow camp skilly!

Raya had a much harder time of it than Tatyana Mikhailovna and I: blackmail, isolation, violence and then torture by thirst. She was separated from us for all the remaining days of the hunger strike. It was much easier for Tatyana Mikhailovna and me to keep our spirits up. The authorities left us alone, only appearing three times a day to deliver our food. By their rules, food is left in a hunger striker's cell for two hours before it is removed. In our tiny box-cell this food stood literally under our noses a total of six hours a day. In an effort to minimize hunger-triggering food odors, we covered the dishes with bits of plastic bags, which we had had the presence of mind to bring from the Zone. There was no proper ventilation in the cell. I kept getting attacks of nausea, which I initially ascribed to the smell of the food. Later, however, I learned that nausea is one of the accompanying symptoms of concussion. The attacks of nausea passed fairly soon, though, and we divided our time between talking and reading Ecclesiastes:

> Two are better than one; because they have a good reward for their labor. For if they fall, the one will lift up his fellow: but woe to him that is alone when he falleth; for he hath not another to help him up.[1]

We counted the days. Not only the days of the hunger strike, but the days remaining before Tatyana Mikhailovna's departure from the Zone. Her camp sentence was due to expire around the beginning of November, but we knew that she would be taken away earlier. It is "their" standard practice, a sort of farewell gesture, to subject people due for release to several months of transportation. Firstly, this is to ensure that the person in question arrives at his or her exile destination in a state of complete exhaustion; secondly, it stops them from being able to publicize any really fresh information from the Zone.

We made arrangements about conveying information from the Zone in the future: it is vital to be devising new means all the time, in case the KGB uncovers this or that method. We even thought up a number of very workable, totally new ideas. Igor would certainly travel up to see Tatyana Mikhailovna after she reached her place of exile, and these ideas would be a valuable guide for him in his future activity. I tell Tatyana Mikhailovna about Igor at great length. The picture that emerges, I notice, seems to be too good to be true. Still, when they finally did meet, there was instant understanding and rapport between them, these two people who are dearer to me than anyone in the world.

We shy away from sentiment, especially when we are young, and because of this often forgo the opportunity of expressing our affection for others in warmest words. I probably missed the opportunity to do so with Tatyana Mikhailovna. But I daresay she knew anyway—she, who always understood everything. Are there people who have no faults? Yes, there are. If you had shared time

1. Ecclesiastes 4:9–10.

in the camp with Tatyana Mikhailovna, you would have seen the proof for yourself, but as it is, there is no point in debating the issue. Different people can have differing views about this axiom. But I am convinced that when there is so much light in one person, its brilliance obliterates all shadows.

For the benefit of skeptics I must admit that Tatyana Mikhailovna has one great failing—she is completely unmusical. She always joked about being tone deaf, but regretted it nonetheless. I can only sympathize, because the same applies to me. Neither of us has dared sing in the presence of witnesses since we were old enough to realize this lack of talent, and just as well! But here in the box-cell, Tatyana Mikhailovna tends me as though I were a small child, stroking my head and singing softly:

> I thank you, rusty prison grating,
> And you, sharp glinting bayonet blades,
> For you have given me more wisdom
> Than learning over long decades.
>
> I thank you, light of feeble tapers,
> And you, hard bunk beneath my rib,
> The comfort that you bring reminds me
> Of distant childhood's gentle crib . . .

That is how I best remember Tatyana Mikhailovna: a thin, frail hand stroking my head, and this song. Never have I heard anyone sing more sweetly.

Day twelve of the hunger strike. Natasha should return to the Zone tomorrow, Tanya should have come back yesterday—that is, unless they had their time extended. If that happened, we shall simply prolong our hunger strike. If the authorities want to finish us off, let them finish off all of us together, not just one of us. The door opens to admit Captain Shalin and an unknown lieutenant. This does not look like another attempt at force feeding: Shalin actually works in the men's zone, and only began appearing in ours after we started ignoring Podust. He is invariably careful and polite, and the administration sends him to conduct "diplomatic" talks with us. Both Shalin and the lieutenant greet us courteously, and then break their news: "You can call off your hunger strike. Lazareva's back in the Zone."

What? Back from SHIZO a day early? Shalin explains that Natasha was not returned because of our hunger strike, but because today is a "transport" day between camps. These occur three times a week, and today is such a day, whereas tomorrow isn't. All right, all right, fine—we get the message.

"Where's Rudenko?" we demand.

"In the Zone, in the Zone. They're all waiting for you there."

We set off. They even help us carry our bags of zek gear. And everyone really is back in the Zone. How emaciated Tanya looks. She had conducted a hunger strike in SHIZO in support of Natasha, too. Luckily, they did not try to force-feed her, and on the sixth day even issued some bedclothes, which are normally not allowed in a punishment cell—such generosity. It's time to call off the hunger strike, but that is not as easy as it might sound. As you have probably guessed, the superb food offered to us during the hunger strike is no longer in evidence. It's back to the black bread and skilly for us. It can be dangerous to throw yourself on to food straight after a hunger strike, nor is it advisable to eat just anything. Raya is our specialist on "coming out" of hunger strikes: before they were arrested, she and her husband specialized in dietetics. According to her, no solid foods should be eaten during the first few days, one should only drink fruit juices. After that, one graduates to grated apples and carrots, then dairy produce ... There is no way, of course, that we can carry out this program. Things might have been different had we still had our vegetable patch, but as it is ... Well, we shall just have to improvise.

Raya devises a kind of thin soup by straining out the bits of potato from our skilly, picks some wild goosefoot ... In the evening we can all eat a small bit of bread, but it must be thoroughly dried out on the stove first, and then chewed ever so slowly before swallowing. We cut up the hunk of bread delivered by a warder. What's this in the middle of it? A lump of salt the size of a large strawberry! From another slice we extract a piece of string. Thank heavens there are no baked cockroaches, at least.

We recall how a few months ago we found a shoe nail in a loaf. The following day the skilly is unbearably salty, so we send it back to the kitchen. In fact, there is not a great deal of difference between the times when we eat and our hunger strikes. Still, we'll manage. We are all overjoyed to be together again. Pani Jadvyga says grace, and we dip our spoons into Raya's soup.

19

Only now do we get to hear about the most important happening of these days of the hunger strike. Now that we are gathered together once more, Tanya and Natasha proceed to tell us all about it. As the account unfolds, we are unable to suppress whoops of delight, and then laughter. It was all due to Podust's haste to send Lazareva and Osipova into SHIZO. She barely waited until the end of my meeting with Igor to act: the only consideration that held her back even that long was that I might, somehow, manage to convey the information to Igor. And that would result in the very publicity "they" are always so anxious to avoid . . . But our meeting ended at 8:00 p.m. and the last "cuckoo" left Barashevo for Potma an hour earlier. So Igor, Alya and both our mothers (they had come, too, but were not allowed to see me) had to stay overnight to catch the first "cuckoo" the following morning. The very same "cuckoo," as it turned out, in which Tanya and Natasha were being taken to SHIZO. There's not much standing on ceremony in Barashevo: prisoners and non-prisoners all travel on the same train, but in different carriages. As the non-prisoners are all jailers, there's no need for secrecy or camouflage; it's not as though the sight of zeks is something new to them. Relatives come here for meetings very infrequently, so there's no question of providing a special train for occasional visitors.

With great glee, we visualized the scene that took place. Natasha and Tanya, escorted by two guards armed with submachine guns, were brought to the platform where Igor and the family were waiting for the train, along with a handful of off-duty camp personnel going to Potma or on to Moscow. It probably never occurred to our administration that Tanya or Natasha might recognize my relatives. How wrong they were! It's true that none of them had ever met, but the absence of identity tags was enough to tell Igor that Tanya and Natasha were from the women's political zone. He opened his mouth to say something, but Tanya was faster:

"Hello, Igor," she greeted him.

She had recognized him just as easily as I would have recognized her Ivan after all the hours we had spent poring over their photographs. Igor bounded across to them: "Where are they taking you? Quick, your names."

Tanya rapped out everything quickly and precisely: who they are, where they are going and why, who is on hunger strike and who is refusing to work. She even remembered to say how many days she and Natasha had to spend in SHIZO each. The guards were in a quandary. Should they shoot? But the prisoners are not trying to escape. And then the rest of the camp staff on the platform (mainly women), irrespective of the fact that they were off-duty, threw themselves on Igor to separate him from Tanya and Natasha. He shook them off with ease (carefully, to give nobody a pretext to claim assault) and tried to get closer to Tanya in case she had any more information to impart. But she had already given him the key facts, so she contented herself with calling out: "We all love your wife very much."

"Very much," affirmed Natasha.

These two words cost her dearly: she was deprived of her next meeting with relatives, just as Tanya was for "disgracefully publicizing internal camp matters."

Finally they were dragged apart and travelled in different carriages: Tanya and Natasha buoyed up by this unexpected piece of luck in one, and my family in another, both mothers barely holding back tears, Alya weeping openly because of her youth and inexperience, and Igor. Now, recalling that incident, I ask him: "What did you feel?"

But he doesn't like airing his emotions.

"I spent most of the journey back comforting Alya," he says. "The poor kid was in a state of complete shock. I knew what to expect, but for her, this first time . . ."

Naturally, the first thing he did upon arrival in Moscow was to take steps to ensure that the information was disseminated as quickly and as widely as possible. So the outside world knew what had happened while Tanya and Natasha were still in SHIZO and we were on hunger strike.

That was a real triumph; ordinarily, it would have taken the information weeks to reach its destination, written out on a tiny scrap of paper or by one of our other means, all involving much planning and difficulty. Yet instead, we had this amazing stroke of luck. Bravo, Tanya. Quick thinking, indeed. Had she hesitated for a moment, the opportunity might have been lost altogether. We express our appreciation with customary banter: "How do you like that? She doesn't get meetings with her own husband, so she grabs one with someone else's."

"Irochka, don't you think you should enact a jealous scene?"

"And how! I'm going to pull out every hair on her head."

"Poor Podust—just think what a blow this must have been to her."

"And what about the KGB?"

We laugh gaily, then the talk switches to our families, out come all the photographs for the hundredth time . . . But now we study each face with new intensity: when will we see them again, by God's grace? All these unknown people are almost like our own kin by now; we know how they are loved by those with whom we shall spend the long years of our sentences.

Funnily enough, when Igor and I met Tanya in the United States, he couldn't believe what a little thing she is. On that faraway platform in Barashevo, flanked by two armed guards, her regal bearing made him think she was very tall. In fact, like any real queen!

The information Tanya gave Igor was only part of the news

that managed to find its way out of the camp during that partic- ularly difficult August. Ironically, this was again due to the un- bridled punitive fervor of our "blonde fiend." Even before the major events, on August 11, she found nothing better to do than to deliver a "disciplinary" homily to our Pani Jadvyga in the presence of the latter's relatives. It is not hard to imagine what our steadfast Jadvyga's son and sister thought of the following exchange: "Bieliauskiene, you're an elderly woman, your health cannot but give cause for concern [here she listed all of Jadvyga's ailments]. You could at least spare a thought for your relatives' feelings. If you persist in refusing to wear an identity tag, you'll land in SHIZO, and that is enough to undermine even the most robust constitution."

"I would rather die than go against my conscience."

"You'll have to give in finally, no matter what you think."

So Jadvyga's son Zilvinis returned to Lithuania with a very clear idea of what they would do to his mother if she refused to compromise her conscience. Naturally, Igor met Zilvinis, and they swapped notes. War had been declared on our Zone, but apart from the two opposing sides, ourselves and the KGB, there was a third side involved in the conflict: all those people who were campaigning for our freedom—in Russia, the Ukraine, Lith- uania, Britain, Sweden, the USA . . . Oh, that I could list them all, and name everybody by name. But that is impossible—the names of some must be safeguarded from the KGB, the names of innu- merable others I will never know, for none of the thousands of letters sent to the camp were ever given to us, all were burnt by the camp censors. The remaining names would make up two or three large tomes. As for the countries from which they wrote— open the atlas at just about any page, and you can be sure that there were people in those countries who demonstrated outside Soviet embassies, gathered signatures under petitions, prayed for us. It was this third side which decided the ultimate outcome of the war, forcing open the gates of the camp and allowing us to emerge one by one, until the Small Zone ceased to exist. But not every one of us gained freedom: Tatyana Velikanova and Yelena Sannikova are still serving terms of internal exile. And I, who am now on the other side of the Soviet border, strain my voice to breaking point in repeated appeals: help them! Let us secure their release! Believe me, you of the third side: it all depends on you, and you are capable of achieving much more than you may think.

Slowly, we were recovering from the effects of the hunger strike. We all had huge edemas and tended to faint from any abrupt movements, but we were improving. On September 1, they came for Tatyana Mikhailovna.

"Prepare for transportation!"

Closing ranks, we put all our energies into pressuring our "doctor/executioner" Volkova. I cannot resist mentioning in passing that Dr. Volkova (the surname derives from the Russian word for "wolf") later married a man called Zverev (deriving from "beast"). So Dr. Wolf became Dr. Beast. I swear that I am not making this up—my imagination wouldn't stretch that far. Our Vera Alexandrovna is a living, breathing person, and there is no need to hide her name from the KGB under a pseudonym. She and the KGB are old friends. We refused to let Tatyana Mikhailovna be taken away and demanded to see the doctor.

"It's not two full days since the end of the hunger strike," we told her when she arrived. "You are prepared to excuse Velikanova from work, but not from transportation? Bear in mind that if you maintain that she is fit to make the journey and something happens to her, we are all witnesses of your culpability. And we'll see that you don't get away with it."

It worked. I don't know whether it was what we said or the letter we wrote to the Procuracy that did the trick, but in any case, it was clear that Tatyana Mikhailovna would be leaving the Zone very soon. On one hand we were glad, but it was gladness mixed with regret. We set about preparing her for the forthcoming journey. Pani Jadvyga made her a pair of slippers out of scraps of cloth: hard-wearing, elegantly styled, the result of loving, patient zek craftsmanship. She decorated the slippers with complex embroidered symbols of us, the past, the future, stars, barbed wire . . . I wrote out all those of my poems which might possibly be passed by the camp censor, poems from the "children's cycle." If Tatyana Mikhailovna were to say that they were a present for her grandson, there might be a slim chance that they would not be confiscated. Tatyana Mikhailovna herself is taking her impending departure very hard: "Once I've gone, they'll probably start on all of you with renewed force."

And indeed, it looks like it. They're probably holding back their main "surprises" until Tatyana Mikhailovna leaves, and won't be able to pass on the information. Still, we'll be in touch; not for nothing did we devote so much time and thought to devising our means.

Chin up! We'll manage.

Tatyana Mikhailovna shares out all her belongings: Tanya gets a dictionary, I get a Bible and a small volume of Mandelshtam's poetry, clothes are distributed evenly all round. Those going into exile are allowed to wear their own clothes, and there is a parcel with civilian-type clothing from home waiting for Tatyana Mikhailovna in the guardhouse. We try to persuade her to take at least some item out of the warmer clothing, but she refuses to listen: "I'll have everything I need, whereas you've all got next to nothing," she says firmly.

So that is how she left us when they came for her on September 5—without even a jacket, carrying a small, homemade bag. That bag contained our farewell presents and a piece of camp bread which Raya slipped in at the last moment. Everything has been said, but how hard it is to part! We all sit down in silence for a few minutes, in keeping with the old Russian custom before the commencement of a journey. Then we accompany her to the camp gates and, again in accordance with tradition, each one of us kisses her three times. Pani Jadvyga makes the sign of the cross over her, Catholic-fashion, we cross her the Orthodox way. Then her thin, grey-haired little figure passes through the gates, and they clang shut.

That's that. She's gone. The next time I was to speak to Tatyana Mikhailovna came after my own release, when I telephoned her in her distant place of exile, and then later from London, when I read out a poem I had dedicated to her. But we have not seen each other again. After my release I was in no condition to undertake the long journey to Kazakhstan in Soviet Central Asia, and now I can't stop reproaching myself: I should have gone, no matter what. Who cares about heart trouble and bronchitis? Even if I had collapsed halfway, Igor would have got me there somehow. As it is—when will I get a chance to embrace her? Forgive me, Lord, for succumbing to such weakness, please let it happen!

In the meantime, I frequently reread those of her letters which reached me in the Zone, and which I always kept by me.

"Irochka, my dear, Bella Akhmadulina[1] once wrote the following lines about Pablo Neruda:[2]

> Did this all really happen?
> But we, when we're reflected
> In a poet's brilliant eye
> Become what we must be.

"When I read them, I recalled how you and I read Ecclesiastes."

And on another occasion: ". . . I remember each one of you, always and without fail, hold imaginary conversations with you, even argue. After all, there are so many subjects we never finished debating." Then again: ". . . try to safeguard your health, and learn patience and tolerance. I'm not saying you don't have them, but you need more in order to understand those who are different from you."

No doubt about it, Velikanova was a bad influence on me: all her advice ran counter to the Moral Code of the builders of communism . . . And I strove, strove and strove again to learn patience. There was plenty of time; those who determined the years I had for learning had been generous with their terms.

1. A contemporary Soviet poet.
2. Chilean poet, winner of the Nobel Prize for Literature.

20

We did not know it then, but Tatyana Mikhailovna was not sent immediately to her place of exile; she was given two months in PKT—internal camp prison—for "refusal to wear an identity tag and for malicious infringement of camp regulations." So she spent September and October in an unheated solitary cell in the criminal zone and, of course, without any of the warm clothing her family had sent for her release. And the frosts were already upon us by then . . . It was in this cell that she conducted the eight-day "Madrid" hunger strike we had agreed on earlier in defense of the rights of her fellow citizens.

To the Heads of States Signatory to the Helsinki Agreement

We, women political prisoners in the USSR, testify that human rights are violated in our country.

Soviet citizens are deprived of freedom of speech, of the press and of assembly. They do not enjoy the right to choose their own place of residence, nor freedom of movement even within the borders of their own country. Soviet citizens are subject to discrimination on national and religious grounds, and are persecuted for their convictions.

We testify that the lives of not only political and ordinary prisoners, but the lives of all citizens are ruled not so much by law, as by secret instructions. Therefore, Soviet citizens cannot even know their rights and obligations, let alone realize them.

They are without rights before the totalitarian machine of the Soviet state. We are prepared to supply evidence to back up all our assertions to any international commission.

We believe that only a government which respects the rights of its own citizens is worthy of trust in the international sphere. We affirm our solidarity with all those who have the courage to oppose lies, tyranny and violence.

Lacking any other means of defending our fellow citizens, we intend to conduct an eight-day hunger strike from September 7, 1983, in defense of their violated rights.

ABRUTIENE, BARATS, BIELIAUSKIENE, VELIKANOVA, LAZAREVA, OSIPOVA, RATUSHINSKAYA, RUDENKO.

September 6, 1983

The rest of us only realized what a hunger strike in PKT means when we experienced it for ourselves. But for us in the Zone, this second hunger strike, the "Madrid" one, was relatively easy, even though it came so soon after the first one. Moreover, the camp administration unwittingly did us a favor by admitting Vladimirova into the hospital; so there were no hysterical outbursts, and nobody to spy on us. Along with Vladimirova's departure we missed a couple of ballpoint pens, which were in short supply in the camp and therefore a prime object for barter. The Zone was quiet, the flower beds blazed with the last asters and dahlias, and the berries of the rowan tree reddened overhead. Nyurka padded around on soft paws, and the warders fed her now as a matter of course. Autumn sunsets streaked the Mordovian sky with brilliant colors long after the sun had dropped below the Zone fence. No attempts were made to either isolate or force-feed us. Podust was nowhere to be seen. In the evenings, we would gather around our "fireplace": the door dislodged by Tanya's unsuccessful fly-swatting was not put back on the stove until around August 1985. However, we even preferred it this way—the open fire brought living warmth to our frail bodies, and the embers changed color gradually as the flames died down. Hunger strikes have the effect of sharpening your sense of smell and perception of color, your eyesight becomes keener and the small details of your environment stand out in unusually bold relief. I remember standing once over our well, and studying a yellowed poplar leaf in its dark brown waters: and this leaf seemed so breathtakingly beautiful that I deliberately delayed dipping my bucket into the water.

On the first day of the "Madrid" hunger strike we were visited by a KGB official, surrounded by our own camp brass. Obviously, information about the goings-on in our rebellious Zone had come as a bolt from the blue back in central headquarters. Actually, he made no attempt to talk to us, realizing at once that we wouldn't respond. In the matter of communications with the KGB, each one of us had her own position: some would talk to them, others wouldn't, but it was our unanimous opinion that they had no business coming into our Zone. Officially, the camp is administered by the Ministry of Internal Affairs (MVD), and the KGB has no right to stick its nose into it. We were not sentenced to any obligatory dealings with the KGB, nor did we invite its officials to visit us. The envoy from Moscow poked around the Zone for a bit, then went away.

On September 14 we had a more interesting visit from the head of the "operative sector" at the Central Administration, Gorkushov. The same Gorkushov who had expressed such touching concern about our probable inability to bear children after incarceration in SHIZO. He asked about our complaints, and then assured us that all our efforts were doomed to failure, because our treatment was in accordance with orders "from the top." Our hunger strike, said Gorkushov, is a malicious violation of camp regulations: by law, prisoners do not have the right to defend one another or their fellow citizens. We told him what we thought of that law, and on this note we parted. Nevertheless, on that day we were all examined by the doctor for the first time.

The last day of the hunger strike brought us a surprise. A group of women from the hospital zone was brought to weed and hoe the "forbidden" strip. We were on opposite sides of the barbed wire, but eyed each other with covert interest. They were not allowed to talk to us, and we made no attempt at conversation, not wishing to get them into trouble. And then, quite unexpectedly, two of them stepped right up to the wire when the patrolling warder was at the far end of the strip.

"Hey, girls!"

We moved over to them. Quickly, quickly, they pulled out a couple of small parcels from under their uniform smocks, thrust them at us, and retreated. Picking up their hoes, they explained from a safe distance: "We heard that you're on hunger strike for rights. And that they keep you half-starved all the time, anyway. So we passed the hat—everything that's in those packets will do you good. Eat it when your hunger strike's finished."

Returning to the house, we unwrap the parcels. Carrots, white bread, a couple of cubes of butter . . . a whole packet of sugar! Who were these women who gathered such gifts for us, bit by bit? What motivated them—they, who barely knew anything about the "rights" for which we struggled—to support us despite the risk of being caught? And in the light of their action, what price the theories aired by some that our people are unaware of their oppressed situation and feel no need for civil liberties? When I was much younger and thought myself unique in my wisdom, I, too, was guilty of such an attitude toward those who grew the bread I ate or sewed summer dresses (little did I know that just such dresses are sewn in the camps). At that time I yearned to emigrate, "to get out of this swamp." Now, finding myself an émigrée by force of circumstances, I have come to understand that which I did not comprehend then.

Thank you, O Lord, that it fell to my lot to endure the rigors of prison transports, to hide poetry and books from the KGB, to languish in punishment cells and to starve. Only when I entered into open combat did I realize how much help I received from almost everyone I encountered. This quiet support brought my poems to freedom, assisted Igor with the typing, duplicating and dissemination of my poems, helped to convey my work abroad in the form of *samizdat*. So many different hands—young and old— slipped us bread when we were exhausted by hunger, so many different eyes smiled at us—grey, brown, blue . . . And in the wondrous realization that they were on our side, and not on the side of our tormentors, I shed my youthful pride, and the arrogance which might have destroyed my soul melted away. At the same time, Igor was being helped by the ordinary Kiev workers who labored alongside him, by former zeks, by Moscow professors, and even by some of my jailers. There are not many dedicated sadists among the jailers, after all; the majority of them are none too bright but cunning functionaries, who are only too glad to leave certain orders unfulfilled. Somewhere at the back of their uniform-encased hearts there are stirrings of shame, and conscience, and compassion—all those qualities which will be the salvation of my people one day.

Thank you, women of the criminal zone. I don't know what brought you to the camps. I don't know how many of you were involved in gathering that gift of food to us. But to my dying day I shall remember the names of the two who passed it to us: they were clearly marked on their identity tags. I cannot identify them. And to whichever KGB official is charged with sifting through this book for any secrets I may let slip, I say this: how many hundreds passed through the hospital zone in the autumn of 1983? You would like some clues to identify those two? By all means: both were wearing faded blue dresses, black uniform smocks (or would you call them jackets?), white headscarves and tarpaulin boots.

We stowed the food away in a hidey-hole, for our last day of hunger strike would end only at midnight. On the last evening of the hunger strike we all sit around the table with cups of hot water. Pani Jadvyga reads us some poetry she has written. She wrote it in her native Lithuanian, but she has translated it for us into Russian: how the Lord comes to us unseen this evening. If we could see Him, we would move up the bench so that He could sit down with us. But although we don't see Him, He sees us. And not just us, but our hearts. The sentiments are simple and naïve, the Russian grammar a bit shaky. But Pani Jadvyga was not writing for literary critics, and we are warmed by the shining sincerity of her unpretentious words. They are reminiscent of the carved and sculpted decorations one sees in many Lithuanian Catholic churches: a little ungainly and out of proportion at first glance, but when you look closer, you realize how much more impressive they are than any perfection of scale and form.

Ten o'clock. Lights out. At midnight, Tanya and I creep out into the "kitchen"—a nook measuring five square meters. One of us was Cinderella that week—I can't remember which. Our idea was not to wait until morning, but to make a meal for everyone right now. The hunger strike is officially over. To be more precise, it was not a meal we were planning, but a small snack, so that it would be possible to eat a bit more in the morning. We grate the carrots on a grater Natasha made by cutting open the side of a tin can and piercing holes through it with a nail. The handle is a piece of steel wire attached to one end. A couple of energetic scrapes has to be followed by a brief rest. Then a few more scrapes. Heavens, how little strength we have left in our hands. But we manage, eventually. The grated carrot is divided into seven equal portions, each portion measuring about two tablespoons. Excellent! We brew tea out of rowan berries and sweeten it with a whole three teaspoons of sugar. To round off the banquet there is a small bit of dried black bread each, and three candies the size of peas. These small colored sweets are sold in the camp kiosk and our benefactors in the criminal zone included some in their parcel.

We go to wake the others, confident that nobody will object. It turns out, though, that they are all awake. They had guessed what we were up to, and were lying quietly in their bunks, waiting to be called. What a superb feast that was! Color crept back into our faces, either from the food or from high spirits. Our voices became stronger, we laughed after practically every word. Fortunately, the watchtower faces the other end of the house, so the guard cannot see the light in the kitchen.

Footsteps! Who can it be at this hour? Oh, of course, it must be Anya, one of the warders, doing her nightly round. How will she react to this unauthorized midnight feast? She grasps the situation at a glance, shakes with soundless laughter and wags a plump finger at us.

"Just be very quiet, women, or you'll get me into trouble. And turn off the light as soon as you finish eating. The duty officer may well take a walk around the perimeter strip."

Our "Madrid" hunger strike is over. What comes next? That will depend largely on what other little surprises the KGB has in store for us. If they leave us alone, we will peacefully resume sewing gloves and writing our two permitted letters a month home. But if they start any "disciplinary work" with us, we shall have to react. Do they think we don't have the strength? Oh, but we do! We don't know ourselves where it comes from. Or maybe we do?

> So tomorrow, our little ship, Small Zone,
> What will come true for us?
> According to what law—
> Like an eggshell over dead waves?
> Covered in patches and scars,
> On the word—the honest word—alone—
> By whose hand is our ship preserved,
> Our little home?
> Those of us who sail to the end, row, live to the end—
> Let them tell for the others:
> We knew
> The touch of this hand.

21

"Women! To the kiosk!"

Our right to buy from the kiosk has been withdrawn for this month, too, but by law we may still purchase essentials such as soap and toothpowder. The punishment applies to the buying of foodstuffs of any kind. It's against the administration's own interests to forbid the purchase of soap, because that would mean that all the zeks would get scabies and need medical treatment. To balance out this reluctant concession on the part of the authorities, the kiosk only sells the most expensive soap available—it's six or seven times dearer than average soap. Few people would even buy this very dear soap "out there," but we have no choice. So our miserable five rubles a month go on trying to observe basic hygiene.

When we enter the kiosk, we stop in amazement: it is full of vegetables, fruit, biscuits, jam, even some kind of cheese. What on earth does this mean? Things like that just don't happen in the camps.

"None of you can buy any of this," we are informed with unconcealed triumph, "because you have all forfeited your kiosk privileges."

So what? We'll simply buy our soap. And what's that cosmetic cream over there, augmenting the picture of plenty? But we're told we can't buy that, either. A violation of the law? There's only one law here—the word of the camp commandant. This charade must have been his brainchild, otherwise why were we brought here? Was it an attempt to unsettle us? The warders don't know: they were ordered to march us to the kiosk, and then back to the Zone, without allowing us to buy anything. Just a little exercise in psychology, a challenge to our stomachs. Keep trying, folks! How pathetically primitive are all your methods! Throw a good scare into them, you reason, and then taunt them with what they're missing. Your temptations are a telling reflection of your own scale of values. If they epitomize the peak of your desires, what can be expected of you?

We chuckle over this as we return to the Zone. They want to "reform" us so that we will be like them. They cannot grasp that all they achieve is to increase the revulsion we feel for them: seeing them in action makes it physically impossible to side with all these "operatives," procurators, KGB functionaries ... The very thought makes the bile rise to your throat. Better dive into a cesspit than adapt to their standards.

But all things considered, wasn't this latest gambit a bit on the expensive side? It must have taken considerable time and effort to obtain all these goodies we saw in the kiosk. Well, perhaps someone else may benefit from them, if only the warders ... There has to be more to it than meets the eye, though. We sit around trying to puzzle it out as our stomachs scream for food. This is because we have been issued no bread for the past three days, and the skilly has been so oversalted that we've sent it back untouched. We make do with the goosefoot growing outside, and some porridge saved from the day before yesterday. But how far can you stretch a camp portion of porridge? If only we still had our nettles. Pity ...

Suddenly, our dinner is brought around. Heavens, what's this? Unsalted semolina and pats of real butter. Where did all this bounty come from? There's sugar here, too: we do get sugar, albeit in minute quantities, yet there's at least three times the usual amount on this occasion. And why the butter? It's only ever issued in special rations for the sick, and the authorities insist that nobody in our Zone is ill, not even Natasha, Raya and Pani Jadvyga. So what's going on? True, there's no bread, but with all these luxuries before our eyes, we don't notice its absence.

We sit down to eat. Then, just as we reach for our spoons, we hear the stomping of boots up the path, and in come about ten officers of various ranks. Half of them are total strangers, but we certainly know the face of the head of our camp's "operative section," Shlepanov. He hurries into speech: "You see, citizen colonel, they've got everything: sugar and butter."

Now we know the reason behind today's mysterious events: it's all an act for the benefit of a commission from the Central Administration of Corrective Labor Institutions (GUITU) in Moscow. The commission must be shown that there are no grounds for all our complaints and petitions.

Oh, how I exploded! I leapt up from the table to confront this colonel before whom all our camp bosses were bowing and scraping. "Yes, look at that butter. Look at it. We're seeing it for the first time, too. See the size of the portion? It must be all of sixty grams! Whereas we have three invalids among us. Look at it, don't miss your chance. Nobody in this Zone will ever see the like again! All this is for your benefit, not ours! Shall I make you a sandwich?"

"Ira, don't offer something you cannot provide," interjects Galya reasonably, "how can you make a sandwich when we haven't been given any bread for three days?" But I am beyond silencing: "If you're so influential, perhaps you can see to it that we get the bread ration to which we're entitled? And organize some medical treatment while you're about it? So that butter won't be a one-time deception, but regular issue for our invalids."

And I wave the plate with the butter menacingly under his nose. He, poor man, retreats before my advance. Emaciated and furious, I must have looked like a cobra prepared to strike. Realizing belatedly that it's better to rein in, I switch to a conversational, social tone: "Anyway, do sit down. Let's talk."

Natasha said later that for a few moments it had seemed that I would smear that wretched butter right down the front of his dress uniform. Such a thing had not entered my mind, but it's a good thing that it had seemed that way. This was the first and last time I lost control over myself before a representative of the authorities: one's adversaries should be addressed coldly, politely and calmly. Otherwise, one should refrain from speaking to them altogether. There's no need to let them see your emotions. But on that occasion, I was simply caught unawares; I didn't expect to fly off the handle like that. However, my outburst had its useful side, because it made it possible for the commission to accept our administration's window-dressing at face value. Our physical appearance must have spoken for itself, too. Naturally, the commission had no intention of listening to our complaints. Not a single commission from Moscow ever bothered to try to speak to us, and some of them never even entered our Zone. We always knew when there was a commission in the camp, because at such time the warders wore their red and white armbands. Usually, they didn't bother with them. The commissions were not interested in gathering information on violations of the law and the cruelties perpetrated in the camp; they only came to get assurances from our oppressors that our living conditions are worthy of a sanatorium, and that we only badger Moscow with complaints out of sheer bloody-mindedness. Yet on this occasion—like it or not—they heard our side. Of course, they hurried away, but that evening we got our bread, and were allowed to buy soap and even the skin cream. Furthermore, for a while they stopped oversalting the skilly. Podust barely showed her face in the Zone, and when she did, she was civil and made no attempts to provoke any conflicts. There was some improvement in our rations. So the noise must have helped, and, in any case, as the camp commandant himself put it, "Nobody knows how to cope with that damned Zone!" We had no intention of making any concessions, and nobody really expected any by now.

Even the wording in the documents concerning our various "forfeits" changed. The administration started writing things down as they were: for instance, "deprived of the right to buy foodstuffs for the month of October for refusing to wear an identity tag." Previously, they would always add a few more alleged violations, such as: "On such-and-such a day, Osipova was without an identity tag. Apart from that, at noon on the same day—in working hours—she was discovered engaged on personal tasks in the sleeping quarters." In fact, Osipova was "discovered" in the kitchen, washing dishes and the pots which had to be returned to the hospital kitchen. The warder who wrote that report knew the truth, but what could she do? She had her orders . . . Or they would write: "On such-and-such a day, Barats was without an identity tag, and wearing a non-regulation skirt." They knew full well that it was their own fault that we had no regulation clothing, and that camp commandant Pavlov had said to us: "You'll be issued some mattress ticking, and you can make it up into anything you like, so long as it's not indecent."

And that mutineer Barats decided that rather than going around just in her underwear (which, you must agree, could hardly be regarded as "decent") while waiting for the issue of a uniform, she would make herself a jacket and skirt. Regulation skirts are black, but the ticking we were issued was grey. Oh, that malicious violator of camp regulations, Galya Barats! And the rest of us are no better. We're all wearing things made out of the same grey ticking. But the administration had no qualms about cynically distorting facts in their reports to justify our punishments. And because of these falsehoods we lost kiosk rights, meetings with relatives, Tanya and Natasha were sent to SHIZO . . .

But now it all suddenly stopped. The lies were dropped temporarily, and the truth—that we refuse to wear identity tags—remained. What's the difference? you may ask. Didn't the repressive measures remain unaltered? Yes, that's true, but it was the lies we objected to more than the punishments. It's impossible to tolerate brazen lies, told straight to your face. Human nature rebels against it.

"What is the worst thing in the camps?" I asked Tatyana Mikhailovna at the end of my first week in the Small Zone.

And she, who had already experienced SHIZO and suchlike, answered without a moment's hesitation: "The perpetual lies."

When everyone who is in any way connected with your imprisonment—from the supervising procurator through to the censor and the doctor—persists in lying day in, day out, you begin to feel as though you are in some huge lunatic asylum. The only difference is that here it is the overseers who are the psychopaths, who try to incorporate you into a hideous, contrived reality. Shalin's insistence that we do not exist is a case in point: "There are no political prisoners in this camp," he would aver. Yet at the same time, he and all his colleagues invariably referred to us as the "politicals." The pots in which our skilly was delivered from the kitchen had the words "Polit. Zone" marked on them with brown paint. And Shalin himself, in an attempt to make us see reason, would say: "Everyone in the men's political zone wears identity tags, so why can't you?"

But if the Party claims that there are no political prisoners in the USSR, Shalin will still insist that we don't exist . . . Is this any less bizarre, than, say, proclaiming "I am a teapot," or "There's a Martian in disguise among us"? This sort of idiocy can drive an unprepared person to fury and loss of self-control. Luckily, we were all ready for this even before our arrests: we were prepared for it by the Soviet press, by the KGB, by the "political briefings" in our places of work. We were tempered to this madness by the entire official style of life in our country. And we rose against it. How could Pentecostal Christian Galya have possibly remained a Communist and at the same time carried out the Party's bidding to assert that there is no God, whenever and wherever she was ordered? Could Tatyana Mikhailovna have possibly read the mandatory "political information" at work? Could Pani Jadvyga "wholeheartedly support the policies of the Party and the government" after being consigned to the camps as an adolescent simply because she happened to be Lithuanian? Yes, we got our sentences. We know what the camps mean: cold, hunger, tyranny, separation from our families. But instead of direct reprisals, we encountered reprisals masquerading under a "humane" mask. For instance, they asked us in SHIZO: "What are you women complaining about? This radiator is hot." And to "prove" it, the person who said these words calmly laid a hand against the ice-cold pipes: see, it's working perfectly! The temperature in the cell was 8°C, but we could hardly pull out our hidden thermometer just to expose the lie . . .

So even a temporary cessation of all these unnecessary lies

was a small victory for us. Admittedly, this state of affairs did not last long; no visiting commission can really change the established practices of Soviet institutions. The situation with medical care was particularly grim. We were all in very bad shape by that time: edemas, constant temperature, fainting spells through physical weakness. At the same time, we were officially cautioned that any one of us not producing her quota of gloves would be consigned to SHIZO. Natasha was stripped of her classification as a Group III invalid,[1] although no medical examination was carried out to justify this action. Wasn't it enough for them that Natasha had already collapsed twice right there, at the sewing machine? Vasili Petrovich brushed the official warning aside: "Do as much as you can, and don't worry. Leave the rest to me." In fact, nobody was actually punished for not fulfilling the quota, the administration limited itself to threats. They could not institute punitive proceedings without Vasili Petrovich's signature, and while we did not refuse to work as such, Vasili Petrovich backed us to the hilt. Of course, he was powerless to protect us when we declared strikes, because our intentions would be set out in written form. All he could do then was to cluck ruefully.

The medical staff, though, were cast in an entirely different mold: how could they reconcile it with their conscience to pass someone with a temperature of 38°C as fit for work? You'd expect them to treat the sufferer first, and then send them back to work. But the doctor was away on leave, the nurse could not and would not do anything, and so it transpired that by September 19, of the seven inmates of the Small Zone, four were seriously ill. Without any doubt, immediate medical assistance was vital. Our Zone is adjacent to the hospital, surely there must be a doctor on duty? Volkova would have been useless even if she were not away, because she knows less about medicine than Tanya the nurse. So why should we wait for her return? For twenty hours, from six o'clock in the morning until two o'clock at night, we tried every method we could think of to secure a visit by a doctor: we yelled

---

1. Group III invalid: One who has lost 50 percent of his capability to work, e.g., as a result of serious injuries to wrists, head injuries, etc.

to the guard in the watchtower, we made our request to the warders and to all the officers (except Podust) who came into the Zone that day. Lights out? Not on your life! We will neither go to bed nor switch off the lights. We demand a doctor right now: we can't wait a month.

A doctor finally arrived at 2:00 a.m.

"I can't hold nighttime clinics," were his opening words.

"Well, where were you until now? We've been trying to get you here all day."

"Nobody told me anything about it."

"All right then, will somebody come in the morning?"

"I don't know. I'm not on duty tomorrow . . ."

"Well, at least examine the ones whose condition is worst."

"Yes, but not more than two."

He examines Raya and Pani Jadvyga—they're sicker than anyone else. He takes their temperatures, checks their hearts. He doesn't deny that both are in a bad way, but what will he write in their medical records? As for that, it emerges that he is not authorized to make any notes; he's only the duty doctor, and it's not his responsibility to make diagnoses or to keep medical records. He can give an injection or issue some tablets, but has no authority to prescribe a course of treatment. Sign a release from work? Sorry—that's not within his power, either, only the senior doctor can do that . . . She'll only be back in a month's time? Well, she'll do it then.

"Do you mean to say that they must work in such a state tomorrow?"

"I didn't say that."

"Then release them from work at least for tomorrow."

"Women, you must understand. I don't have the right to do that."

They all lie, but in different ways. Some of them derive a perverted sense of pleasure from the process: the more cynical and barefaced the lie, the more they enjoy it. These will watch your face as they mouth their falsehoods, and their greatest achievement is to make you lose your temper. Their trick is to present an innocent front while provoking you into a state of stress; it's easier to break someone whose emotions have got the better of him. Our KGB men, procurator Ganichev and Podust belong in this category. We make a point of treating them with cold disdain; they are not worth any display of our feelings.

Others, like this particular duty doctor, are forced to lie. But they can't look you in the face as they do it, and are clearly miserable themselves. If they had their way, none of us would be here. From time to time, their conscience drives them to admit it to us in as many words. Yet what can they do? Where would they go? One of our warders, Sveta, put it this way: "What else could I do, then? I was born here in Barashevo, and I'm registered for residence[2] here. I could try working as a milkmaid, but that's a hell of a job, worse than hard labor from morning till night. As for a job in the local kindergarten—well, there aren't enough places there for all the women in Barashevo. The only other place is here: three days on, two off. The work's easy, and the pay's great. But you have to sign on for five years, and the officers for twenty-five. Later on, you won't ever get away from here, even if you want to. I don't do any of you any harm, do I? I know you're not like them other criminals . . ."

All the same, Sveta will write a report full of lies that will see you into SHIZO if she's ordered to do so. Even though the next time she comes into the Zone she will be shamefaced and will try to avoid everyone's eyes. Yet she never sneaked on us or did a single thing against us on her own initiative. On the contrary, she would whisper a warning: "You be careful, Ratushinskaya, don't get caught. Don't sit outside sunning yourself, and don't watch television after lights out; you've got a meeting coming up, and we've been told to start gathering information against you . . ."

This is true of the majority of our jailers, and we feel rather sorry for them, albeit with a trace of disgust. Those poor, miserable people. Is their life all that much different from the zeks'? They spend all their working life in the camp, they can't dispute

2. Soviet citizens may not live wherever they want. They must receive permission from local authorities to move from one town to another. Failure to comply is a criminal offense.

any orders. They're better dressed and fed than the zeks, but that's about the sum of their advantages. Of course, they live with their families, but what's the guarantee that one day their grown son or daughter won't say to them: "Aren't you ashamed, Mom and Dad, that you oppressed people for a living? How can I help feeling ashamed of the fact that my parents were jailers?"

On the other hand, the son or daughter may well follow in the parents' footsteps, go through Ministry of Internal Affairs (MVD) training, and become a warder, too. The brighter ones may even become procurators or camp commandants . . . Working as a jailer is an inherited profession in many families in these parts. One thing with which we cannot reconcile ourselves is that, were there no such reluctant overseers and liars, this whole monstrous system of tyranny and spiritual oppression would not last a single day. They are its victims, yet they work for it, out of weakness and out of fear. They would be only too glad to be free of it, but what would they do? And are they any worse than those "Soviet workers" who vote unanimously "for" something at meetings (try voting "against"!) and prefer to know nothing of repressions which do not affect them personally, or who give political speeches which they themselves find every bit as tedious as their audience? And who then, emerging into the corridor, sympathetically squeeze the arm of the one who may have dared, despite everything, to vote "against," and say: "Well done, old man, you really let them have it. We're all for you." But they will whisper these words, glancing around furtively to make sure that nobody can hear. Then later, when the "collective" is summoned to publicly reprimand the one who voted "against," they will keep well away from him, sympathizing from a safe distance. However, in a circle of trusted friends they will boast a little: "Yes, I knew such-and-such personally, we worked together. He was a nice guy, we all liked him. When does his sentence expire?" Oh, the unfortunate, thrice unfortunate citizens of my country! Do not lose at least that sense of shame and the supportive whisper! Maybe your children will be braver than you.

In the meantime, one of our warders, escorting us to wash after a spell of SHIZO, has this to say: "Sure I understand everything. So what? No sense in bashing your head against a brick wall, is there? If I put a foot wrong, I'll be in the same cell with you."

She cannot grasp that not a single one of us would ever change places with her. For we have breathed freedom—if only freedom from fear.

22

On October 20, Pani Jadvyga was finally removed to the hospital. Dr. Gunkin, in whose care she was placed, examined her and then asked a truly mind-boggling question: "What proof is there that your gallbladder was removed? Oh, the post-operative scar. But maybe they just cut you open and then sewed you up without taking anything out?"

And on the strength of this assumption, he refused to prescribe either a course of treatment or a special diet. Shortly after that, Pani Jadvyga received a visit from several officials from the political sector of the Central Administration. Their visit was occasioned by the official request Pani Jadvyga sent to the Central Administration concerning the disposal of her body after she died: she wrote that it was her wish that her body be given to her relatives for burial. What, asked her visitors, is the reason for these sudden deathbed wishes? Pani Jadvyga explained that the doctors who had performed her gallbladder operation had warned her that she must observe a very strict dietary regimen in order to go on living. Almost everything that we are given to eat in the Zone is just what she should avoid at all costs. Without the prescribed diet, her chances of survival for much longer are virtually nil. That, she said, was the reason for the request to Central Administration: as a Catholic and a Lithuanian, she wants to be buried by her church in her native land. She has no wish to lie in the camp cemetery, which is surrounded by barbed wire, and where the graves are only marked with numbers. If she must die, she wants at least a proper funeral. "If you don't want to give me the required diet," she added, "then don't. But my body is to go to my family!"

Podust, who tagged along with the officials from the Central Administration, intervenes at this point, even though Jadvyga ignores her: "There are any number of people here who are just as sick as you. If we give you a special diet, they'll all start demanding them!" Pani Jadvyga remains silent. In fact, she didn't say another word to any of them. But our camp administration must have been a bit worried, because Pani Jadvyga did receive some medical treatment, and returned to the Zone in a somewhat better condition than she left it. Our authorities did not go as far as allowing her the special diet, but for a month she received 40 grams of sugar, 30 grams of butter, 450 grams of milk and 15 grams of dried fruit daily, in addition to normal zek rations.

Our stubborn Pani issued us with an ultimatum: either this additional food is shared out between everyone, or she won't eat so much as a mouthful of it. She will simply fast, and pray to God that He would bring us to our senses. As a matter of fact, whenever we managed to get additional sick rations, we always divided them equally. Dr. Volkova came to take this for granted, and would simply say: "I can issue sick rations for two people this month. In whose names do you want them?"

But that was in the period of relative peace and quiet, when the pressure on us was less intense, and before we started hunger-striking. In those days there would be the occasional sick rations, we had our vegetable patch, and could buy from the kiosk now and then. But things have changed now, and our Pani Jadvyga is fading away without extra nourishment. We're all physically stronger, we can get by.

"No," says Pani Jadvyga in a tone that brooks no argument. "The Lord will sustain me."

We had no choice but to bow to her wish, and everything was divided into equal parts. Even Vladimirova, who ate separately from the rest of us, got her share, just as she always received her share of the few packages and parcels to reach the Zone. To do her justice, when she was a recipient of the sick ration, she, too, would demand that we all get equal shares. Moreover, when my Igor and Olga Matusevich (who had been released from the Small Zone by then) sent Vladimirova a parcel in 1986, she shared it with the others in the Zone. You may wonder why a parcel was sent to her at all: the thing is, she had nobody of her own to send her anything, and everybody must eat, even informers.

At the end of October, the censor came around with our mail, and we all retreated into various corners to read our letters from home. Suddenly, Edita gave an anguished cry, and burst into tears. At first we couldn't make out what was wrong—every bit of Russian she knew went out of her head, and our knowledge of Lithuanian consisted of a couple of phrases. We had to wait for Pani Jadvyga to tell us what had happened. From her letter Edita learned that her husband and small son had come to the camp on October 14 for the three-day meeting Edita had been yearning for so much. But our camp officials informed him that both this long meeting, and the next scheduled short one, had been cancelled. We couldn't believe our ears. Edita had not been told anything of the kind, nor had she been issued with a written notification, as she should have been . . . How must her husband have felt, after making the arduous journey from Lithuania to Mordovia with a small child, when he was sent away without even seeing Edita? How her little boy must have cried when he realized that he would not see his mother. And she had not even known they were here . . .

Edita makes a lightning decision: "This is too much," she cries. "You can do as you like, but I'm going on strike until both meetings are reinstated."

We agree that the situation is quite extraordinary, but we can't understand why there was no written notification about the cancellation of the meetings. Maybe there has been some genuine misunderstanding? Maybe Edita's meeting was not cancelled, but some fool of a duty officer simply looked in the wrong column? We persuade Edita to wait with the strike until we can get official confirmation that what has happened is not simply a very regrettable error. If it turns out that the meeting was in fact cancelled without Edita receiving the statutory no-tification, then we will all go on strike with her. Not Vladimi-rova, of course. In the evening, we send queries to the Procuracy, the Central Administration, and our camp comman-dant. Our letters explain what happened, and ask for clarifica-tion. If there was a genuine misunderstanding, then it's not too late to make amends.

We wait one day, two days, a week . . . Edita's nerves are at full stretch, she wants to know when we are going to start the strike. Patience, we tell her, let's have official confirmation of their cheating. Even a quite unexpected excursion to the kiosk doesn't cheer us up; contrary to recent practice, nobody was barred from the kiosk for November. Wonders will never cease.

It's perfectly obvious that a new round of illegalities has be-gun, though, and with it, presumably, a new stage of the war. They're dragging out time before replying quite deliberately. But we are still determined to have a legal basis for any action we may take—in other words, we need their explanation in black and white. While we wait, we carry on our lives as usual, with no outward changes. At present, we're locked in conflict with our jailers against dirt. It's autumn, so the muck and mud outside is unbelievable. All the paths are a churned-up mess. Verbal protes-tations having failed, I turn to methods of "visual agitation." Taking the center pages of a school exercise book, I design a poster with the words:

FRIEND OR FOE, WE KINDLY ASK:
WIPE YOUR BOOTS! IT'S NO GREAT TASK!

This I fasten to the outside door. The warders tear it down and hand it in to their bosses. I do another one; it won't do the camp commandant any harm to learn about this simple courtesy.

One day, we hear the familiar stamping of warders' boots, but today they are not alone. They usher in a terribly thin woman, with huge eyes and straight hair. She's not wearing boots, but special camp issue half-boots with high lacing. It's hard to imagine any footwear clumsier or uglier than this. In the camps, these half-boots are commonly known as "come now, come now!" shoes, and they are equally hated by male and female prisoners alike. At least, boots have the advantage of keeping out the muck (until they start cracking and leaking, that is) but it's not an easy task to get the ghastly "come now, come now!" shoes exchanged for a pair of boots. The newcomer smiles at us: "I read your poster, and would like to be a friend. I wiped my feet . . ." We all laugh, and take to her immediately. The identity tag on the breast of her carefully washed zek jacket reads: "L. Doronina, Brigade No. 2." So they seized their chance and got her to put the tag on in the guardroom.

Despite her Russian surname, our new companion speaks with a slight accent: she's Latvian. Born Lasmane, she married a Russian geologist whom she met in Siberia. She's a widow now, and had been living on her pension in a small village not far from Riga with her small dog Sames for company. Some friends took him in and promised to look after him when she was arrested. As for herself—Lidija Doronina has few worries; she's serving her third sentence. Lidija was born in 1925, when Latvia was still an independent country. Her first encounter with Russians came when Soviet troops invaded her country. A Soviet officer was riding on horseback along the edge of a forest when he saw Lidija, then a young girl, coming out of it with a basket. He dismounted, intending to rape her, and threatened to shoot her if she resisted. But it all worked out quite differently. Lidija, a peasant's daughter, leapt on his horse with ease, and galloped off. He didn't shoot—either because he was afraid of killing her or of wounding his horse. After she had gone what she judged to be a safe distance, she released the horse, knowing that a good steed will always find his master. Subsequent developments followed the usual pattern which marks the arrival of Soviet power in every country.

Rather than attempt it myself, let this written statement of Pani Lida's tell her story:

To the Presidium of the Supreme Soviet

I was born into a religious peasant family in independent Latvia in 1925. My education was in accordance with the spirit and laws of my country.

Two terrible events overshadowed my youth: the forced exile of my people by the Soviet government in 1941, and the mass execution of Jews by the Gestapo in 1942. Among those who fell victim to these events were many of my school friends, people close to me, people I knew. I realized then that my country had become an arena in which two powerful states battled each other.

Eighteen months after the end of the war, my whole family, including myself, was arrested on charges of treason. It was alleged that we had connections with "bandits." These so-called bandits were friends of my father's, to whom he had offered the same help as he had to Russian refugees, prisoners of war and others in need, without once betraying his country or his people. Nor was I ever guilty of betrayal. Nevertheless, I was tried and sentenced to five years by the Military Tribunal of the Baltic region. The proceedings were conducted in Russian, a language I did not know at that time. After the trial I was sent to the Urals, and after that—to Vorkuta.[1] I was released in 1951, ill, with cavities in my lungs, but as one of the "war" prisoners, I had to stay in the Komi Autonomous Soviet Socialist Republic. I was unable to return to my native land until 1954, after Stalin's death, when there were positive changes in the country. However, my husband, my daughter and I had nowhere to live. By working in the Far North, my husband and I managed to save enough money to buy a cooperative flat in Latvia only in 1962. It seemed, then, that my life was finally secure.

But in 1970 I was arrested and tried under Article 183–1 of the Latvian republican Criminal Code.[2] This article was only in-

1. The Vorkuta camp complex was founded in 1936. After the partition of Poland by Germany and the USSR in 1939, tens of thousands of Poles were sent there to work in coal mines. In 1940 they were joined by thousands of Soviet soldiers who had been taken prisoner in the Soviet-Finnish war and then repatriated. In the same year began the influx of tens of thousands of Latvians, Lithuanians and Estonians whose countries had been annexed by the USSR. By the end of the 1940s there were some 150,000 prisoners in the Vorkuta camps.
2. Art. 183–1 of the Latvian Criminal Code: "Circulation of deliberately false concoctions, slandering the Soviet state and social system."

troduced into the Code several years before my arrest. The Supreme Court of the Latvian republic sentenced me to two years for disseminating *samizdat*. I contend that there is no ethical justification for this article, because according to Article 18 of the Universal Declaration of Human Rights, everyone has the right to freedom of thought, conscience and religion; this right includes the freedom to adhere to one's convictions and to seek, receive and exchange ideas and information ... irrespective of state frontiers.

After spending two years among imprisoned criminals, I returned to my family, resumed working and tended to my paralyzed husband and very elderly parents (their combined state pension was ten rubles a month).

In 1977, the newspaper *Padomju Jaunatne* published an article by J. Kalnajs and F. Licis entitled "Tell Me Who's Your Friend." This article slandered members of my family—my father, my late brother, his wife—and myself. The refutation I sent to the paper was not published, and the slanderers remained unpunished.

In 1983, I was arrested for the third time, and tried by the Latvian Supreme Court on charges of "anti-Soviet agitation and propaganda." The charges against me were unfounded and unproven, but that did not deter the court from sentencing me to five years' strict regime camps to be followed by three years of internal exile. In other words, I was unjustly condemned to another eight years away from my homeland. As an elderly woman and a Group II invalid[3] in a labor camp, I have no particular expectations of returning home alive.

On January 17, 1984, I was again slandered by the central Latvian press in an article by V. Silins. This article claimed that I am working in the interests of some "masters" abroad. I must stress that I consider myself free even in imprisonment, and have no "masters" anywhere. I have been a loyal Soviet citizen always. I worked, I raised a daughter and grandchildren, paid my taxes and obeyed the law. I sought no privileges and received nothing apart from my state-paid wages, therefore I do not consider myself to be under obligation to anyone.

---

3. Group II invalid: One who has only slight disabilities, e.g., missing a finger, suffering partial loss of sight, etc.

It seems, though, that by being a religious believer and trying to observe the ethical principles of religious morality, I have been, unwittingly, undermining the Soviet system.

The thought of emigrating had never entered my head earlier, but now, finding myself without protection against slander, being unable to live in my native land, being denied the rights delineated in Article 18 of the Universal Declaration of Human Rights and Article 19 of the International Convention of Civil and Political Rights, I HEREBY RENOUNCE MY SOVIET CITIZENSHIP.

I ask the Soviet government to allow me to emigrate to Switzerland to join my late brother's family—his widow Valentina Lasmanis and their three daughters. I do not think the Soviet authorities need my death in Mordovia rather than in Switzerland to consolidate their position.

Lidija DORONINA

March 6, 1984

Having served two sentences in criminal camps, she did not consider the identity tags a matter worthy of conflict: there are things much worse than that. She pointed out that in Stalin's time, everyone in the camps wore identity tags, and, although there were uprisings, they were not over this issue. So for the time being, she would wear the identity tag, and only remove it if she felt it was becoming a burden. We did not try to dissuade her, as this was a matter for individual decision. We explained our stance—or rather, we showed her a copy of the document which set out our reasons for refusing to wear the tags—and left it at that.

Podust, needless to say, was delighted: "You see, women?" she crowed to our unresponsive faces. "Doronina is the eldest here, and probably the wisest. You'll all be going to SHIZO and having your meetings cancelled, but she won't."

We, of course, said never a word, but Pani Lida did. "By drawing comparisons between me and my fellow prisoners," she said calmly and politely, "you are making me consider removing the identity tag. I will keep it on for the time being, but if anyone is punished because of it, I shall take it off and burn it."

That's just what she did do later on, for that very reason, and set everything out in writing. It was not wise to fool around with Pani Lida: although she is incredibly kindhearted and accommodating, there is a limit beyond which it is better not to push her. After we brought her up to date on the situation in the Zone and the impending strike, she said that she had no intention of working anyway. The state could be content with the thirty-two rubles a month it was saving on her pension. She's reached retirement age, so that's that. As for boycotting Podust, she will wait: "I have to make up my own mind about her. Don't think I don't believe you, but I will feel better in myself when I've seen and heard her in action. Maybe she's not an entirely lost soul?"

Podust has been keeping a low profile lately; it's possible that her conflict with the Zone has not helped her career, and her position is somewhat insecure. She makes no further attempt to take Pani Lida in hand—the first rebuff seems to have worked. Pani Lida is the only straw a floundering Podust has to grasp, so she can't afford to antagonize her. Sensibly, therefore, she leaves everyone alone. Vladimirova, too, quieted down some time ago. She finds her isolation in our midst difficult to bear. She no longer threatens us, but reiterates that one night she will hang herself. We don't take this too seriously: those who continually threaten to commit suicide are the least likely to actually carry it out. But she is clearly having a hard time. Now that she has abandoned her histrionics, it's obvious that her nerves are, at best, very shaky, or, at worst, that she is seriously disturbed psychologically. Her occasional hysterical outbursts, though no longer directed at us, occur without rhyme or reason. In the grip of one of these fits she can either launch herself, screaming, at the warders, or clamber over the wire fencing and chop through the signal wires with a shovel before scrambling through to the territory of the hospital. From time to time we really fear for her: if any one of us were to try something like that, it would be treated as an escape attempt. But Vladimirova gets away with it.

Some three hours later, looking subdued and dazed, she is invariably escorted back by a solicitous Podust, who tucks her into bed. We guessed that they gave her tranquilizing injections of some kind. With her aggression spent and her inner turmoil plain for all to see, we feel more and more sorry for her.

The days pass as we await developments. That was the situation until November 14.

23

"Vladimirova and Lazareva! Transportation!"

SHIZO? But in that case, why Vladimirova? She is not subject to administrative punishments no matter what she does. They don't even forbid her to use the kiosk . . .

"No, no, not SHIZO," the warders assure us consolingly. "They're going to Saransk for re-education."

Re-education means that you are placed into a KGB isolation cell, and then taken periodically for discussions with Mordovian KGB officials. Actually, this is quite illegal: by law, you can only be transferred to a KGB investigation cell if new proceedings have been instituted against you, or if you are being called as a witness in someone else's case. But when has the KGB bothered to observe the law? Vladimirova starts gathering her things, but Natasha lies unmoving in bed. She's running a temperature, and is having some kind of abdominal trouble again. She refuses to budge. A couple of doctors arrive with Podust and an officer called Shishokin. Podust and Shishokin accuse Natasha of malingering. The doctors take her temperature twice, and are unable to deny that it's way above normal. They don't transport her, but they won't sanction her admission into the hospital, either. Yet how can she be treated without an examination? Pani Lida, who is a trained nurse, has no problem diagnosing Natasha's trouble: ulcerative colitis. Who, though, is going to pay any heed to the words of a prisoner? Still, Natasha remains in the Zone for the present.

The next day we finally get a long-awaited visit from Pavlov, the camp commandant. We surround him at once, demanding to know what's happened about Edita's meeting with her husband. He hems and haws at first, then resorts to threats that he will punish us for coming to one another's defense.

"Abrutiene's meeting was cancelled quite legally," he declares finally.

"Why?"

"I don't know why. All I know is, that it was done legally."

Fine, that's clear as crystal. The time has come for us to start our strike. We write the necessary notifications, and the sound of sewing machines stops. All except for one: Pani Lida is a superb seamstress, and, indeed, this talent helped her to survive in exile. Of course, it is not gloves that she is making now, she has decided to do something about our clothes. Different stitches, stylish pockets, quilted yokes—all this and more. Pathetic amateurs that we are, we can only stand around and wonder at her creations. Very soon our warders start coming to her with their sewing needs: one needs a new uniform skirt, another needs to have her greatcoat taken in, yet another needs a dress for a social occasion . . . Pani Lida never refuses, and, in exchange, they bring her surreptitious offerings of sugar, sweets and biscuits. Our marvellous dressmaker is very happy; she has not received any money from home yet for the kiosk, and it upsets her terribly that she has been unable to put anything into our pool of supplies, even though we laugh off her misgivings: there can be no reckonings between us.

"Not reckonings, no, it's just that there's practically nothing left of any of you," protested Pani Lida, then changed the subject. But now, a pile of sweets appears temptingly on the table, and we prepare to feast.

"How many shall we have each?"

"Two," decided our strict "Cerberus," Tanya Osipova. It's her job to allocate our supplies so that there will be enough not only for today, but for next month. She gives the Cinderellas their weekly portions of tea, items bought in the kiosk, and sunflower oil. They have to make what she gives them last the whole week, come what may. Otherwise we'll run out, and then what's to be done? The remainder stays in a suitcase, which we have had to start locking since Vladimirova's arrival.

Two sweets in one go is a generous allocation, but we start demanding second helpings: waging joking warfare with "that mean Cerberus" is one of the Zone's favorite games.

"What's two sweets? All good things should come in threes."

"As for that troublemaker Ratushinskaya—she won't get anything until she writes ten lines of poetry," retorts Tanya immediately.

This is another of our games. Tanya seizes every conceivable pretext to make me write a certain number of lines of poetry, and somehow it always works out that I owe her ten or twelve lines. Mostly I pay my debts by writing jocular little ditties about the fantastic exploits of Tanya Osipova, which are then declaimed to the whole Zone. Tanya loves them. She calls them "libels," and treasures every one. Periodic searches of the Zone enrich the KGB archives with literary masterpieces such as:

> Why do I sing
> This Snake
> A song?
> Because my virtue
> Is so strong
> Why must I suffer
> Endlessly
> Without reward
> To sing
> To she?

"All right, all right, I'll do ten lines if everyone gets another sweet right now."

"Twelve!" insists Tanya.

"Ten!"

"Fourteen! For extortion!"

"Who's the extortionist, I'd like to know?"

"Sixteen!"

Things are going against me, so I switch tactics. I write an official demand:

TO CERBERUS FROM THE SMALL ZONE:
COUGH UP!

Laughing, everyone adds their signatures. Tanya bows to "the will of the people," but adds threateningly that this is going to cost me at least thirty lines. Of course, she's really only too happy to dole out the extra sweets: it's easy to talk her into parting with that little bit more, but the rules of the game must be observed.

Tanya has not abandoned her penchant for terrorizing a poor poet to this day. When she and her husband came to visit us in Chicago, she was barely across the threshold before she found some excuse to demand seven lines of poetry from me, to the appreciative laughter of our spouses. All jokes aside, though, this simple game was her way of trying to keep me in shape professionally. Inspiration can come and go, yet this way, even when there was none, I still had to use my brains to rhyme Tanya's "libels." She understood how difficult it is for a poet to be cut off from literature and to be isolated from the world—so she kept me on my toes. Not a day without a line—it was due to her that I was able to carry out this far from simple ambition in the camp.

But it wasn't just sweets and games. At long last, we received an official explanation for the cancellation of Edita's meeting. The reason, we learn, was "for not working on August 20–23." The warders who came into the Zone did not find her sitting at a sewing machine . . . Good Lord, but those dates were the fourth through the seventh day of our hunger strike in defense of Natasha! We were even excused from work for two days after the hunger strike ended. In any case, the sewing machine was neither here nor there, for Edita had been assigned housekeeper instead of sewing gloves. On August 23, Dr. Volkova had assured us that Edita's health was giving cause for serious concern, and because of this we persuaded Edita to come off the hunger strike on its seventh day.

We set about unravelling this bundle of lies. Dr. Volkova, of course, claims that she remembers nothing. Shalin, the officer in charge of political education (how's that for a title?), asserts that Abrutiene has never done any work at all. We drive him against the ropes by pointing out that a glance at the camp's accounts will show him Abrutiene's "earnings" for September and October. This throws him for a moment, but then he rallies and produces a new version: our Zone is not eligible for a housekeeper, so the job doesn't exist. Since when? Since November 15, he tells us. Very well, we are on strike now anyway, but we were eligible for a Zone housekeeper in August, weren't we? He dithers, blushing painfully. Later, as his career advanced and he received promotions, he gradually lost the ability to blush. We write detailed appeals to the Procuracy of the RSFSR, asking that the matter be resolved. Our own officials are totally entangled in their own lies. Of course, nobody wants to be involved: you can't gainsay the KGB. In the meantime, we're on strike.

"Lazareva! Prepare for transportation to Saransk!"

When the deputy camp commandant arrives, we greet him with a chorus of protests: "She's ill. Call a doctor!"

"Come on, come on, get ready. You'll be examined by a doctor in the guardhouse. If he says you're running a temperature, you won't be taken anywhere."

A temperature is the only symptom of illness that they're prepared to accept.

But we have no great faith in his promises of a doctor in the guardhouse: let the doctor come here, there's no sense in dragging a sick person out of bed unnecessarily. Volkova appears with a thermometer. Yes, Natasha has a high temperature. Perhaps now they'll stop bothering her? But no. The next thing to happen is the arrival of a group of hefty men: Major Pazizin, Colonel Shlepanov, several junior officers, Major Shalin—not the Shalin who's a captain and is still capable of blushing, but another Shalin. One frequently encounters the same family names in these parts.

"Come on, now. Either you come by yourself, or we'll drag you."

We find it hard to believe that they will drag a sick woman bodily out of bed, but, just in case, Tanya and I link hands and stand between them and Natasha's bed. We are seized, our hands are twisted behind our backs, and we are hauled into the dining area. Natasha, clad only in a blouse and briefs, is seized by her hands and feet and dragged out of the house into the freezing cold of the yard. She is towed through the snow which already lies on the ground, and thrown into a cart. The gate slams shut. Natasha screams for help. Major Shalin kicks her with a heavy boot once, twice, three times. Then they all fall on her, kicking her into unconsciousness.

After that, they come trooping back—to get Natasha's jacket. But here they encounter Raya, usually so quiet, and now beside herself with rage. She stands squarely in their path, clucking like a small, ruffled hen defending her chicks: "How dare you? How dare you drag a sick woman half-naked through the snow? God-less, that's what you are!" And with all her might, she hurls Natasha's ragged old quilted jacket right into their faces.

So that was how Natasha was dispatched to Saransk: the last kick came from Major Shalin, when they were hustling her onto the train. Upon arrival, she refused to talk to any of the KGB men, but kept repeating that she was beaten up.

"Nonsense, Natalia Mikhailovna! All they did was help you along," asserted the Saransk officials, their fat faces split in com-placent grins.

"I want a doctor. I want treatment for my injuries."

A doctor came to see her a week later, but she was still black and blue all over.

"Maybe you hurt yourself through your own carelessness?" he asked. "Or, perhaps, got into a fight during transportation?"

It is hard to imagine how someone could kick themselves in the back, let alone with enough force to leave huge, angry bruises. The KGB could hardly have devised a less successful start to "re-education." Natasha was too angry to speak to them at all. But the assault on Natasha had one very unexpected result: Vla-dimirova wrote a statement testifying that Natasha had been severely beaten up when she was brought to the cell. They both returned to the Zone burning with indignation. Who would have thought it? Our stoolie had done her first humane deed. Nobody was optimistic enough to read some kind of spiritual rebirth into this act (we knew that our troubles with Vladimirova were far from over), but, nonetheless, we decided to lift our boycott. Heavens, how she blossomed! She chattered without pause, so we were driven to finding ways of channelling her energy into something constructive. Raya volunteered to teach her how to grow decorative peppers and other house plants, and I volunteered to teach her embroidery, a skill I myself acquired in the camp. I even drew up some patterns for her to embroider with cross-stitch. Everything she attempted was done sloppily and haphazardly, but it kept her occupied. Things quieted down, but we knew that this would not last for long.

Natasha lodged a petition to the court against the officials who had beaten her up, and was trying to ensure that something was done about it. Useless, of course. We wrote a letter in support of her demands to the Procuracy for the record, and another one destined for "out there." Publicity was Natasha's only real defense:

APPEAL TO WORLD PUBLIC OPINION

We, women political prisoners of the Small Zone, bear witness to the systematic persecution to which the camp administration subjects Natalia Lazareva, one of our number.

We know that the KGB tried to coerce her into becoming an informer, and repeated this demand when she arrived in this camp. When Lazareva made it plain that she would not act against her conscience, she became a target for persecution. Particular efforts in this respect were undertaken by brigade supervisor Lidia Podust. She made a personal crusade out of finding fault with Lazareva on the slightest pretext, threatening and humiliating her whenever she could. Even though the administration was aware that Lazareva was suffering from a chronic inflammation of the Fallopian tubes, a condition she developed in the camps, she has still been placed twice in SHIZO—the standard Soviet camp method of torture by cold and hunger. The camp's medical staff did not protest against this, but acted as accessories in this shameful campaign. Lazareva is constantly ill, yet despite that, and in violation of the law, she was stripped of her classification as a Group III invalid, because invalids in this category have lower production quotas. Lazareva is denied medical care on the pretext that the doctors "can find nothing wrong," and resort to all sorts of excuses to avoid admitting her into hospital for a proper examination.

Lazareva and the rest of us have been demanding such an examination since September 1983, but Dr. Vera Volkova, who is officially responsible for our Zone, falsely claimed that there were no free beds in the camp hospital. Bieliauskiene, who was in the hospital at the time, testified that there were beds available. Lazareva's examination kept being deferred until November 16, on which day she was told by camp officials to prepare for transportation to a KGB isolation cell for re-education.

We summoned Dr. Volkova, who measured Lazareva's temperature in our presence. A high temperature is the only symptom of illness which Dr. Volkova considers valid. On that day, as on others, Lazareva was running a high temperature, and refused to let herself be taken anywhere.

She was then dragged out of bed, despite our attempts to protect her, and hauled almost naked into the snow outside. This operation was supervised by Majors Shalin and Pazizin. In order to silence Lazareva, they subjected her to brutal physical assault, and when she reached the KGB isolation cell, she was jeeringly told that she had not been beaten up, but merely "received help."

We do not know what other plans the KGB may have for Lazareva's re-education, but we hope that she will be left in peace.

We call upon world public opinion with an appeal for support for our fellow prisoner, whose only fault lies in her unwillingness to betray her friends by acting as a KGB informer.

ABRUTIENE, BARATS, BIELIAUSKIENE, OSIPOVA, RATUSHINSKAYA, RUDENKO.

November 25, 1983

World public opinion, where are you? Do you hear the appeals made to you now by prisoners driven to the edge of despair? Do you know how incredibly difficult it is to get such an appeal out from behind barbed wire? Natasha is still alive. She completed her four-year sentence and is trying to restore her shattered health in Leningrad. But human rights champion Anatoli Marchenko perished before release, the Ukrainian poet Vasyl Stus was brutally murdered, nor did seventy-five-year-old religious prisoner Tatyana Krasnova survive to the end of her sentence: she died in exile just three months after release from camp. We must remember the dead, but let us save the living. If we don't, then who will? All their hopes are pinned on us . . .

24

"Ratushinskaya and Rudenko! To the hospital!"

The order comes several hours after Natasha has been dragged off to Saransk. At last! I have had edemas and been running a temperature since April. I also have inexplicable pains in my right side. Maybe they'll diagnose the trouble. Unfortunately, this is not the best time to leave the Zone; they're obviously trying to scatter us so there'll be fewer strikers in the same place. But in this instance there's no choice, so we prepare to go.

"Stop! What's all that stuff you've got with you? What are these envelopes? Letters? The orders are that you're to leave your letters in the Zone."

We are distinctly alarmed by these "orders." By law, prisoners may keep by them all letters that have been passed by the censors. It's also a well-known fact that anything left in the Zone may be confiscated during a search; the others will be powerless to stop that, because it's not their personal property. So you can't even give your letters to someone else for safekeeping. Moreover, the KGB has been showing intense interest in my correspondence over the past few months, making inquiries all over the place and even questioning a woman awaiting birth in a maternity ward. Clearly, they think there is some kind of secret code in my letters, and want to see if they can crack it by studying letters which have been sent to me. They were nowhere near the truth, but I had no intention of telling them that; let them stay on the wrong track. So I dug my heels in: "You have no right to touch my letters."

"If you don't surrender them, you won't be admitted into hospital."

"That's up to you . . ."

Raya leaves her letters and goes into hospital, while I remain in the Zone. I can't say that I am particularly upset; they'll examine me anyway if they really want to. But if this is all a trick just to get their hands on my mail, I wouldn't get any medical treatment in any case. Why, you may wonder, do I cling to these letters so tenaciously? Because letters from home are a zek's most treasured possession. Our dear ones, if only you could know how your letters warm our hearts! But they do know, and that is why even the most reluctant letter-writers make the effort. Half of our mail never reaches us at all—it remains in the hands of the "operative" section, the censors or the KGB. Why should they get the other half, too?

They hover around me for the next eight days: "Maybe there are forbidden subjects in those letters? We have to check."

"Go ahead. But in my presence."

No, that doesn't suit them. Dr. Volkova utters righteous reproaches: "You see? You're refusing medical treatment."

"No, I'm not. I've been demanding treatment for more than six months."

"If you were really ill, you'd agree to anything in order to get medical care."

But that's just it—I am not prepared to agree to anything: you make one small concession, and then you may well find yourself with no choice but to "agree to anything." That's how they tried to get the better of Tanya Osipova in Lefortovo prison in Moscow. Before her arrest, she was undergoing a course of treatment for infertility, and demanded a continuation of that treatment in prison. Investigator Gubinsky offered her a deal: "If you give the required evidence, the treatment will go on. But if you don't— well, you'll have only yourself to blame." . . . And then, "quite by chance," he switched on a tape of a radio program about the joys of motherhood, how wonderful it is to hold your baby in your

arms. Tanya wept, but refused to cooperate with the KGB nonetheless. Maybe Western doctors will be able to help her to realize
her dream now, even though she clocked up more than 160 days
of SHIZO, to say nothing of other privations . . .

After eight days, they give in: "All right, take your letters with
you."

About time, too. This is my first visit to the hospital of ZhKh-
385/3. That's the official designation of our camp. What do the
letters "Zh" and "Kh" stand for? Why, the Russian words for
"Railway Property."[1] That's because, officially, there are no concentration camps in the USSR! And the number "385"? Well, the
authorities must keep count of the non-existent camps, mustn't
they? Our camp was not the last on the Mordovian list.

I am taken to the therapy block. It is a wooden building divided into four wards. It also contains a dining room, a storeroom,
a toilet and doctors' offices.

"Hand in all your things to the store, and put on that gown.
Hang your jacket on the hook over there, and don't wear it inside.
If you do, it will count as a violation of discipline."

It's freezing cold in the block, but it would be against my
interests to commit a deliberate violation of the regulations. I've
been cold for so long now, I can bear it a while longer. There are
already twelve people in the ward to which I am directed, I make
up the thirteenth. Raya is there to greet me with a hug: "Ira.
Thank God!"

She immediately starts rummaging around for something for
me to eat. Raya has very definite ideas about poets: she's married
to one, after all, and it was her devotion to him that landed her in
the camps. To her, poets are like small children who are incapable
of looking after themselves. She is convinced that if food is not
placed before them, they will forget to eat, or that if they are not
forced to go to bed at a reasonable hour, they will sit up all night
communing with their Muse . . . She was like a nursemaid to me
in all the years we spent together in the camp. Also, she liked my
poetry, and we would spend hours reciting to each other; she
would read her husband's poems, and I would read mine . . .

1. *Zheleznodorozhnoye Khozyaystvo.*

Now she manages to assemble a huge sandwich: white bread spread with butter and jam. Class! Apparently those in hospital get supplemented rations; slightly less for those who have already been diagnosed, slightly more for those who haven't. This is not Raya's first stay in the hospital, so she already has her diagnosis. We knew about the white bread in the hospital, because on several occasions we even got some of it; that was when the black bread had not been delivered for some reason, and we insisted on getting our statutory ration. Those few occasions were a high treat.

I cast an eye over the other patients while I give Raya a summary of Zone news. There are three pregnant women in the ward, all close to giving birth, one with pneumonia, three with stomach ulcers and two who have something wrong with their legs. Actually, you could say that this is a lucky ward, because everyone in it is mobile. Paralyzed prisoners are kept in Wards Three and Four, lying there steeped in their own excrement, because the sheets are not changed for weeks on end. Some of them get "decreed"—in other words, sent home to die, rather than raise the camp's mortality statistics. Never fear, they have paid the penalty for their misdeeds, the Motherland has not been cheated of her due. Those who do die here are buried in the barbed-wire-enclosed cemetery. Igor told me later about this cemetery, which he was unable to enter.

"Who stopped you?" I asked.

He only smiled at my naïveté: "To the right of the camp—if you stand facing it—there's an ordinary cemetery. But the zek cemetery is on the territory of the camp itself, surrounded by barbed wire. It's impossible to get into it, especially with armed guards in the watchtowers looking on." He told me that when he came to the camp for a cancelled meeting, he spent the night in the "Visitors' House" with a family which had come here for a funeral. The deceased, as a young woman aged twenty-one, had gotten a job as a booking clerk with Aeroflot. A year later, a book of unused tickets for which she was responsible went missing. "Humane Soviet law" went into action: she was charged with embezzlement to the sum of the maximum estimated value of the tickets, and sentenced to eight years. She went into the camp leaving a one-year-old son. At the age of twenty-five she died in this very therapy block from untreated pneumonia. This is not surprising, when you consider what it takes to secure admission into hospital from the camp. The doctors accuse everyone of malingering until they become incapable of doing any work at all. And when they reach that stage, not all of them even manage to reach the hospital alive. The mother of this young woman poured out the whole story to Igor during the night, weeping bitterly. In the morning, they parted ways: she to the cemetery, Igor to the camp offices where he was told that our meeting had been cancelled.

I said this in the camp, and I say it now: everything was much harder for our families than it was for us. Igor travelled to Barashevo eight times—and was only allowed to see me twice. And that's not counting the times when I managed to warn him that a scheduled meeting had been cancelled. Every time he was in that Visitors' House, he encountered two or three families who had come to attend the burial of a relative. They were not allowed to claim the bodies for burial elsewhere: if you die in the camp, you shall remain behind barbed wire even in death. Igor started gathering statistics, questioning hospital workers. On the basis of the information he assembled, it emerged that the annual zek mortality rate is 8 percent, and the Mordovian camps are not the worst in the Soviet Union . . . However, let us stick to the figure of 8 percent: there are some four and a half million prisoners in the USSR, so that means one thousand of them die every day—in other words, forty zeks die every hour of every day of the year . . . How many will die by the time you get to the end of this chapter? Calculate it for yourself, depending on how quickly you read.

We were specifically barred from entering the wards where the paralyzed were kept. The reason for this was Pani Jadvyga's stay in the hospital this autumn. Her time there was an endless round of arduous voluntary labor. She removed the soiled bedding from under the paralyzed, plucked lice from their bodies with her bare hands. A true Christian, performing a Christian labor of love. But there was nobody to help her, and her strength began to fail. In an attempt to secure some assistance, she appealed to the hospital administration: "What are your notions of hygiene? How can you justify keeping people in such appalling conditions?"

The senior staff could not care less, so Pani Jadvyga wrote to the Central Medical Administration . . . That's why she was discharged so quickly: the hospital staff hurriedly gave her the minimum amount of treatment possible, and sent her back to our Zone. I met women in the hospital who remembered her.

"She was one smart lady, that one. How's she doing? Still alive?" They meant no disrespect—this was their normal way of speaking. They had become very fond of Pani Jadvyga, and were sincerely concerned for her.

The refusal to issue the bodies of dead zeks to their families is a violation of the law. What threat did the authorities see in a zek corpse? In the case of political prisoners—well, there could be potential problems: an elaborate funeral, attended by dissidents, funeral orations, and then, before you know it, young people coming to the grave with flowers . . . But if the deceased is just an "ordinary" zek? Nobody is likely to come on pilgrimage to his grave! However, just stop and think a moment: one thousand deaths a day calls for the supply of an equivalent number of coffins. These would have to be delivered to the camps by rail, spending many days in transit. Is this not an unnecessary strain on the national economy? No, comrades, let us not overburden the nation's railway network! The dead are beyond caring, anyway, and we have to get on with the business of building communism . . .

25

The morning is temperature-measuring time. The medical aides hand out thermometers, and you report your temperature to them. If it's above normal, you have to go to the duty nurse's room, where it's measured again. As an added precaution, the nurse uses two thermometers, just in case you've done something to your armpit to make it hotter than the rest of your body. I have to endure this ritual twice a day, and the medics are obliged to record an average of 37.5° C in the morning, and 38° C in the evening. This may not seem drastically high, but when it lasts for months on end, it's terribly debilitating. Your knees become weak, there's a constant buzzing in your head, and the slightest exertion makes you gasp for breath as though your head were trapped in a plastic bag. At the same time, life must go on: you have to carry buckets of water, cut firewood, load and unload the dray with the gloves, launder your sheets in a small basin. And conduct hunger strikes. And laugh, and maintain a cheerful demeanor; nobody else in the Zone is any better off. Everyone is ill, and that makes it all the more vital not to lose heart. Camp regulations don't promote positive emotions, only negative ones, so Heaven only knows what will become of you in seven years if all you do is fret and fume.

For this reason, we don't let a single day go by without jokes and mirth. We try to recall all the good and happy times in our lives. Yet the flesh weakens, and it becomes harder and harder to control the treacherous unsteadiness of your legs. Maybe they'll patch me up a bit while I am in the hospital. I must confess that while I was not opposed to sewing gloves, I could not help feeling a purely physical sense of relief when we began our strike.

"Ratushinskaya! To the oculist!"

What? There's nothing wrong with my eyes. They, at least, are in order . . . There must be some mistake.

"Hurry up, now. We're supposed to give you a full medical examination."

Well, if they insist . . . I am taken to the oculist's consulting room. There are charts on the walls, glass gadgets of all descriptions lying around. The oculist is elderly, and looks to be an intelligent man.

"What seems to be the trouble?" he asks.

"Nothing. My eyesight is fine."

"Well, why have you come here, then?"

"I was told I had to. I find it surprising, too."

"What's your illness?"

"No idea. I have a constant temperature, and edemas. But all that's outside your field."

"Then you should be examined by a doctor."

"But they made me come here. Perhaps I should go back now?"

"Well, since you're here, I may as well check your eyes. Can you tell me what this letter is?"

We run through the charts. Obediently, I try not to blink while he studies my eyes through a magnifying lens. Such stupidity! Our poor Galya, who ruined her eyesight in the Rostov KGB prison, has been trying to secure an examination by the oculist for months without success. She did get to see him eventually, and he prescribed glasses. She sent the prescription to friends, who had the glasses made up, and posted them to her. The package was returned, marked "not permitted." By the time Galya learned what had happened, by the time she managed to get permission to receive the glasses, by the time they were sent again and by the time she finally got them, her eyesight had deteriorated even further, and the glasses proved to be too weak. So the whole process had to be started again—examination, prescription, request to friends, receipt of new glasses. In the meantime, Galya had to manage as best she could, until the chance discovery that she could see quite well with Pani Lida's spare glasses.

Yet here is the oculist, wasting time over my perfectly good eyes. It's not his fault—his job is to examine everyone who is sent to him. Nor can he visit our Zone just like that: he would need a whole pile of passes. In fact, there's a lot of bother involved for any doctor to enter the political zone, and just as difficult to bring one of us out of it. The procedure calls for signed authorization from the regime supervisor, the "operatives," Dr. Volkova, the KGB . . .

The oculist is keen to chat about literature. He is an educated man, and must be bored to death in Barashevo. Yet I can't help feeling that I am personally robbing Galya of this half hour. I return to the ward with an official certification that my eyesight is excellent. Little did the oculist know, as he tested me with his charts, about the microscopic script in which I conducted our clandestine correspondence. He would have needed his magnifying lens to decipher it. Luckily, this is not our only means of conveying information out of the camp, or I would have certainly become blind by the time of my release.

The ward is being mobilized for work.

"Women! Time to do the chores!"

You're surprised that sick people have to work? Who else do you think carries coal supplies to the boiler room and removes piles of slag? Jackets go on over our hospital gowns, we pick up buckets, and off we go. Coal must be carted from this pile over to Block Twelve, way over there. It's not wise to try to evade these duties—if you do, you'll find yourself discharged forthwith. Lugging our buckets, we plod along in line: ulcer and lumbago sufferers, lame old women, those with diagnoses and those without. A patient may have a hernia which will be diagnosed tomorrow, but today she will carry heavy buckets with everyone else. It's only for two hours—that won't kill her. Other chores, such as washing the floors in the wards, the dining room and the corridors, and keeping the stoves burning, are done by us on a rotation basis. This is a little easier, because the staff don't care who does this work so long as it is done. Therefore, we don't let the older women attempt it.

"Now you simmer down, Granny Katya. Just look at you— barely keeping body and soul together, and you think you can do the floors? I'll do them for you. No way you'll manage that bucket." The speaker is Shura, who is serving a sentence for murder. She's in the hospital with pleurisy. Now, how do you go about judging human nature after her offer?

After two hours of carrying coal, your clothes, your hair and your skin are covered with a thick layer of coal dust. Bathing, however, is permitted only once a week. You can wash your hands and face under the tap in the toilet. You expect them to build washrooms for you? Do me a favor! As for your clothes— well, the hospital gowns are black, so the coal dust doesn't show. In any case, you may as well stay as you are, because the same chores will have to be done tomorrow. And don't even think of complaining—just thank your lucky stars that you were admitted into the hospital at all. Why, you even get a 30-gram pat of butter for breakfast . . .

"Being in the hospital is Heaven," I was assured by Lyuba, an embezzler who had been planted as a stool pigeon in my cell in Kiev prison. As sinners have no place in Heaven, I was driven forth quite soon. I had only had time to hear Granny Masha's account of her personal encounter with Saint Nicholas (she was arrested for vagrancy) and write out a literate clemency plea for black marketeer Auntie Vera (I believe she was completely illiterate) when the door opened, and a hospital aide beckoned to me: "Ratushinskaya. Come and get your injection."

"What injection?"

"That's none of your business."

Oh-oh, I don't like the sound of that . . . Who is to say what they've got in mind? The shadow of the KGB hangs over me as it does over all political prisoners, and that injection could contain any number of things brewed up in their psychiatric hospitals: they like using dissidents as guinea pigs. They'll inject you with some solution or other, and for the next two hours you'll sit there babbling without a break, or become so stupefied that you won't even be able to remember your own name. Or they'll pump narcotics into you . . . You can expect absolutely anything, but one thing is quite clear to me: I have not been diagnosed yet, no treatment has been prescribed, so the injection can have nothing to do with any of my ailments. In that case, why should I agree to it?

"I shall not allow you to inject me with some unknown substance," I tell the nurse. "Show me the ampule."

"If you're refusing medical treatment, say so."

"I'm not refusing medical treatment. But I want to know what is being used to treat what."

"I can't give you that information. Ask the doctor."

So I go to the doctor. This is the first time I'll be seeing him. He turns out to be Dr. Gunkin, the one who accused Pani Jadvyga of pretending not to have a gallbladder. By the time I get to him, he has been forewarned.

"It's my business what the injection is, not yours," he declares.

He also permits himself the use of the familiar "thou" form of address. A bit premature, isn't he? I point this out to him, and add: "What do you propose to treat me with, when I haven't even been examined yet?"

But Gunkin is used to being a sort of omnipotent little god around here. It's for him to either transfer a zek to light duties or send him back to the camp without any treatment at all. Gunkin is not accustomed to any questions or objections, and he uses the familiar form of address with everyone, even though he can hardly be over thirty. He replies in keeping with the spirit of his institution: "It's none of your [the familiar form again!] business. Any more trouble out of you, and I'll have you discharged immediately!"

Talking to someone like that is a waste of breath. I refuse to let them administer their mysterious injection: this is not a psychiatric hospital. After writing a protest to the hospital superintendent, and pointing out that covert medication is forbidden by law, I return to the ward.

I arrive in the middle of a fascinating discussion about the various forms of self-mutilation practiced by zeks to gain admission into the hospital, or, at least, secure release from work for a week or two. Liza, one of the pregnant women, is holding the floor: "Our girls grind sugar into a very fine powder, put it in a bag, and then inhale it. It settles on your lungs so that when they X-ray you, it shows up as dark patches. If you do it regularly, you get real tuberculosis, and they transfer you into the TB wards in the hospital, where you get issued with milk. And if they put you into SHIZO with tuberculosis, they're supposed to give you bedding and feed you hospital rations every day. It's great!"

"Why don't you inhale sugar powder, then?"

"I'm a bit scared to," admits Liza frankly. "After all, tuberculosis . . . I've still got five years to serve, and could die in that time, even on hospital rations. No, it's much better to have a 'quickie' with one of the alcoholics—their camp is right next door, and they're in and out of our Zone all the time. So I figure I'm better off as I am—I'll have the kid, and get out the next time there's an amnesty."

"We had such a good nurse back in '56," says Granny Katya wistfully. "She was a zek herself, so she understood everything. We were doing tree-felling then, and that's work that had even the men dying like flies. When she'd see that you were about to drop, she'd inject about 3 ccs of milk under your skin, and in a hour or two you'd be running a temperature of 39°. Or even higher. They'd release you from work for a few days, and that'd give you a chance to rally a bit . . ."

"Our girls in Number Two cultivate scabies. Anyone with scabies has to go into quarantine until they recover. The best way to do it is to use a needle: the one who's got scabies will prick one of her blisters with it, and then you prick yourself with that needle right away. I've got myself into quarantine three times that way: terrific!"

They describe cunning fractures, how to give yourself stenocardia with the lees of tea brew, how to keep ulcerous sores on your feet from healing . . . To what lengths must they be driven to do such terrible things to themselves? What kind of work makes tuberculosis seem preferable?

Shura, the one who's in for murder, explains: "I'm the brigade leader in the sewing room, so it's up to me to make sure that everyone produces more than the quota. Then you get a productivity bonus—a whole two rubles a month to spend in the kiosk. If someone in the brigade doesn't do the norm, that means more work for the others. You get them from time to time—some useless cow who can't pull her weight. Okay, you give her a week, thinking she'll learn. And she's probably some damned good-for-nothing intellectual. Well, then I just have to use my fists to teach her. My girls know better than to mess around with me. I'm strict, I am."

But of course, how else would the Soviet government set about reforming a killer like Shura? What better than to put her in charge of others, and let her use her fists to show some "damned intellectual" what's what? That is bound to purge them both of criminal inclinations! Yet at the same time, that Shura is genuinely kind to Granny Katya; admittedly, Katya is no threat to Shura's monthly two-ruble bonus.

Talk like this goes on until dark. The next morning, just as the temperatures are being taken, they come for me: "Ratushinskaya, back to the Zone! You're discharged."

"Why?"

"For refusing treatment, Dr. Gunkin says."

I check my temperature—37.5° C, the same as it was when I arrived. I've also caught a cold while I've been here in the hospital. The edemas are worse than ever, my legs are like inflated balloons. Thanks for the cure. I'm glad to get out of here.

The ward is very upset on my behalf, though: "Irisha, why don't you go and have a word with Gunkin? He might let you stay after all."

"I wouldn't ask Gunkin for anything. It's his job to give medical treatment, not a favor."

"Going back to the Zone could really finish you off, though!"

"Too bad. At least it's warmer there, we go around in our jackets, not in these flimsy gowns."

"But how will you be able to work?"

"I won't. We're on strike."

They know about our strike and sympathize with it. But they

are amazed by our daring: "One of you has a meeting cancelled, and the others all go on strike! How about that?"

"So what? They're right. I wish the lot in our camp were like that."

"Where? In Number Two? Don't make me laugh. I served my first sentence in Number Two, half of them do nothing but lick the bosses' asses. Why, even our Number Fourteen's better than that."

Raya is terribly upset to see me go. She quickly pulls out all the butter and sugar that she's been hoarding in her bedside locker. "Take it to the Zone."

I kiss her goodbye, and head for the door.

" 'Bye, girls. Look after yourselves."

"Good luck, Irisha. Hang on!"

Larisa from the neighboring ward catches up with me in the corridor: "Ira, wait up. You have a harder time in the 'strict' than we have in the general zone. No offense, but I'd like you to have these." She hands me a pair of socks. They're made out of thick, good-quality synthetic fiber, and are quite new. I wore those socks until the end of my time in camp, and I was wearing them when I was finally released. In exchange, I give her a bookmark I have embroidered as a keepsake.

Goodbye, hospital!

26

How good it is to be back in the Zone! And bringing butter and sugar as well. The others, however, are not at all pleased with the results—or rather, lack of results—of my brief stay in the hospital. Well, it can't be helped. I'll simply have to resume writing to the Central Medical Administration, demanding medical treatment for the condition to which they've reduced me here. It's better to be back home in the Zone than to stay any longer in the icy, filthy hospital. The others heat up two buckets of water for me, and I wash off the hospital's coal dust. I throw my jacket and underwear into the snow outside to kill off any germs they may have picked up in the hospital compound. I'll wash and clean them tomorrow. Washed and dressed in clean clothes, I settle down by our "fireplace." Pani Lida brews tea. I already feel much better within these walls, but even better than the walls of this our home is our friendship.

Five days after my stay in the hospital, we try to get a concrete answer out of Volkova: are they, or are they not, going to give us medical treatment? Tanya's kidney troubles have become more acute and her temperature is higher than mine. It's hard to tell what's wrong with me; as for Natasha—she's in a dreadful way. "But women!" complains Volkova, "your rations have been improved, haven't they?"

That is true: they are certainly better than they were at the beginning of autumn. But what about actual treatment? Finally they examine Tanya and prescribe a course of antibiotics. Then they promise me an examination too. However, half an hour later we hear: "Ratushinskaya and Osipova to SHIZO! For going on strike!"

Well, it was only to be expected. We can't figure out, though, why I have been given twelve days of SHIZO and Tanya fifteen. We all started our strike at exactly the same time.

"Don't worry about it," laughs Tanya, "you'll have lots more SHIZO yet."

The others bustle about trying to find the warmest things that could possibly pass as underwear. We put on about three layers. You couldn't call us thin now. Surreptitiously, we sneak an alcohol thermometer into our things, in the hope that we might be able to smuggle it into SHIZO with us and keep a record of the temperature in the cell. We kiss the others goodbye, and are escorted to the guardhouse.

"Wait here!"

Apparently, the "cuckoo" has already gone and we'll be delivered to SHIZO in a van. This is called "special transport." Meanwhile, we sit in the room in which I had my meeting with Igor, and a couple of sympathetic warders bring us dinner from the officers' mess: a huge pile of rissoles, mashed potatoes, and fruit pudding.

"We'll never manage all that."

"Go on, eat it up! You won't be getting anything over there."

They're right, of course, and we make a conscientious effort to chew through as much as possible.

Our mood is a happy one: first, we'll be together, and secondly—none of the others have been taken. Thank God they've left Pani Jadvyga and Natasha in peace. The "special transport" van arrives and we are bundled inside into minicompartments designed to hold one person. These are popularly known as "glasses." You sit on a tiny bench surrounded by iron on all sides, your knees pressed against the door and your back and shoulders to the wall. It's vital to hang on to the bench as tightly as possible, because Mordovian roads consist mainly of ruts and potholes, and the van veers and bumps like a bucking horse. Ah, we've arrived at Number Two, that is, women's camp ZhKh-385/2. This is where we'll be put into SHIZO. We are taken through admissions into the zone itself. The camp motto is "Back to freedom with a clear conscience!" An excellent ambition, isn't it? To be released without having been broken, without renouncing your views, without informing on your friends, without co-operating with the KGB ... Camp either cleanses your conscience, or destroys it forever. People emerge either much better than they were, or much worse, depending how they were predisposed. But I fear that we interpreted that motto far too literally. It's not likely that the "operative" section, which specializes in this kind of agitation, meant it quite that way.

It soon becomes evident that the campaign being conducted under that motto bears absolutely no resemblance to our understanding of the sentiments the motto might imply. It is occasioned by the mountains of unsolved criminal cases clogging up the work of the criminal investigation departments. What price the public assertions that no case remains unsolved? Then someone had a brilliant idea: let's get the zeks to lend the militia a hand! You're caught committing a burglary—what do you know about other break-ins? Maybe some of your friends were involved—give evidence, help stamp out crime. Or maybe you, too, have committed a misdemeanor or two that hasn't come to light? This is just the right time to go to the "operatives" and make a clean breast of everything. It's highly unlikely that your sentence will be extended: one burglary or three makes no difference to the law. But you may well be allowed an unscheduled parcel from home as a reward. Even if you have nothing to confess, it's worth considering taking the blame for some other unsolved case. The duty "operative" will advise you on the choice of an appropriate felony that's wasting valuable militia time. With your assistance they can declare the case closed and improve their success rate. You will be given a glowing testimonial in the camp newspaper *Accelerated Tempo*:

> For the past six months, Prisoner K could not sleep peacefully. He was tortured by recollections of two car thefts about which he

had not confessed during pre-trial investigation on other charges. It was as if he could hear the voice of his aged mother: "My son, live an honest life. And if you should chance to make a false step, then confess, and see how much happier you will feel." Yet it is possible that, even despite this, Prisoner K would have kept his guilty secret were it not for the tactful, profound educational work of operative section head V. P. Korytin in the bureau headed by Comrade Gorin. With great patience and gentleness he frequently urged Prisoner K to clear his conscience before the law. And then one evening Prisoner K walked decisively into the operative section: he could not bear to conceal his past misdeeds any longer. Now Prisoner K is firmly on the path to reform: he exceeds production quotas by 20 to 30 percent, observes camp regulations of internal order . . . His exemplary behavior has been rewarded by an unscheduled parcel.

We read any number of such heart-warming effusions while we were in camp Number Two. The paper was not available in our Zone, it was published by the ministry specifically for the camps, and may not be taken out of them. Giving it to us would be risky: who knows, we might smuggle out a copy or two to our friends and relatives. All Soviet zeks are obliged to subscribe to this paper, whether they want to or not. With the exception of political prisoners, that is; it would be easier for them to take out a subscription to the practically unobtainable journal *Foreign Literature* than to get *Accelerated Tempo*. Luckily, fine ideological considerations like that were unknown at Number Two, and when we were later put into camp prison there, the librarian gave us huge folders of *Accelerated Tempo*. By studying them thoroughly we acquired a great deal of information about the various "educational" campaigns in recent years. But that was six months later. You may not have newspapers in SHIZO, indeed, no paper of any kind—not even toilet paper.

We pass through Number Two zone escorted by an officer and a warder. The prisoners here don't look to be in any better shape than the ones in our camp. Grey faces, grey or blue jackets, grey barracks and grey fences. Even the snow, powdered over with coal dust, has lost its whiteness. The only splashes of color are the red armbands worn by some of the zeks, with the letters "SVP"[1] standing for the Russian words for "Section of Internal Order." It is their responsibility to ensure order and discipline in the camp, and to report any breaches. They are virulently hated by their fellow prisoners. Zeks decipher the letters "SVP" not quite as its members would like: "Bitch Out Walking."[2] The camp authorities are well aware of how the SVPs are detested, and that suits them fine; it's sound tactics to set zek against zek, that makes them easier to handle. This was the reasoning that made Podust try so hard to sow discord among us. Had she succeeded, we would have destroyed ourselves much more effectively than she could hope to do.

The whisper "Politicals!" follows us as we go through the camp.

One brave soul calls out to us from a safe distance: "Hey girls! SHIZO or PKT?"

"SHIZO. Osipova and Ratushinskaya!" we call back.

The warder, knowing it's no use saying anything to us, shakes a fist in the general direction of the inquirer: "Oh, Derkayeva, are you asking for trouble." Then she mutters discontentedly all the way to the cell: "They keep bringing these damned politicals. As if we didn't have enough of our own rabble. You'd think they could build their own SHIZO at Number Three, but no, they bring them here, so we have to waste time on them!"

They have no clear idea of how to handle these mysterious politicals. It's a strain for them to address us formally, instead of by the familiar "thou." Later, when the corresponding instructions were handed down by the KGB, they would strip off our clothes, and once even tried to give us a "gynecological search." But that met with such resistance that they didn't have the nerve to try it a second time. But at this stage, they're still careful in their dealings with us. They take our bags and lock us into the cell with a minimum of words. The cell is not a large one, for four people: six steps long, and not quite four across. The wooden floor

1. *Sektsiya Vnutrennego Poryadka.*
2. *Suchka Vyshla Pogulyat.*

has rotted from damp. In one corner the boards have disintegrated, leaving a large hole. A damp-basement smell issues from it, as well as countless woodlice. There is a huge window, though, about a meter by a meter and a half. Barred, of course. It consists of thin wooden rods into which squares of glass about the size of both my palms have been set. As the window frame is crooked and the bits of glass have been set in anyhow, there are cracks the width of a finger all over. I measured the length of these cracks later, and the sum total was thirteen meters. But it's not cracks we are worried about, two squares of glass are missing entirely, and the December wind drives snow in through these holes. We bang on the door: "Transfer us to another cell!"

That's not as simple as it may sound. Cell Number Seven is specifically reserved for politicals. It serves both as SHIZO and PKT. The ordinary criminals are in neighboring cells, and it is categorically forbidden to let us mix with them. "Wait until morning, they'll put some glass in then."

Yes, we know what that "wait" means. We could freeze to death here overnight. Also, if we agree to wait, we may as well forget about being moved elsewhere. Nobody will come to fix the window in the morning, and we'll be told to "wait until tomorrow."

"Take your food. It's 'hungry day' today."

"Hungry day" means that no skilly is issued, only 150 grams of bread. At least, you're supposed to get 150 grams, but how can you tell how much there is in the two damp, misshapen lumps they push through the flap in the door? As it happens, we have no intention of trying to gauge their weight.

"We're not going to eat until we're transferred to another cell."

"Right, I'm going for the duty assistant camp commandant."

This official strikes terror into the hearts of zeks. He can consign them to SHIZO and, in general, decide their fate. But he is just the person we need to see. He appears, a thin, rather ungainly figure. His name is Vasili Ivanovich Kochetov. I remember his surname at once not so much because of the zek habit of doing so, but because at the back of my mind there's a conviction that I've come across that name many times, but where. . . ? After he leaves, I suddenly remember. Of course! Our school math textbooks were compiled by a Kochetov. I remember their ink-stained covers . . . But that would have been another Kochetov: nobody could suspect our Vasili Ivanovich of academic endeavor. He is remarkably obtuse, even for a jailer. He's just marking time until retirement here, his ears propping up an officer's cap. There, it's sliding off again! Yet he, poor soul, must be responsible for deciding whether to transfer us to another cell. And he's got to decide quickly, because he remembers Tanya only too well from the four-month hunger strike she conducted right here in this cell. He cannot help having vivid recollections of how the ordinary prisoners rallied to her support, either.

"Wait a moment, I'll have to phone."

Smart move: Shift the responsibility for the decision onto someone else. Well, run along and phone, it's minus 15° C outside. We breathe on our hands to warm them, and wait.

"Women! Transfer to Number Eight cell!"

Number Eight cell has the same system of locks as Number Seven: first, two locks and a bolt on the outer door, and then a door made of crisscrossed iron bars.

"Settle in!"

The window in this cell is unbroken, but your breath still comes out in puffs of vapor. We are told that the camp heating pipes have failed, but will be fixed tomorrow. This is a traditional state of affairs in all the camps: as soon as the frosts begin, pipes start bursting all over the place. There's nothing deliberate in this—it's just that camp inefficiency and ramshackle equipment are the warp and weft of camp life all over Mordovia. There's a drastic shortage of qualified labor, for the jailers are incapable of doing anything useful. A good workman is worth his weight in gold around here, but gold is just what the camp management doesn't have. That's why broken windows abound, the power supply and the water supply are unreliable, so there's nothing surprising in the breakdown of the heating system . . . The camp commandant can hardly clear the block over trivial quibbles like that. Let the zeks be without water or light for a bit—this is not a holiday resort. There's not enough bread? They can make do on reduced rations for a week. Luckily, there's never a shortage of paint, so everything can be given a fresh coat at short notice in the event of a visit by some commission or other. Our SHIZO-PKT block is being constantly repainted, either grey or institutional green. The warders walk the corridors with smears of paint all over them, fuming, but give us civil warnings: "When you go out to empty your slop bucket, don't touch the walls. They've just been done again."

The slop bucket is made out of three-millimeter thick iron, and is officially known as a toilet tank. There is no sewage system around here, naturally. Recalling the specific weight of iron and the formula for calculating the capacity of a cylinder, I once calculated the weight of an empty slop bucket: it came out as 12 kilograms. The slop bucket is attached to the wall by a thick metal chain at the end of which there is an iron bar one meter in length. This bar is passed through a special aperture into the corridor, where it is fastened to the wall with bolts. For some reason, prison regulations stipulate that the slop bucket must be fastened to the wall, and the warders, cursing loudly, have to unscrew the bolts each morning, and then fasten them again after the bucket has been emptied. The bucket has a 30-liter capacity, so when it's full, it would weigh around 44 kilograms when you add the weight of the chain and fastening rod. It takes two of us to carry the slop bucket: it simply can't be lifted by one person. The bucket has handles on the sides for carrying.

You may wonder why I am devoting so much space to this repellent "convenience." But it was a very important aspect of our daily life! I spent a total of seven months in PKT and four in SHIZO, and every one of those days began with the laborious process of dragging the slop bucket the length of the corridor, down ice-covered steps, and then across the snow to the cesspit and back.

"Women, you haven't let the fastening bar through again. It's stuck? Well, come on, give it a push. You out of strength or something?"

So we had to push it through on "hungry" and "eating" days

alike, we had to do it even if we were hunger-striking. The rest of the time, we inhaled the slop bucket's odors.

"Lights out!"

A warder comes in, jangling keys, and unlocks our flimsy wooden bunks (they are raised like flaps and bolted flat against the wall in daylight hours). We are not entitled to any bedding, nor may we change clothing for the night. We settle down as best we can on the bare boards, using our slippers for pillows. It's impossible to sleep properly: you doze lightly from time to time, then wake because of the cold. You keep trying to find some position in which you may feel a little warmer. By the morning you are completely exhausted, and this is when you see brief but incredibly vivid and beautiful dreams. You often hear marvellous music, smell delicious aromas. In just about all these dreams you can fly. I have never had such dreams anywhere except in SHIZO, but I can fly to this day: I had plenty of practice.

"Time to get up, women! Empty your slop bucket!"

27

There are rumors that efforts are being made to repair the heating, so we entertain hopes of thawing a little this evening. Meanwhile, we do the routine morning chores: wash ourselves and clean the cell. To enable us to wash, they allow us to take our toothbrushes, toothpowder, soap and towels out of our things. The warders are half-asleep, so we seize the opportunity to remove the alcohol thermometer and a plastic bag with cotton wool. Tanya is an old hand at this sort of thing by now, and has packed the most necessary things. The regulations state that one mug of water per prisoner is issued for washing, but on her previous stays here Tanya had managed to get this increased to a kettleful. But this is a concession just for the stubborn politicals. Tanya pours out a bit of water, I lather my face with soap. Then we reverse roles. After our ablutions, we have to hand all the wherewithal back: you may not have any personal articles in SHIZO. You can even comb your hair only once—at 6:00 a.m.

While still in our own Zone, we managed to stitch two thin, wafer-textured towels together. We now separate them, and return only one. We wrap the other one around Tanya's midriff: she needs any extra warmth she can get because of her kidney trouble. The next morning I get the "second" towel. It's little inventions like this that help you to keep going. The alcohol thermometer is cunningly concealed. Where, you ask? But you, my readers, are never likely to find yourself in those cells! And if,

God forbid, you do, then you will learn for yourself soon enough, just as we did. Think of a place where they're least likely to look for anything, and hide it there. The cell is searched rather cursorily: the warders run a hand around under the small table which is fixed firmly to the floor and under the bench . . . As there's nothing else in the cell, that's it. True, they look under the slop bucket now and then . . . Very unimaginative lot, the warders. Naturally, they will run their hands down your sides to make sure that there's nothing under your smock, and immediately feel the towel you've wound around your midriff. But they will pretend not to notice out of compassion. That is, unless they happen to be warder Akimkina and regime supervisor Ryzhova: those two will gain enormous pleasure in stripping it off you.

The cell has to be cleaned with a bucket of water and a filthy piece of burlap. In recognition of our political status, they usually give us a mop as well. We pick up grit and dirt off the floor as best we can with the wet rag. It's dark; the lamp behind its grille gives virtually no light. Dawn is still two hours away.

"Women, breakfast! 'Food day' today!"

That means there will be skilly with our bread today. There will be a little piece of unscaled and ungutted fish in the skilly. We are supposed to get the equivalent amount of 60 grams of raw fish, but you get cooked bits of whatever has not been stolen. The "food day" ration is designated Ration 9-B, and here it is in its entirety:

Rye bread	450 grams
Flour	10 grams
Grains, various	50 grams
Fish	60 grams
Meat	0 grams
Fats or vegetable oil	6 grams
Potatoes	200 grams
Cabbage	200 grams
Tomato paste	5 grams

What you get in practice is half of a potato, and a shred of cabbage in your skilly. The camp personnel will find other uses for the fats and tomato paste without your help. Mind you, their reasoning on this matter is not without a certain logic: you're not going to be able to taste those 5–6 grams anyway, but if you put together all these small rations which are supposed to be issued to everyone in SHIZO, you get a reasonable amount of oil and tomato paste. As for the potato, we only realized our present luck later. When I was sent to SHIZO in another camp, Number Fourteen, they only gave you one eighth of a small Mordovian potato! Grains? Here the proportions are reversed: instead of getting the cooked equivalent of 50 grams of dry grain, you just get 50 grams of wet mush. They try to make sure that you don't overeat and forget that you're being punished. They cheat on the rye bread too, by cutting each loaf into ten or eleven chunks instead of seven. That I worked out quite easily by measuring the average thickness of each slice, knowing the size of the standard loaf. I had no ruler, of course, but I did have a carefully prepared piece of thread with knots tied at regular intervals: try finding that! We don't see the loaves of bread, but there's no reason to suppose that they're different from the ones delivered to our camp, and those we get to divide up ourselves.

On a "hungry" day you get nothing but bread. They alternate, so by the tenth day you are dizzy from hunger. The official (but not actual) calorie content is allegedly 1150, with an average 30 grams of solid protein. When normal, the official calorie intake is supposed to be 3000 for twenty-four hours.

If these statistics don't bother you, pay no attention to these figures, which were compiled bit by tiny bit, and go back to that nice steak you were planning to cook for dinner. With my own ears, I once heard a Leningrad student say derisively: "They claim that they were hungry? Why, during the Leningrad blockade people got only two hundred grams of bread a day. I can go without eating bread for a few days quite easily."

Actually, I believe she could: her parents were important Party bosses, and she had never known a day's hunger in her life. Why bother with bread when there's always meat on the table? She is even far from understanding why no ordinary family in the Soviet Union sits down to eat without bread. Igor and I lost the habit of eating bread with everything during that first month of living in England. But how well I remember that soggy prison slice, its taste and its smell . . . Still, don't be in any great hurry to pity us just yet: we had that really solid meal thanks to the warders in our camp yesterday, and the bread issued on our first evening in SHIZO we had put by for today. Later on, however, any bread we tried to save for the next day would be confiscated from us during the morning searches of the cell.

"Drying bread, are you?" they'd say, taking it away. "That means you're planning an escape, eh?"

But that was still to come.

Furthermore, with truly inspired genius, Tanya had concealed broth cubes in the cotton wool she had taken with her things. When our stuff was searched upon arrival in SHIZO, that cotton wool was, of course, unwrapped and shaken out, but nothing was found. This was because the small stock cubes were concealed between the layers of the cotton wool. We meant to use these cubes on "hungry" days only. Thirteen cubes in all. We had got them in small packages which don't rate as "parcels." Such cubes are not available in the Soviet Union, but they had come in parcels received by our families from the West . . . Obviously, the émigré friends who sent these parcels were still getting to grips with everyday life abroad and had not yet acquired Western fastidiousness: the foil cover of each small cube features a picture of a friendly-looking dog surrounded by English words, which, when we decipher them, state that these cubes are for cooking pet food! Thank heaven for pampered Western pets. We have no objection to the fact that the cubes are for dog food; the people who bought them didn't know enough English to distinguish the purpose, so they bought the ones of which they could get more on their slender means. These cubes will turn our "hungry" days into feasts. Throw one cube into a mug of hot water, stir it with Tanya's hairpin—and voilà! When the mug is empty, it must be wiped inside with a bit of bread, so that no traces of fat can be discovered during cell searches. The process is repeated in the evening, so that uses up two cubes a day. This illegal method of "dietary supplement" lasted until August 1985. The "blushing"

Shalin (promoted to the rank of major by that time) personally examined a roll of cotton wool, and triumphantly extracted twelve stock cubes which were meant to last four of us for a week . . . How he boasted to us about his success at "catching us"! May God forgive him . . .

The only activity permitted while you're in SHIZO is work, and the criminal prisoners from the neighboring cells are taken out daily to sew gloves. Despite the reduced rations of the SHIZO, they are expected to meet the usual production quotas. They are delighted when there are power failures, because the sewing machines are electric, and work has to stop until the power supply resumes. The delight, however, is premature: "What, you've made nothing in eight hours?"

"But, supervisor, there was no electricity."

"You could have pushed the machine wheel around by hand."

"By hand? But how many could we make that way?"

"You'd have done about sixty percent of the quota if only you'd tried. But no! Well, you're all guilty of deliberate evasion of work."

We are not taken out to sew. There's only one workroom for the whole SHIZO block and it's not permitted for us "especially dangerous" prisoners to mix with the ordinary criminals.

We have our own concerns, anyway. We're busy keeping a record of the temperature in the cell. By law, the temperature in SHIZO may not fall below 16° C. The local administration interprets that instruction as that the temperature may not be above 16° C. We make an official demand to have the cell temperature measured, and they bring along the famous camp thermometer: "There you are. You can measure it for yourself."

The thermometer is famous throughout SHIZO because its pointer invariably shows 15.5° C, anywhere, any time. This is considered "acceptable" by local standards. Now there's optimism for you. Maybe the Procuracy ought to hear about it?

"Warder! Give us paper and pencil, please."

"You're not supposed to have them in SHIZO."

"We want to write to the Procuracy. By law we can do that from SHIZO."

"Goddamn politicals. All they ever want to do is write complaints. Why do we have to have them? There's no paper."

"There's some in our things. Look in the side pockets. There are some envelopes there, too."

The warder disappears, and we can get no response from anyone until dark. The duty deputy camp commandant does the evening round with a new shift of warders. They search our cell.

"We asked for paper to write to the Procuracy, but didn't get any."

"Lord, more complaints! Why can't you settle down?"

"Because it's cold, and you're cheating with that thermometer."

"Cold? Nothing of the kind! The temperature in here's quite normal."

They all stand there in greatcoats and warm hats, well-nourished and red-faced, ignoring the puffs of steam which are their breath. No, they're not cold, that's obvious.

"But you agree that we have the right to write to the Procuracy?"

"Only during the day shift, and the night shift's only just come on. You can write tomorrow."

In other words, tomorrow another deputy will be on duty, let him handle it. And we'll have to start from scratch trying to get pencil and paper from him. "What are you on about, anyway, women? The heating's come back on, you'll soon be warm."

It's true—the pipes become slightly warm. They run along the floor, so we lie down lengthwise, pressing our bodies against them. Our own thermometer shows that the general temperature in the cell is 12° C, but it's a little warmer near the pipe. We clasp the pipe with fingers which are blue from cold and feel the tingle of returning circulation. Bliss! An hour later the pipes are stone cold again, but we stay where we are, because we know that the stokers run hot water through the pipes in fits and starts. They'll throw some coal into the furnace when they feel like it, then go off to rest, or sleep, or play cards. A while later they'll stoke the furnace again. You have to catch the moment.

But it's not just water that flows along these pipes; so does life, in the form of conversation through drinking mugs. The same pipes run through all the cells, and as we are lying right up against them, we become involuntary eavesdroppers on other people's personal concerns: "Hey, third cell! Third! Did you find the *makhorka*[1] in the workroom?"

"No."

"Idiots! We left it for you under the unsewn stuff."

That means cell Number Three missed finding the tobacco during its work shift, and *makhorka* in SHIZO is in terribly short supply: smoking is not allowed here, and you have to be a real virtuoso to smuggle in tobacco and matches. The *makhorka* is not divided up evenly, but by some incredibly complex scheme of reckoning. And Number Three cell has missed out. Idiots indeed.

"Hey, Eight! Politicals! Tanya, it's Tishka from Number Six here. D'you remember me?"

"Yes, yes I do."

"Well, how're things, Tanyusha? Who's with you? What's her name?"

"Ira. She's from our Zone, too."

"What's she in for?"

"Do you mean in camp, or in SHIZO?" Tanya is a great stickler for precision. She learned to give attention to detail while working on the clandestine human rights bulletin *Chronicle of Current Events.*

"Her and you, too."

"Ira—for writing poetry."

"Ah, she's a poetess, then."

"As for why we're both in SHIZO—we went on strike."

"You're both striking?"

"The whole Zone's striking, not just us."

"That means Natasha'll be along soon. How is she, anyway?"

"Sick."

"Well, girls, hang on. Everything'll be all right."

"Everything will be all right" are standard zek words of comfort. How many times I was to hear them over the years, from

1. A cheap kind of shag tobacco.

people I barely knew or from complete strangers during my time in the camps. And each time the senselessness of this utterance struck me anew: how do they know whether everything will be all right for me or not? Yet the amateur prison prophets turned out to be right in my case. Things were difficult, I was cold, and—to tell the truth—even afraid at times. Nevertheless, everything did turn out all right: I survived, I did not betray my conscience, and the man I love was waiting for me when I came out . . . What else can one ask for? If only it could be the same for the countless others who have heard the same prophecy . . . I daresay it helped me. It was like a short prayer for us by those who have never been taught to pray.

Tanya and I argue about the fate of Russia: where did we begin to go wrong? With Peter I?[2] Earlier? Later? Like all similar discussions, this one has no end. It's time to bed down, but neither of us feels like it. I recite poetry to Tanya: first other people's poems, then my own. Then I fall silent, and Tanya, ever sensitive, pretends to be asleep. She knows that the poems composed this night will be read to her tomorrow morning.

> I sit on the floor, leaning against the radiator—
> A southerner, no-gooder!
> Long shadows stretch from the grating, following the lamp.
> It's very cold.
> You want to roll yourself into a ball, chicken-style.
> Silently I listen to the night,
> Tucking my chin between my knees.
> A quiet rumble along the pipe:
> Maybe they'll send hot water in!
> But it's doubtful.
> The climate's SHIZO. Cainozoic era.
> What will warm us quicker—a firm ode of Derzhavin,
> A disfavored greeting of Martial,
> Or Homer's bronze?
> Mashka Mouse has filched a rusk

2. Peter I, also known as Peter the Great (1672–1725). Initiated radical changes in all spheres of Russian life in order to bring Russia into line with the leading European nations of that time.

And is nibbling it behind the latrine pail.
A two-inch robber,
The most innocent thief in the world.
Outside the window there's a bustle—
And into our cell bursts—
Fresh from freedom—
The December brigand wind.
The pride of the Helsinki group doesn't sleep—
I can hear them by their breathing.
In the Perm camp the regime's
Infringer doesn't sleep either.
Somewhere in Kiev another, obsessed,
Is twiddling the knob of the radio . . .
And Orion ascends,
Passing from roof to roof.
And the sad tale of Russia
(Maybe we are only dreaming?)
Makes room for Mashka Mouse, and us and the radio set,
On the clean page, not yet begun,
Opening this long winter
On tomorrow.

I managed to send this poem off during transportation back to the Zone from SHIZO. First it went to "unnamed" people, and then to Igor. This poem reached him before I was to go into SHIZO again. What would my "possessed" one think of these lines, I wondered, as I scribbled them down hastily in the shaking, rattling carriage of the "cuckoo." But during the night I did not pause to ponder this question. Igor is carrying his part of the burden, and I am carrying mine. While I composed I was, like Tanya, concerned with precise formulation . . .

28

Even more than by mice and woodlice, more than by the deliberate freezing of SHIZO inmates, hunger and ubiquitous dirt, I was amazed at that time by the daily life of a criminal women's camp. The mores of this life extended to all the neighboring cells, even though there was a constant turnover of inmates, and twelve days were enough to become fully *au fait* with all camp events. Later I became accustomed, but at first I couldn't understand why so many male names figured in the incessant conversations "on the pipe." Why the jealous tirades? After all, the camp is a women's one . . .

I had heard, of course, about lesbianism in the criminal camps, but I had had no idea of how widespread it is. These women, mainly young, who were torn away from normal life, compensated by seeking substitute love and creating substitute families. Yes, families—with grandmothers and grandfathers (those were older zeks), mothers and fathers of under-age children. The "children" were young girls who had been transferred from juvenile zones upon turning eighteen. But they still had to learn the women's lore of the adult camp.

"Masha, Masha. Second cell. What's new in the Zone?"

"Oh, Zina, it's you, is it? They brought in a transport of 'juveniles' yesterday. We went to look them over: beautiful, they are! One of them's in our brigade. We've taken her on as a daughter."

Men's names were assumed by "stallions"—women who play
the male role in lesbian sex. Those who took the woman's role
were referred to as "pickers." Of course, such activities were
strictly forbidden, of course anyone who was caught was punished and if all they got was a public denunciation, they could
count themselves lucky. Nothing could stop them, though, punishment only seemed to fan the flames even more. If one was sent
to SHIZO, then the other, according to camp mores, had to do
something that would ensure that she, too, would be placed in a
punishment cell. If she didn't, this would give rise to jealousy and
endless intrigue.

"Hey, Ted! You're in here, and your Liza is running around
with Eugene."

"What Eugene?" demands "Ted" in a ringing mezzosoprano.

"From the sixth brigade."

"Are you lying?"

"No, why should I? You ask Mikhryutka, she only came in
here today."

"Mikhryutka, Mikhryutka! First cell. Is that true?"

"How the hell would I know? I don't stand over them with a
candle. They did go to the kiosk together, though."

"Oh, I'll show her . . ."

And "Ted" will beat up Liza after leaving SHIZO, or, better
still, will slash her/his wrists before that, to bring the treacherous
Liza to a sense of her "betrayal." The camp doctors, fed up with
these constant slashed wrists, sew them up without any kind of
anesthetic: "Yes, yell your head off, go on. Next time you'll think
twice about doing anything so stupid."

Some, indeed, might not. Yet I recall how forty-year-old Xenia
in our hospital showed me her wrists which had scars upon
scars—and all from "bad luck in love." Like everyone else, the
"stallions" have to wear headscarves in camp, but they tie them
in a way which makes them resemble a man's cap. They try to
deepen their voices, walk with a rolling gait and tattoo themselves. They don't wash clothes: their "other halves" do that for
them.

Even those who had perfectly normal families before they

were arrested get drawn into this madness. I once heard a mind-boggling scene during one of my spells in SHIZO, when the brigade supervisor of one of the women in a neighboring cell came to persuade one such "half" to come out of PKT to see her husband and two-year-old son, who had been permitted a meeting with her. Strictly speaking, prisoners being punished by a spell in PKT are not eligible for meetings with relatives, but in this instance either the administration showed a flash of humanity, or decided to use this opportunity to break up a "pair of cohabitors" in the camp. The arrival of a husband on a visit to a criminal camp is quite a rare occurrence in itself. Most men don't wait for their unlucky wives to be released, but apply for divorce. There are exceptions, of course, but they're very few. It's the political prisoners who wait for each other, even up to twenty years. The husband who came on this occasion must have been one of the few faithful ones, and, against all the odds, was told he could see his wife.

But she didn't go: she flatly refused to leave the cell to see her husband and child. All the persuasions of the brigade supervisor—who could clearly hardly believe her ears—were in vain; the prisoner now had a new, camp love! And her "Alec," listening to all this from the neighboring cell, could be satisfied . . .

Certainly not everyone becomes involved in lesbian affairs in the camps, nor would I even say that this could be said of the majority. But it is certainly the most popular theme for discussion in SHIZO and PKT. It is a sticky mess of gossip, intrigue, lies, quarrels and reconciliations. Sometimes you will get two of them, sitting in different cells, sorting out their personal relations "on the pipe" for hours on end. The same pipe to which you are pressing your frozen body. In fifteen days, the "lovers" will quarrel and then make up at least ten times. It occurred to me that the basis of these relationships was not their "love," but a physiological need to run through a full gamut of emotions in camp: hatred, jealousy, the desire to be admired as a woman, the thrill of running the risk of engaging in something forbidden. The liver produces so much bile a day, and that triggers off the need to have a quarrel or a fight with someone. A desire to weep?—well, one can either seek reconciliation with the erstwhile adversary, or sing a song full of heartrending pathos.

Sounds primitive? But if only you could hear one of these endless, identical scenes which drag on as tediously as a prison day! You could predict in advance who would be pouring out effusions of affection to whom by lights out, and who would be quarrelling with a monotonous exchange of curses and obscenities—only to make up in the morning. All this in sum makes you want to shout with pity: you poor creatures, you poor creatures! To what have they reduced you? It's all very well to say that you lack self-control, have not known real love, that all your camp sufferings have only one outlet—aggression—and that "culture" is just another word to you. But are you the only ones to be blamed for that? Indeed, is any of it your fault? Or does the greater share of the blame fall on those who make you live in pigsty conditions, set you against one another, humiliate and debase you just to pass the time—in order that you will always feel their hand on the bridle? Your work is made to be no less than a hated burden, to escape which you are prepared to mutilate your bodies or induce tuberculosis. They want to reform you? To re-habilitate you so that you will become decent people? Rubbish—they don't want anything of the kind! They simply want slaves—pathetic, helpless and always to be blamed for everything. And when you emerge into "freedom," with a warped psyche and with an annotation in your passport about your imprisonment, you will be visited by your area militiaman, whose job it is to keep an eye on you. And when he says, "Jump," you will have to respond, "How high?", for it is within his power to have you charged with, say, "hooliganism," and land you back in the camps. If you're very lucky, all he'll demand of you will be money. If you're not, he can demand things that will make lesbian sex in the camps seem like the pinnacle of chastity! And the fact that some of you, indeed, many of you, manage, despite everything, not to lose every vestige of humanity and kindness, can only make one won-der at the quiet feminine fortitude, of which you are sometimes unaware yourselves, that survives in your hearts.

Much later, in the summer of 1986, I was able to have an

"unrestricted" discussion with a brigade supervisor of camp Number Two. This was a "chance" discussion arranged by the KGB. When I brought up the matter of the camp cruelties, with which she was directly connected, she looked at me in honest astonishment: "You simply don't know these women. They're not human, they're animals! You can't treat them otherwise."

And I, who knew you, my SHIZO neighbors, in your tears and your joys, in the desperate misery of your quarrels and strange songs, in your unexpected acts of kindness—I do not believe her claim that you are not humans. All I could do was look at her and wonder: And you, my fine one, are you sure that it is not you who is inhuman? Are you not just a simulacrum? In the folklore of every nation there are stories of soulless beings who only masquerade as people. And in every legend they are aggressive and incapable of anything but evil . . . Yet that young, light-haired law graduate did not look like a robot or a zombie. And looking into her clear, untroubled eyes, I realized yet again how little we people know about each other.

29

I completed my first twelve days of SHIZO, feeling as though I had passed through eternity. So much had happened in that time: the ongoing battles over the temperature in the cell, and freezing sleepless nights when mice tried to crawl into our sleeves or under our gowns for warmth, and talks with our neighbors ... Never mind the worsening edema, which means we have to prise our eyes open with our fingers in the morning; never mind the cold and hunger: I'm still young, and I can put up with any place if it means learning something new! With zek cunning, I have concealed a scrap of paper with the table of our illicit temperature measurements in the cell, and our secret results are set against the official readings: for instance, actual temperature in the cell 12° C, official temperature 26° C. How's that? Easy: when we finally managed to make the authorities produce an alcohol thermometer instead of their "standard" pointer one, it also registered 12° C. But the experienced warder took it gently into her hands, as one would a newborn babe.

"Twelve degrees, you say, women? Wait a moment—let me take a look." Not only did she close her hands around it, she even breathed on it "to see better." "There, you see? Twenty-six degrees Centigrade."

We were only surprised that she didn't try to get it up to 36° C. Now, however, I have priceless objective data: night temperature in the cell? 9° C to 11° C. That can't be waved aside as figments of the imagination of a hungry person; figures are considered more convincing in our day and age. Temperature in the bathhouse? The same 11° C. And so forth. A procurator is not likely to pay heed to these figures, but we're not collecting the information for him. Our tiny thermometer (which got smashed in the end, unfortunately) did not know how to lie, and could not be intimidated; not in vain did it go through SHIZO with us, where it bravely laid down its head—sorry, its bulb of alcohol! Day after day, four times every twenty-four hours it exposed the lies of our tormentors, without knowing that the evidence it provided was the sort of thing that is classified as "subversion aimed at the weakening of the Soviet system." The truths told by our little thermometer, when we sent them to the Procuracy, were described in the Procuracy's reply as "anti-Soviet slander." They gave that appellation to everything that they didn't like . . .

I say my farewells to Tanya—she still has three days to go. How I hate the thought of leaving her here alone . . . It's warmer together: do you know that 50 percent of our energy is used up in emission of heat? Now it's into the red zek carriage for me, and back home, to the Zone. I'm surrounded by a noisy throng of other prisoners being transported; these periods of transportation are the most valuable feature about going to SHIZO. If there had been at least one transport on which I had not managed to pass poetry and information to those who "fronted" for Igor, I would have said that zeks are not zeks, and guards are not guards. Or that I must be out of my mind . . . There was one occasion when a young guard whom I had picked out as a possible helper refused: "It's not allowed."

He whispered those words, this close-cropped youth with an open, uncomplicated face. I was honestly astounded.

"Good God! There really is no hope for Russia."

He shied away as if I'd burnt him, and went to the other end of the carriage. Half an hour later, he came back, and silently extended a hand. Silently, I pressed my hastily addressed letter into it, and we exchanged a smile with our eyes only. No, transportation is a gift from God!

As I write these words, I can imagine what the KGB official checking through this book for his superiors will think when he reads them: "So. The thing to do is clearly to transport them separately, and not in the train with others."

A fig for your reasoning! Even special transports are manned by people. There are no robots capable of doing that job yet.

"In that case," he may rejoin, "you should be under convoy with our own, trusted people in charge, instead of ordinary soldiers."

But there aren't enough of your own trusted ones to go around, are there? And even they defect to the West and tell all your secrets once they've been granted political asylum. Their number may not be enormous, but sufficient to make you view your own ranks with suspicion: who knows what is going on in whose mind?

But even more important, every generation contains more and more of us, those who are not afraid of you, and we shall be your downfall! Because for decades your strength has lain only in the fear you generated . . .

"She's overoptimistic," will say some clandestine Soviet readers into whose hands this book will inevitably find its way. Maybe. I don't know. But I have always thought that optimism is only a cheap substitute for faith, and have no time for optimism myself. Now faith—that's another matter altogether. So forgive me, skeptical Soviet reader, that I believe in you more than you do yourself!

But you surely will feel no surprise to learn that as I climbed out of the train in Barashevo, I saw Natasha: she was being transported, as I'd had reason to expect, to SHIZO. For fourteen days. Operation "Meat-grinder-83" was in full swing, aimed at bringing the intransigent Small Zone to heel, to crush us once and for all. No longer were any holds barred: you're half-dead? All the better. Operation Meat-grinder-83 is set to become "84": Natasha will be spending New Year in SHIZO. I learn all this upon returning to the Zone, and meet a new resident: Olya Matusevich.

She came to us not from "out there" but from a camp near

Odessa, in which she had been for three years. Her first sentence was for membership in the Ukrainian chapter of the unofficial Helsinki Monitoring Groups. The Ukrainian KGB arrested every one of its members. At the end of her three years, they came and told her she was free to go. She had already said her goodbyes, distributed all her possessions, memorized messages and requests, and was ready to go. She left the guardhouse, and stepped out into a warm spring Odessa street . . . To freedom? Not at all. She was only able to walk a couple of steps as a "free woman." A car full of strapping KGB lads was waiting for her. They detained her and drove her to the KGB prison. Who can describe the feelings of a person who has counted the days until release for three long years, to find herself being trundled along in a barred KGB car? Olya says that she had not had time to grasp the fact that she was free, so it was easier than it might have been. We, however, could imagine what that "easier" was like. Olya was sentenced to a further three years, this time on strict regime. And she has elderly parents, both of whom are constantly ailing, and whose only hope was to embrace their daughter before they died. But now—who can say whether that hope will be realized? In fact, Olya's mother did live long enough. Her father died without seeing his daughter again . . .

Meanwhile, we are preparing to go on hunger strike in protest at Natasha's incarceration in SHIZO. Her health really is giving cause for the greatest concern. Not everyone can join this hunger strike: it will be conducted only by Tanya (who's back from SHIZO), Olya and myself. The others simply could not last out physically if they were to attempt it. They continue the work strike in connection with the demand that Edita's meeting be reinstated, and to that they add the demand that Lazareva be released from SHIZO and given immediate medical treatment. They write an official statement that they offer the hunger strikers their full moral support, and, in fact, give us practical support, too. This is Olya's first hunger strike and she's bearing up very well, but Tanya and I barely manage to drag our feet from place to place. Tanya came back from

SHIZO with rasping lungs and a temperature of 38° C. I'm not much better, but at this stage I have no way of telling that I'll only spend two days in the Zone before being shipped back to SHIZO for twelve days "for refusing to work without acceptable reasons."

They are afraid of the word "strike" and never mention it in any of their documents. How difficult it is, when you're hunger-striking, to clamber up the high step into the carriage. One of the convoy soldiers gives me a boost, and throws my bag in after me. Truth to tell, I don't regret this return to SHIZO: it was unbearable to think of Natasha lying alone and ill on the filthy floor of the cell. How will my being there help her? I don't know—but at least she won't be alone. Furthermore, I might be able to sneak in some extra bit of clothing to put on her. Time will tell; it's always easier to do battle together, and battles there will be aplenty: to get a doctor, and about the cold in the cell. "They" don't let themselves go quite so much in front of a witness, either—remember, they waited until Natasha was alone before they really set about beating her up the time she was sent to Saransk. Immediately upon arrival I am horrified to learn that Natasha has declared a hunger strike until she is taken to hospital. Madness, madness! She's barely alive, and goes and does something like this! Thank heaven the hunger strike is only from the 26th and not from her first day in SHIZO. If only Tanya had been there, she would have talked her out of it, but it's too late now. The hunger strike has been declared, so there can be no going back. On the other hand, Natasha definitely has a point: the medical treatment has to be now or never. Half a year has already been wasted on fruitless correspondence with the Procuracy and the Central Medical Administration. In another six months, Natasha may no longer be there to treat . . .

In any case, there's no point in any post factum discussion. The important thing is to survive. Before my arrival, a doctor examined Natasha, diagnosed cardiac insufficiency, and has not been seen since. So Natasha spends the day lying on the cell floor (after the bunks are raised and locked to the wall in the morning) and on the bunk at night. There's no medical treatment in the offing, and SHIZO rations are practically the equivalent of a hunger strike anyway. So it's not hard to see Natasha's point of view. She is determined to emerge victorious from this situation. If not—what has she to lose? During the night of December 27/28, Natasha has two cardiac seizures. She chokes and wheezes frighteningly. I beat on the door with my cup, raising a racket that can be heard right around the SHIZO block: "A doctor! A doctor! Immediately!"

"The doctor will come in the morning."

"Now! He must come now."

"There's nobody to come now."

"What if she dies before morning?"

"Then we'll write her off."

And there's nothing, nothing I can do. Only hold Natasha's head in my lap and pray: Please God, don't let her die! Need I say that no doctor came in the morning? Moreover, we were told that Natasha would not be getting any medical treatment: "This is not a holiday resort!" And from that time on, they didn't come into our cell. Not even to search it. Every so often someone would take a look through the peephole in the door to check whether we were still alive. All it took to chase them away from the door was one word: "Doctor!"

During that hunger strike I realized how little we know about our own capabilities. Lying on the floor, I watched a woodlouse, wending a roundabout route toward my powerless hand . . . Couldn't it choose some other direction in which to take a stroll? I knew that I should sweep it aside, but with an obtuse kind of certainty knew just as surely that I didn't have enough strength to make the necessary movement. I could move my fingers slightly, but not enough to frighten the wretched insect. Then suddenly there was a groan from over by the heating pipe: Natasha had wakened. The cold had brought on a resumption of her old problem—inflammation of the Fallopian tubes—and she now lay there writhing in agony. And somehow—I don't know how—I was across the cell and kneeling beside her, cradling her in my arms, whispering words of comfort, trying to transmit something of my own life force into her. And now it seemed to me that I had so much strength to share! If I'd had to pick up Natasha and carry her out of the cell that moment, I know I could have done it. From what reserves? I don't know. Strange things happen when you have nothing to depend on except God's help.

Natasha was not in such dreadful pain all the time. There were hours when the pain subsided, and her heart beat evenly, though very feebly. At those times we worked out the details of an amusing idea: a hotel in Paris called "Fifteen Days."

You would like first-hand experience of some aspects of Soviet life? By all means! We guarantee exotic experiences, a broadening of your outlook, and those who are worried about their waistlines will be like sylphs after a week without the fuss of consulting doctors. Our hotel will be very true to life: cells, bunks, skilly and bread rations. We shall, of course, have to import warders from Mordovia; the French would never be able to provide just the correct touch. Skilly cooks would have to be recruited in Mordovia too. It would all be quite costly, but the hotel would be the genuine article, no cheating. How many days would you like, sir? Madam? Ten? It's up to you, of course, but as this is your first time, we would recommend that you take a cell for four days, and see how it goes.

We have amusements and competitions, too: if you manage to pass a note along to the neighboring cell, you win a prize. If you manage to send off a complaint to the Procuracy by using correct legal procedure, you win a prize too, and another if you can sneak a sweater into your cell despite a search of your effects. So give your imagination and initiative full rein ... What are the prizes, you ask? Well, not money, of course, that would be too crude, and would not contribute toward a total appreciation of the fullness of life. How about a fluffy towel to wind around your body under your residential smock? Or a pair of woolen socks? Or—and this is the top prize—a warm jacket for twenty-four hours?

How happy the Parisian clients of our hotel would be! How they would cease to worry about their usual everyday problems!

How delicious they would find everything they ate, how fresh and aromatic the air of Paris! Coming home they would forget all family differences, and everyone they met and could talk to freely would seem so interesting and lovable!

Should they suffer a relapse—welcome back to hotel "Fifteen Days." The hotel operates around the clock, cells can be locked at any time of day or night . . . And don't be unduly apprehensive—the hotel is in a civilized country: anyone wanting to go home before their booking expires will be released. One wonders, however, about the whole new vocabulary our French clientele would acquire. Our warders watch their tongues with us, but they enter freely and as equals into altercation with the criminal prisoners.

"You so-and-so and such-and-such!"

"And the same to you, why don't you do such-and-such!"

This can go on for a long time and the inmates of the other cells listen to these gripping dialogues, because sound carries well in the SHIZO block. With apologies to the late Boris Pasternak, I could not help recalling his line, "A meeting of two nightingales," when I heard these exchanges.

These "encounters" usually ended when the warder, having exhausted her stock of expletives, but not wishing to end up as the loser, would suddenly recall her exalted official status and clinch the argument with the threat: "Shut your trap, or I'll put you on report."

Then, after taking a few turns around the corridor and realizing that there are still one or two things she's got to say, she would go back to the same cell and start the verbal battle all over again. We imagine how this would be conducted in a mixture of French and Russian, but we are too weak to laugh.

We did, however, hold a New Year's celebration. We managed to keep back a box of toothpowder when we returned our washing things, and used it to outline a full-sized Christmas tree on the black metal surround of the unused stove. I did the top and middle part and Natasha, lying on the floor (she was unable to get up by that time), drew the trunk. Actually, not one trunk but two, wearing zek "come now, come now!" boots. We had made a paste out of the toothpowder with a bit of water, so the whole thing came out really well. It was such a happy little tree. And, lying on the floor—Natasha on her sixth day of hunger strike and I on my eleventh—we rejoiced as we looked at it, like a couple of children.

30

Toward the evening of December 31, the heating suddenly came on. The stokers, in the absence of the guards, must have decided to give the zeks a treat. The guards were all celebrating New Year themselves, so there was nobody about. We lay pressed up against the pipes, and for the first time in all these days felt our blood responding to living warmth. It was impossible to warm the cell itself because of the multitude of cracks letting in the freezing winter wind, but our fingers began to move more freely and one side was warm. We cheered up, and singing began in the neighboring cells.

"Number Seven! Politicals! Happy New Year, girls! This next song is for you."

And, for some reason, they started singing one of Bulat Okudzhava's[1] songs. On second thought, I suppose there is no need to be surprised: the musical repertoire of the women's camps is rich and varied. It embraces everything from ancient folk songs through to cheap contemporary pop and the most obscene ditties of the criminal underworld. Why should it not include the songs of the officially unacknowledged bards on whose songs our generation grew up?

---

1. Bulat Okudzhava (b. 1924), a writer and popular song writer who has been in and out of official favor many times. Many of his songs have a political message, and have been widely sung "unofficially" since the early 1960s.

Oh Hope, I shall return again
When "taps" is sounded by the player,
Who lifts the trumpet to his lips
And points an elbow sharply wide.
Oh Hope, I shall remain alive
The grave's damp earth is not my calling,
But rather—all your tribulations,
Familiar world of our concerns . . .

We could sing nothing for them because of my lack of musical talent. In return, I recited some poetry "along the pipe" through my cup. I started out, though, by simply shouting it out by the door: until my voice started to give out, that could be heard in all the cells. Then I had to continue "on the pipe." I was beginning to flag, but they demanded more and more—and again, I was filled with new strength which came from some source I did not know I possessed. I read to them about Christmas, about the hunt for wolves, about the boy who appeals to the prison to give him a nickname . . . About jolly fantastic dragons, who are not voracious, but whose teeth are itchy . . . I needed no other acclaim, nor is there any reward greater than bringing at least a few minutes of pleasure to the driven and the suffering on New Year's Eve in the midst of so much everyday sorrow.

On January 2 Natasha's SHIZO term ended, and they carried her out of the cell. She could neither stand nor walk by that time. Then they set about me: "Call off your hunger strike!"

"I was demanding not only Lazareva's release from SHIZO, but her admission into hospital."

"That's where she's been taken."

"I don't believe you."

"Why?"

"If only because you kept a woman in her condition here for the full allotted SHIZO term. I asked for a doctor for her at least a hundred times, yet nobody came. And in any case, all of you lie all the time, so I can't take you at your word."

"What do you want, then?"

"To see Lazareva in the hospital with my own eyes."

"But you've still got two days of SHIZO."

"And I'll keep to my hunger strike for that time."

I have no real recollection of those remaining two days. I think I slept most of the time. The accumulated exhaustion of the past months seemed to hit me all of a sudden, and here in the cell I was alone, with nobody to wake me. I do remember carrying out the slop bucket every morning with the help of one of the other women—a criminal prisoner who had been threatened with dire consequences if she exchanged so much as a word with me. She had been assigned this duty when Natasha could no longer stand up. This chore done, I would lie down on the floor near the pipe, just in case the heating might come on for a bit. And then I would flee that cell—but where it was that I went to, I don't know. All I can remember is that it was a place of light, and there was incredibly beautiful music which came in waves, and drew me in deeper and deeper. Then I would find myself in a dark tunnel, at the end of which someone was waiting for me. And I would fly toward it, yet every time, just as I neared the end, the realization would come that I had to go back. And, oh, how I did not want to go back! I had to, because it was not yet my time. And, then, what about Igor? So I would go back.

On January 14, when they brought me back to the Zone, I caught a glimpse of Natasha: she was waving to me from a hospital window. Back in the Zone I learned that Olya had called off her hunger strike on the fourth day because Podust assured her that the temperature in our SHIZO cell was 18° C. Poor Olya— she was new here, and still had to learn the true worth of Podust's word. Now the three of us—Olya, Tanya and I—could celebrate our victory: Natasha was finally in hospital.

The refusal to work, however, was still in force. Olya decided not to take part in this strike and took over the duties of housekeeper. As we had expected, this post, which had been declared non-existent, was suddenly reinstated. The earlier decision to cancel it had only been taken because it was Edita's duty. This was a lucky development for the Zone; the cleaning must be done, we could hardly live in filth for the duration of the strike. As it was, SHIZO had been taxing enough. Raya had been taken from the hospital in December straight to the KGB prison in Kiev for "re-education." Natasha was now in hospital. So retaliatory measures for the strike would be borne by those remaining in the Zone. But we were quite prepared for that.

At the beginning of January, we were visited by a beaming Shalin, who informed us that a new article—188-3—had been introduced into the Criminal Code. Under this article, "malicious violators" of camp regulations could have their sentences extended by up to five years. In practical terms, this new article made it possible to turn prisoners into prisoners for life—anyone could be charged with "malicious violation": first give them a term of PKT, then SHIZO, and that gives grounds to bring charges under Article 188-3. Then add a couple of years to their sentence, put them back in PKT, and repeat the whole process again. No wonder the camp bosses were happy. They figured that this would make us call off our strike, for that qualifies as a "malicious violation" of the regulations. They started on Tanya first: "It would be a pity, Osipova, if you're not released in 1985, but in 1990!"

"Your reasoning is quite fascinating," said Tanya cuttingly. "You will break the law, and we won't be able to protest because of Article 188-3. Give Edita her meeting, and we'll call off the strike."

"No, why?" retorted Shalin. "Abrutiene's punishment was quite justified: prisoners are obliged to work even if they're on hunger strike, and if they're placed into isolation, work is provided for them. If the administration forgot, she should have asked for work herself."

Lies again: he knew full well that no work is given to those who are in hospital "boxes" and, indeed, that none could be done there. He knew about the medical release from work, just as he knew that a hunger striker is physically unable to work. But by this time Shalin had lost his earlier tendency to blush when lying, and we had nothing to say to him. As soon as they start lying—that's the time to discontinue any discussion, if only because it would be too sickening to continue. Naturally, we did not call off our strike.

On January 9, they took Edita and Galya to SHIZO for ten days each. They both came back with tonsillitis. On top of that, Galya, who suffered from rheumatic arthritis anyway, had terribly swollen joints, and any movement was sheer agony. Edita told us how she had passed the time by making little flowers and figurines out of the damp prison bread. It was brought to them not even half-baked, and they were afraid to eat it except for the crust. You would think it hardly surprising that all these little flowers and figures were confiscated and destroyed before her eyes, for hadn't worse things been done to us? Yet you never can tell what will be each person's breaking point, and Edita was very badly affected by this wanton destruction of her small creations; they weren't doing anyone any harm, were they?

A new personage appeared in the camp—Lieutenant Colonel Pavel Polikarpovich Artemyev. He began by having each one of us brought to his office. We were not told where we were being taken, just brought there. The former KGB head in our camp had been transferred, and his successor decided to make his presence felt in no uncertain manner. He was quite incapable of conducting a polite conversation; even if he started a sentence with acceptable courtesy, he could not finish it without saying something disgusting either about you, or one of the other inmates of the Small Zone. Galya, Pani Jadvyga, Tanya and I refused to talk to him at all. Pani Lida said she was prepared to talk to him on religious themes only. The others informed him of various objections against the camp administration, but Lieutenant Colonel Artemyev did not let this upset him: complaining to the KGB about our jailers is like complaining to your right hand about the doings of the left.

I was familiar with this KGB style of approach from my time under pre-trial investigation: "You can talk about anything you like."

But the real meaning behind this magnanimous offer is this: Yes, talk, and we shall turn your words to our advantage. You're bound to slip in a few bits of information, you'll hear us out when we confide a few nasty details about your fellow prisoners, and then we can blackmail you into doing anything we want.

For that reason, I preferred to say nothing at all. Indeed, I had nothing to say to him: talking to an unmannered swine was out of the question in any case, and I was not sufficiently sure of my not-so-great zek experience to be absolutely certain that I might not give someone away with a chance word. Or, rather, not so much by anything I might actually say as by some involuntary movement—body language, if you like—or expression which gives an experienced inquisitor his answer to an unexpected question. Maybe I underestimated my own abilities at that time, and overestimated theirs. But I have never regretted my silence: it is invariably better to err on the side of discretion. Artemyev really did his best to find some kind of a lever. Having read my file, he knew that I was totally opposed to any kind of conflict on the basis of nationality, so he tried to play that card against me: "I am a son of the Mordovian people, a national minority. Your refusal to speak to me is an insult to my nation."

But as far as I was concerned, he was no true representative of Mordovia. A much worthier representative of Mordovians, in my eyes, was the broad-faced warder who would surreptitiously push bits of bread or a few caramels into Tanya's and my SHIZO cell during the night. It was she who pleaded with us when we arrived for our second SHIZO term: "Girls, don't not eat, please! Hurts me to look at you!" And then, pushing a bit of bread through the grille: "Go on, eat it. I won't tell no one. Really, I won't."

Of course, we observed our hunger strikes strictly, and did not eat anything that she pressed on us. But she acted out of kindness, and, with God's grace, she would eventually come to an understanding of the concept of honesty. Artemyev spent three years in attempts to get at least a word out of Galya, Tanya and me. He failed. By the end, however, he and his assistant Yershov had rendered themselves so odious that nobody in the Small Zone would speak to them.

Toward the end of January, Procurator Ganichev, who was responsible for camp ZhKh-385, came to see us for the first time in several years in order to "sort out" the matter of our refusal to work. Like all the other officials, he lied and then got tangled up in his own falsehoods. First he would maintain that strikes are forbidden in the USSR altogether, then he would claim that "hunger strikers must still produce their full work quota, march in formation, and not flaunt the fact of their hunger strike." He could not quite grasp the connection between the hunger strikes and Edita's meeting, and that annoyed and frustrated him even more. There was nothing to be gained from his visit, but it did show that our strike was causing the camp administration a considerable amount of worry, and that the next stage of the bureaucratic process would bring the matter to the attention of the central authorities in Moscow.

In the meantime, Edita had petitioned the court again with a demand that Podust be tried for slander: she was not content to accept the lack of response to her first petition. Oh, that at this point I could use that phrase so favored by novelists in days gone by: "How great was our surprise, when . . ."! But I can't, because we were not really surprised to find out that Edita's second petition was confiscated by the camp censor "for unacceptable use of bad language." We were, however, very interested in finding out just what was this alleged bad language. It turned out to be one word, "prostitute." This was what Podust had called Edita in front of all of us, and Edita quoted it in her petition. That would teach us not to repeat the names we're called by our "citizen supervisor" in complaints against her! So what, if you feel insulted? If every zek went around lodging petitions every time he was sworn at or slandered by his overseers, you'd have to imprison practically the whole camp administration if these petitions were taken seriously. For pity's sake, can't these politicals find something better to do with their time?

Try to put yourself in our administration's place for a moment, and you'll see why I refer to them as "poor creatures," and similar. They really were caught between two hazards: on the one hand, we were refusing to back down, on the other, they were being pressed by the KGB. They really were in a no-win situation. Our camp commandant would have been only too glad to get rid of Podust, she was uniformly hated by all the guards and warders—but she was their local Party organizer! Unlike us, they did not have the option of refusing to have any dealings with her.

The head of the escort taking Tanya and me to one of our

spells in SHIZO (she had thirteen days and I had fifteen that time) spent the whole trip standing on the other side of the bars asking about our battles with Podust. He positively beamed when we told him how we refuse to hear her or speak to her and how she is forced to lurk between two fences as a face-saving measure because she lacks the courage to enter the Zone. I swear that he envied us at that moment!

They had a packed program lined up for us for that stay in SHIZO. When, after seven freezing days, we had reached what the authorities judged to be a suitable condition, Deputy Procurator Osipov came to our cell. Just a little friendly visit to see how we were. We did not find it necessary to discuss our condition with him, but suggested he send along a doctor to get a qualified medical opinion. We were, however, prepared to discuss violations of the law.

"By law, you cannot discuss other people's affairs, only your own," he objected.

"What about the Constitution?" burst out Tanya.

"Never mind the Constitution!" retorted the guardian of the law, and Tanya decided there was no further point in pursuing the discussion. We were not to know then that Osipov had been in the Zone the previous day and had thrown a positive tantrum when Pani Jadvyga raised the vexed question of Edita's meeting: "I'm not listening, not listening, not listening!" he screeched at the perfectly calm Pani Jadvyga. Not surprisingly, Pani Jadvyga and Edita joined us in our cell a day later, for ten and fifteen days respectively. That evening we managed to insist on having a properly functioning thermometer brought into our cell. It registered 8° C.

31

We could not help noticing that our local authorities were agitated over something, and we had yet another visit from a KGB official, one Tyurin. After letting him conduct a monologue for a while, Tanya and I made an exception to our usual role, and told him that there was one matter which we were ready to discuss with him.

"What is it?" he asked eagerly.

"Jadvyga Bieliauskiene has been in SHIZO since yesterday. She is an elderly woman and an invalid. If you must torment somebody, let us sit out her time in SHIZO on top of our own, but send her back. If you like, we'll put this offer to the KGB down in writing immediately."

"That's out of my sphere. The KGB doesn't handle matters pertaining to SHIZO."

"Then what are you doing in this building? It looks like there's nothing more for us to say to each other."

And, no matter how he tried, he didn't get another sound out of us. But we returned to our cell convinced that some developments were taking place in connection with our strike, something had given somewhere. Probably, the publicity had spread, and they had to take action. If we hold out—they will have to give in. Their insecurity was plain in their overly threatening tone, and in the repetition of their threats: they had nothing to scare us with except possible life imprisonment or that they would finish us off by repeated incarcerations in SHIZO. We were certain that we only had to hold out for a little bit longer, and our tormentors would have to concede defeat.

In the meantime while the four of us sat in our cell and Pani Jadvyga recounted the sad story of the Lithuanian Prince Jagail, the others in the Zone were writing a declaration whose content was identical to what we said to Tyurin: either Pani Jadvyga is returned to the Zone (they volunteer to do her SHIZO term for her) or they will all go on hunger strike, each one for as long as she can in view of the fact that everyone is very weak. Galya and Pani Lida for one day, Natasha for three, Olya—until Pani Jadvyga comes back. Our virtually identical reaction probably surprised nobody by now: it was just another manifestation of the spirit of our Zone. In fact, it would have been surprising had this unity been absent. Natasha had only just emerged from the hospital where she had been diagnosed as suffering from five specific illnesses, all of which needed specific treatments. Galya had a personal grief to contend with: in November, her husband had been taken away from his camp in the Perm region, and she had no idea where he was. She heard about the move in a letter from friends, but they had written in such veiled terms (to avoid confiscation by the censors) that Galya feared that her Vasili might be dead. We all took turns at deciphering the meaning behind the deliberately vague allusions in the letter and decided that what her friends were trying to tell Galya was that Vasili was alive, but his precise whereabouts were unknown. Galya spent a month writing to various government bodies in attempts to get some news of her husband. The amount of grey hairs on her head doubled by the end of that month. Finally she received a reply that he had been taken "for further investigation." Hardly a comforting thought.

Olya worried constantly about her parents: her additional sentence was the greatest blow to them. She was also worried by the identity tag. When she arrived in the Zone she had decided to wear it, just as she had during her preceding three years of imprisonment. We had told her our position, then left it to her to make up her own mind. After all, Pani Lida wears an identity tag, and that doesn't make any difference to our relations. But Olya couldn't simply let the matter rest: again and again, she would initiate discussions on this theme, seeking justifications for our position, or hers. But we were powerless to help her, for in such matters each has to reach her own decision, and only an act done in accordance with inner conviction will enable one to defend it in the face of pressure. Olya did finally stop wearing the identity tag, almost simultaneously with Pani Lida, when both reached the conclusion that this was what they really wanted. Yet despite their individual sorrows and ailments, they all united in their defense of Pani Jadvyga. Probably this is the best way to retain one's humanity in the camps: to care more about another's pain than about your own. We were not seeking to perform heroic acts; if anything, these were acts of self-preservation. Having lost the ability to set another's concerns before your own, you lose everything. We were to see proof of that very soon.

The four of us continued in SHIZO, huddling against each other for warmth, wrapping "illegal" towels around each other under our smocks, learning the history of Lithuania from Pani Jadvyga, and, occasionally simply fooling around to keep up our spirits. One evening, a warder came into our cell: "Women! To the bathhouse!" She took us there, remained while we undressed, skillfully managed to overlook the illegal extras under our smocks, and then, lowering her voice, broke the news: "Have you heard? Andropov's died!" She left immediately, rattling bolts and locking the door.

The scene that followed defies description: Pani Jadvyga, without a stitch on her, began dancing around the room, we cavorted around, splashing water and doing any number of childish things to express our joy at such welcome news. We did not see anything improper in that rejoicing, nor do I see any now, when I look back on that evening. Andropov, the former head of the KGB, was personally responsible for the crushing of Hungary in 1956, and later, upon reaching the pinnacle of government power, was undoubtedly the most repugnant leader since Stalin. The "raids" on shops and cinemas, the escalating arrests, the totally unchecked power of the KGB—all these were the hallmarks of his tenure.

Now he's dead, and will come before God's judgment, having had his fill of persecuting his fellow men. He will drink no more blood, be it Hungarian or Russian or Lithuanian. We had no illusions about the future, as yet unknown, Party boss: whoever he will be, he, too, will be no sweet innocent, but a confirmed Communist. But they won't find another Andropov, that's for sure. It's unlikely that anyone in the present Kremlin Old People's Home would be able to emulate his personal initiative and perverse imagination.

While we were splashing each other with water and recalling all the Andropov jokes we'd ever heard—they constitute a whole body of Soviet folklore—a new addition was on her way to our Zone. It was Lagle Parek, who was scooped up in the last "Andropov intake." She was awakened on the train that night by shouts of "Hurrah!" by all the zeks in the carriage. In their exuberance they rocked the carriage, while the guards stood around grinning (Andropov's death was no loss to them, either), and pelted Lagle with questions: "You're a political. You should know who's going to be the next one!"

Lagle knew no such thing, and who could guess who would emerge on top out of the behind-the-scenes jockeying for power between the Kremlin "leaders"? It's likely that they, too, would not know until the last minute. But the following day, in the shop queues and crowded buses, in the cramped hutches called communal flats, a new joke was doing the rounds: "In February 1984, at the age of seventy-one, after a long illness and without regaining consciousness, Konstantin Ustinovich Chernenko became the leader of the Soviet Union."

When Tanya and I returned from SHIZO, we joined the hunger strike in defense of Pani Jadvyga. I don't know whether it was the effect of all our protests or simply the desire of our camp authorities to lessen the number of strikers, but in February a medical commission acknowledged Pani Jadvyga and Pani Lida as Group II invalids, and Natasha as Group III. This meant that both our Panis were no longer obliged to work: the camp had no suitable work for Group II invalids, and Vasili Petrovich, beaming with pleasure, removed their names from his work sheets. We, too, breathed a sigh of relief; at least our elderly inmates would no longer be dragged off to punishment cells for striking. And Natasha, once the strike is over, will be able to cope more easily with a reduced production quota.

Lagle Parek arrived in the Zone: a cheerful, fair-haired woman with a sentence of six years of camps plus three years of internal exile. She and her friends had been issuing a clandestine (*samizdat*) journal in Estonia, hence the hefty sentence. Her unfailingly good spirits were a great bonus for our Zone, and her calm and unshakable ideological stance a source of constant frustration for the KGB. This was not her first transportation: she was a veteran of the "Estonian exile." After the war Estonians were loaded in their thousands into railway cattle trucks and sent off to Siberia. This tiny and courageous nation, which had experience of democratic government, could hardly expect any other treatment from Stalin. The tragedy did not pass by Lagle's family: her father was shot, her mother sent to a camp, and Lagle, together with her grandmother and sister, was transported to Siberia. Lagle was six years old at the time. She told us that neither she nor her sister really understood what was happening; the fate of their parents was not known to them, and the hurried packing and the prospect of a long journey seemed exciting rather than frightening. They were laughing as they got onto the truck taking them to the station, and their wise grandmother let them be, knowing how much grief was still to come. This carefree, childish laughter, under the circumstances, was given a totally unexpected interpretation by the family's neighbors: they decided that the elder sister had gone mad. So when Lagle's mother returned from the camps years later, that is what they told her. Luckily, she did not believe them.

The grandmother managed to get both girls to Siberia alive, where, standing knee-deep in snow, the Estonians were told that by government decree, they were destined to remain in "eternal exile." Lagle never forgot her grandmother's smile, and pitying comment: "They think that they are masters of eternity?"

After Stalin's death, the exiled Baltic peoples began to return home. Not all together and all at once, but little by little. Lagle returned too, with her grandmother and elder sister. Behind her lay Russian schooling, Siberian goats (which Lagle had to herd with the other children), cold, lice and dirt. But it was not until her own arrest under Andropov that Lagle learned her father's fate: she saw the order for his execution in her file when she was held under pre-trial investigation. Of course, they had guessed that he had been killed, but had no way of knowing when and on what charges. The Soviet government saw no reason to advise an orphaned family of such trivial details.

Lagle refused to wear an identity tag, but the camp authorities left her alone for the time being; they had enough on their plate with our strike. Our lexicon of foreign phrases was expanded by a new one: how to say a greeting in Estonian. And if I ever meet Lagle again, I will say to her, just as in the camp: *"Tere!"* And she will answer in Russian: *"Privet."*[1] Then we shall both laugh before throwing our arms around each other.

1. Greetings.

32

They brought Raya back from Kiev. She never did get to see the orders setting out the aim and reasons for her removal to the KGB prison in Kiev. KGB officers Gonchar and Ilkiv were not inclined to give explanations, they preferred asking questions. They seemed to be interested mainly in Olya and myself, as we had been "processed" by the Ukrainian KGB. Needless to say, they got nothing out of Raya; she refused to tell them anything, and, in any case, extracting information out of Raya was a hopeless task.

So the "re-education" degenerated into the usual KGB tricks: "Aren't you sick of being in camp? Your husband's out now, he's in exile. Wouldn't you rather be with him than risk another sentence for anti-Soviet activity?"

"What anti-Soviet activity?"

"Well, that strike, for one thing. That's anti-Soviet activity."

And so on, and so forth: a reminder of the new Article 188-3, an offer to attend the theater with one of the KGB officials (Raya refused), a meeting with her elderly mother, persuasions and threats. Finally they suggested that she write a plea for clemency: express "sincere repentance" and ask for mercy. Raya didn't write a word, so at the beginning of March they sent her back to the Small Zone. Upon her return, Raya told us honestly: "I am afraid of Article 188-3, so I'm pulling out of the strike. I won't wear an identity tag, but I feel I don't have enough strength left for any more strikes or hunger strikes. Think of me what you will."

Of course nobody thought any the worse of her: she had reached her limit, and had the courage and grace to admit it instead of assuming a defensive stance and thinking up a string of "acceptable excuses." Raya had defined quite clearly what she would or would not do, and there were no misunderstandings between us. She did not become an informer or a "mercy pleader," she continued to ignore all compulsory Lenin anniversary *subbotniks*[1] just as we did, but she knew that an endless round of SHIZO and a possible new sentence were beyond her strength. We all do as much as we can, after all, and who can demand more? For the remainder of her sentence Raya helped us in everything she could, carried around all her husband's poems in her memory, reached the end of her term in March 1986 without any compromises with the KGB, and then, after a separation of nine years, went to join her husband in his exile in the mountains of Altai. We saw her off in peace and accord.

As soon as Raya was brought back from Kiev prison, the authorities began to pressure Pani Lida to write a clemency plea. At the same time, a Latvian newspaper published yet another libelous article about her. There was no way of refuting the allegations: the Soviet press provides no right of reply to such attacks. The results put an end to any hopes the KGB may have been nourishing that Pani Lida would appeal to the authorities for clemency; she rejected Soviet citizenship instead, and that was that. She also removed her identity tag and threw it into the stove.

Meanwhile, my thirtieth birthday was approaching fast. We always celebrated birthdays and name days[2] in our Zone with great enthusiasm. Presents were prepared long beforehand, in deepest secrecy. The one whose celebration was coming up was not supposed to know anything about the preparations, so she had to exercise great care in order not to surprise the conspirators at work. Congratulatory letters and telegrams from friends and relatives would be confiscated in part by the camp authorities, and

1. Voluntary unpaid work on the Saturday closest to Lenin's birthday (April 22) each year.
2. For Orthodox and Catholics—the feast day of the saint whose name you bear.

the remainder would be issued after several weeks. The only greetings you had on the day were from your fellow prisoners. So we made enormous efforts to mark the occasion with style.

When I woke on the morning of my birthday, I was (as Tanya put it) "kissed to death." Officially we start celebrating at midday, but everyone is in a festive mood from the moment of rising. And looking around at these bright faces and happy eyes, you could not allow yourself to feel sad for even a moment on that day. Not even homesick. I knew that friends would gather around Igor today, that they would drink a toast to me, and that Igor, too, would be very gay. He would recite my poems (as we do here), pull out old photos, they'll sing my favorite songs. And only late that night, having said goodbye to the last of the visitors well after midnight, would Igor go into our empty room and bury his face in the pillow encased in a pillowcase I had embroidered. That's what the nights are for—to grind your teeth over your separation, then rise in the morning smiling and ready to face whatever the new day might bring.

"Ladies! Time to dress for dinner!"

Well, what did you think? For a special meal, we make an effort to look our best. Pani Jadvyga wears a grey flannel jacket: you'd never guess that it's made out of footcloths. From the morning on, an absolutely fantastic dress has been waiting for me: it's made out of poor-quality uniform satinette, but the cut and style are superb. Pani Lida can turn even an old rag into a work of art. I'm supposed to come into the dining room last, when everybody is there. Natasha, using a spoon and an aluminum dish, hammers out what sounds like a march. As a poet, I am crowned with a laurel wreath. The bay leaves have been carefully fished out when we chanced to get them in our skilly during the past months: for some reason, the camp cooks don't stint on bay leaves. To a chorus of laughter, I am turned this way and that, and the verdict is that the laurel wreath definitely suits me, so I've got to keep it on until dark.

That laurel wreath was to cost Natasha her right to use the kiosk. It all came about because on the eve of my birthday, late in the evening, she was sitting in the workroom and making the frame for the wreath with some pieces of wire and a pair of pliers. She was found here by Podust, who tried to engage Natasha in conversation. When Natasha remained silent, Podust went off and wrote a report to the camp commandant, claiming that Natasha had been planning to ambush her in the dark with a "heavy object," the object being the above-mentioned pliers. I'll bet the camp commandant laughed about this as much as we did, but he still cancelled Natasha's right to use the camp kiosk—one excuse is as good as any other, when all is said and done. Podust, however, got a lot of unwelcome publicity over the "heavy object": the warders gleefully recounted the episode outside the Zone, and a week later Podust was the laughingstock of all Barashevo.

But the birthday celebrations passed unmarred. Presents were from everyone, and on this occasion, Small Zone Publications Ltd. issued a booklet (I suspect the actual work was done by Tanya and Natasha) of the incredible adventures of little Pegasus, my Zone symbol: these were illustrated and accompanied by rhyming signed entries. The booklet started with a drawing of Pegasus behind barbed wire, and the words:

> "Peggy" sits in Small Zone four,
> As a poet in the law.

Then there he is sitting at a sewing machine, not making gloves, but sewing together huge sheets of poetry; then he's sitting on a stool facing a KGB man who holds a fishing rod. The words underneath read:

> KGB is in a fit:
> "Peggy" will not talk to it!

The KGB man in question has no face—just a large uniform cap perched on a pair of ears; poor Artemyev had no problems recognizing himself when the booklet was confiscated during a search some time later. In fact, he complained about it to me, being under the erroneous impression that the booklet was my work.

Next I am presented with a shirt made out of somebody's sheet, with ruffles and red embroidery. Then a tube of skin cream: "Thirty years is not over the hill yet." And finally, they bring in the birthday cake. Raya and Olya had not been deprived of kiosk rights that month, so they had bought some cheap biscuits and margarine (that was a stroke of luck, because margarine is very rarely available). They creamed this margarine with a full two-week ration of sugar ("Cerberus" is very accommodating on such occasions), and whipped it up into a truly gourmet cream, which they colored with the juice of a chance-acquired beetroot. They then made a layer cake with the biscuits and this cream. Not a bad birthday cake, was it? Tea is brewed with double the usual quantity of leaves, and then I, as the "divider," am ceremoniously instructed to carry out a very special duty: to cut up not just any old thing, but a real lemon. Lemons are a luxury only to be dreamed about in the camps. This one was secretly given to us to round off our banquet by a member of the camp personnel: they're not all monsters like Podust. On days when we have a celebration, the warders and officers usually come round to the Zone out of curiosity to see what the politicals have thought up this time. They stare at our home-made candles, little colored flags made out of old magazines, drawings and cakes, with unfeigned admiration: how's that for making something out of nothing. They are forbidden to accept anything from us, but, on the other hand, feel awkward about refusing. That's why we usually wrap up a bit of cake for the braver ones, and they take it away with them. Today we're rich, today we enjoyed ourselves! In eight days' time, preparing to go into hospital, I had to use a razor blade to divide one soya-based candy into eleven equal slivers—but when we celebrate we don't stint!

In the evening, I have to recite poetry: everyone knows all my poems by now, but they put in requests for their favorites: "Ira, the one about the cherry-red dress."

"The one about the letter to the other world."

"The one about horses."

Before going to bed I sit down to write to Igor: the most tender words I can think of, my hopes of seeing him, everything I can say to cheer him up. This letter was confiscated, as were most of our letters, but as I wrote it I nursed the hope that it might get through.

At the beginning of March the hapless Artemyev showed up in the Zone with congratulations on the occasion of the imminent International Women's Day. Such thoughtfulness! Especially in view of the fact that not a single one of us can say with any degree of certainty where she will be on that day (tomorrow): in the Zone, in transport, or in SHIZO. Realizing that he had not hit the right note, Artemyev changes tactics and goes to the hospital, where the KGB has an office, and has us brought to him there one by one. From Raya he demands a written statement that she is renouncing "anti-Soviet activity" (he doesn't get it), to Olya and Pani Lida he complains that the rest of us won't talk to him, but finally gets a partner for discussion in Edita. She has recently taken to trying to explain to the KGB that they will gain nothing with their punishment cells, that the whole world will despise them, that it is inhuman to torment women by cold and hunger. They are quite happy to listen to all this—they even came to SHIZO to let her have her say—then they tell her that there's nothing they can do, because it is the camp administration, and not the KGB, which sends prisoners to punishment cells. Now if only Edita would cooperate with them, they would try to persuade the camp authorities . . . At the end of their chat, Artemyev gives Edita a bit of chocolate—as a reward—and tells her that he had brought chocolate for all of us, but as we are all so rude and uncooperative . . . We are not happy with this new turn in Edita's behavior: we have reason to fear that her present tirades will eventually lead to searches for compromise. And now—this handout. Then again, Edita is an adult, and what she does is her own business. We have no intentions of trying to tell her how to run her life. When Edita reached the bit about the chocolate in her account of her conversation with Artemyev, I almost blew up: there is something indescribably revolting in these "favors" offered by butchers. I once heard a similar story of how a sadist tortured a cat. He would put a noose around its neck, and tighten it until the cat started to choke. Then he'd loosen it and start stroking the cat just as if nothing had happened. The cat, in blind hope that the torture was over, would start purring with joy—and the noose would be pulled tight again. Over and over. It was on the tip of my tongue to ask the person telling this story how he could have stood by watching this monstrous cruelty, but manners compelled me to leave the question unasked.

Naturally, I said nothing about my misgivings when Edita told her story; in such cases it is better to control yourself. But when my turn came to be taken to Artemyev, I refused to go. There is nothing in the law that says prisoners have to talk to the KGB. I told the warder that under no circumstances would I go voluntarily. If they liked, they could send a detail of armed guards, who would have to drag me to Artemyev by force.

The warder scuttled off to report to Artemyev, then returned: "Artemyev said that if you don't come it will be a violation of the regime, and you'll go into SHIZO."

"Then I'll go into SHIZO on that International Women's Day about which he's making such a song and dance. Do we have to listen to him and accept his chocolates under threat of SHIZO? After all that rubbish he's told Edita? No, I won't go!"

"So are we to get a detail to drag you there?"

"That's up to you."

The warder departed "to get the detail," and we didn't see her again that day. Artemyev didn't bother sending for anyone else, but went away with nothing. They didn't put me into SHIZO that time—it would have been too obvious how "little" the KGB had to do with our punishments.

33

That March, Igor raised an enormous fuss about my health: he had sent frequent inquiries to the camp and invariably received replies stating: "Prisoner Ratushinskaya's health is satisfactory." Then he learned that even as these replies were being sent to him I was running temperatures of 38° C, a fact which was even noted, but given no treatment or a medical examination. Furthermore, the other women in the Zone wrote a letter in my defense, expressing concern that I would not live to see the end of my sentence. The noise made by Igor and the publicity generated by this letter finally resulted in my admission to hospital, where they even did a blood test. I permitted myself the hope that this time I might really get some medical help. This was on March 14, and on the 16th I saw Natasha and Tanya escorted past, on their way to SHIZO: thirteen days for Natasha, fifteen for Tanya. Tanya's SHIZO was calculated so that she would spend her birthday in a punishment cell. That aside, however, I still had to write a letter to the Procuracy that I was going on hunger strike for all the time that Natasha would be in SHIZO; she had seen me and managed to shout that she was being taken to a punishment cell although she was running a temperature.

When she and Tanya arrived at SHIZO, they were stripped naked. They were not even allowed to wear their own slippers: "We'll issue you some of ours," they were told. Everyone in the Zone already knew the results of wearing prison slippers by what had happened to me. They are never disinfected, just passed from prisoner to prisoner, and I had picked up some nasty skin fungus from them. I spent a month in fruitless attempts to get some treatment for it from Dr. Volkova, who maintained that it was merely a "nervous rash." Only after I lost all the skin off the soles of my feet and they were covered with suppurating sores did she finally call a skin specialist. By that time I was unable to stand on my feet, and the doctor could not hide his amazement when he examined them. Luckily, he was a new man, not yet dehumanized by the camp, so he got hold of some medicinal cream which cleared up the trouble in two weeks. I had to move about the house with all the caution of a tightrope walker to avoid passing this nasty bug on to the others, and there were enough incidents connected with this for a stage comedy.

So Natasha and Tanya, not unreasonably, declined to wear the prison slippers and went to the cell in their socks. The next day (Tanya's birthday), regime supervisor Ryzhova summoned them both to check personally whether they had anything "illegal" under their SHIZO smocks. They did. Both had sneaked through an undershirt apiece. Ryzhova confiscated these immediately, as well as their socks and the regulation issue headscarves that prisoners are supposed to wear at all times. These she confiscated because winter headscarves are woolen. Natasha refused to undress at first, and Ryzhova uttered the standard threat that a detail of soldiers would be called in to strip the recalcitrant one. Ah, like that, is it? Natasha promptly removed every stitch, and marched back to the cell stark naked, with warders scurrying beside her and urging her to put something on. But Natasha, sharp chin out belligerently, swept their persuasions aside: "You wanted me to strip—so I've stripped!"

"It's not us. That was orders from the KGB!"

"Well, let them come and look! They are the ones who should be ashamed of themselves, not I."

"Now, come on, Lazareva, put on something at least."

"And pick up scabies and who knows what else from your slippers? No thanks! Outer clothes are put on over underclothes, or not at all."

She stalked along, past SHIZO and PKT cells, whose inmates could only gasp: "Oh, girls, how thin she is! Bones and nothing else. Look what they do to the politicals."

In order to stop a full-scale scandal, they returned Natasha and Tanya's socks, scarves and their own slippers. Clearly, the KGB's orders were to ensure that they were dressed in the barest minimum, to be as vulnerable as possible to the cold.

All the Small Zone inmates, except Vladimirova, who was never really one of us, conducted a twenty-four-hour hunger strike on Tanya's birthday. We had no strength for any more. A one-day hunger strike for a zek is nothing like a day without food for a normal person. It means passing from continual semi-starvation into nothing at all. There were traditional one-day hunger strikes which we observed: August 23, the anniversary of the Molotov-Ribbentrop pact, in accordance with which the Nazis let the Soviet Union seize Western Ukraine, Lithuania, Latvia and Estonia. Then there was October 30—Political Prisoners' Day. And December 10—Human Rights Day. I observed all these one-day hunger strikes every year of my imprisonment; halfway through the day you start having dizzy spells, and by evening you can barely stand. By the end of the hunger strike Pani Lida and Pani Jadvyga frequently lost consciousness. Galya would be pale as death. Lagle never had the strength to venture on more than twenty-four hours of hunger strike. Luckily, she was sensible enough to realize her physical limits. There's nothing worse than having to call off a hunger strike halfway through without achieving its aim. Of course, I am exaggerating when I say that; there are worse things. But at that time, this was how we felt and how we acted. Raya, in view of her chosen position, wrote no notification to the camp authorities about going on hunger strike, but couldn't bring herself to eat all the same. She went through all our hunger strikes with us, but did not declare them officially. So she was no better off than we were. Edita battled gamely against hunger: out of all of us, she was the most "physical," and this cost her great effort. Olya never gave any sign of her difficulties during hunger strikes; the only outward signs were that her eyes would seem to sink deeper into her head, and her cheekbones become more prominent. At those times, she would look absolutely beautiful, and I felt a great deal of affection for her despite our rather complex relations. Olya was an expert in complicating issues, and I was too young and lacking wisdom to make allowances and curb annoyance.

I was approached in hospital by one of the more able local doctors, a surgeon called Skrynnik.

"If you are on hunger strike, we can't keep you in the hospital," he told me.

"But the practice is to isolate hunger strikers right here, in the hospital. I know that from personal experience!"

"In that case, you have to be housed separately, and receive no medical treatment."

"Why, then, remove hunger strikers to the hospital?"

"Irina Borisovna, neither one of us is stupid. You know my possibilities, and I know yours. If you like, I'll write you an affirmation that a thirteen-day hunger strike would place your life in danger. What's more, I'll do it with a clear conscience: in your present condition, it would be no less than the truth."

"What about Lazareva? Don't thirteen days in SHIZO put her life in danger?"

"I can't do anything for Lazareva, but I can help you. So let me write that note and you call off your hunger strike and stay here. We did that for a political prisoner [he named the person in question] from the men's Zone and nobody thought any the worse of him. And nobody will reproach you, either. How long have you been on hunger strike? One day? Well, that's enough."

I don't need him to tell me that nobody would reproach me. I'm not on strike just to avoid censure. A deal like that would be like a chasm between me and God, and this is something Skrynnik can't understand. But I do. He is sincere and well meaning in his own way, and I in mine. We have nothing against each other: we appreciate each other's honesty, and therefore feel mutual respect. Skrynnik could not know that long ago, when I was a child, a gypsy in Odessa looked at my hand and then, staring at me with deep dark eyes, said: "You've got nine lives, girlie. Once, twice, you'll die—yet not die. Only on the ninth time. Like a cat. Here, take this chain, don't give me money. It's a gift."

I wore that copper chain around my neck until I was an adult, long after I stopped believing in fortune telling. But by that time I had already known for several years that it's no great sorrow to lose one's life—be it the first, the second, or the ninth. That, which is the most important, comes later, and in the meantime, it's as though I'm in training for it, testing myself in different situations. And I have no values other than to tell no lies, and to endure whatever I must.

Skrynnik and I parted with polite smiles, and on March 15 they threw me out of the hospital. The next day Edita and I were told to prepare ourselves for SHIZO. The whole Zone, however, was up in arms: "A doctor! We won't let Ira be taken to SHIZO."

A nurse came to measure my temperature: above normal. She hurried away and came back with a "commission" consisting of three doctors. They measured my temperature again with two thermometers: 38° C. Skrynnik, the senior doctor present, refused to sign the order for my dispatch to SHIZO, saying that he was not a murderer. Edita was sent off, though. Oh, God, how much better it would have been if I had gone with her that time.

KGB officer Tyurin came to see Edita on her very first day in SHIZO. Natasha and Tanya refused to talk to him, but Edita agreed. The following day she had a long discussion with another KGB man, Yershov. He treated her to tea with lemon, fed her, and gave her a cucumber and some rusks to take back to the cell with her. When Tanya and Natasha refused to touch any of this, Edita assured them: "Of course, you can think that I've become an informer just because I don't refuse to talk to them, but that's not so! I intend to outsmart them, and get concessions for us out of them."

Tanya and Natasha could only sigh despairingly; unfortunately, it was all too obvious who would win such a battle of wits. All attempts to make Edita see reason fell on deaf ears. And I really shouldn't moan that things would have been different if only I'd been there. It would have worked out exactly the same way, and there was nothing we could do about it. Meanwhile, I was taken away from the Zone and isolated in a "box cell" in Block Twelve of the hospital. I took along a Bible, some sewing, clean paper and my woolen headscarf. I was not harassed, they made no attempt to force-feed me, and even gave me a second blanket (oh, but it was cold in there!). On the other side of the locked door I could hear the warders talking to a new arrival in this psychiatric block: "Now, Korneyeva, we're putting you into a clean ward; nobody pisses or shits in their beds here, so see that you don't."

"Yes, supervisor."

I gloried in my peace: they brought me food three times a day, but didn't stop me from covering it with bits of plastic bag to minimize its tantalizing smell. I read the New Testament and the Song of Songs. I embroidered cherries on a napkin for my mother-in-law, and, by a lucky chance, was able to get it passed on to her later: how thrilled she was that I had been thinking of her, and did not seem to be having problems with my eyesight! I wrote poetry. Nowadays, during sleepless nights far from my native land, I often think that I would give everything in the world to experience again the wondrous dreams dreamed during hunger strikes. But, as Ecclesiastes rightly tells us, there is a time to cast stones and a time to gather stones.

They come for me on the thirteenth day: "Right, let's go! Lazareva's back in your Zone."

And again, they carry my zek bundle, and I walk back to the Zone—slowly, but on my own two feet. Warder Nastya hovers solicitously: "Mind you don't fall, Ratushinskaya. Here, take my arm."

"No, no. Thank you, but I can manage by myself."

And there's Natasha. The kettle has boiled, the others sit around the table. But we can't say our usual "everyone's home" today, because Tanya and Edita aren't back yet. Nyurka, who adored Tanya, would lie in her bed in Tanya's absence, dejected and with her nose buried in the threadbare blanket. Even Pani Jadvyga, who had not time for such feline liberties, did not have the heart to chase her away at such times.

34

At the end of March a stream of officials from the Central Administration visited the camp in order to look into our strike. Someone came from the medical administration to determine whether Edita had been capable of working on the days for which her meeting had been cancelled, and whether she had been assigned any sewing work at all in August. Formerly they had refused even to discuss the matter with us, but now they were only too keen to ask questions, and at all levels, from the camp commandant to the KGB section chiefs. They had even travelled to Moscow for instructions. There was no difficulty in vindicating our stance by referring to existing documentation. All the signs were that we would win our battle if we held out for just a few more weeks. And then Edita floored everyone. On March 31, when everyone gathered in the dining area, she suddenly announced: "I've decided not to defend others any more and be sent to SHIZO for it. I'm pulling out of the strike!"

We sat there, speechless. It wasn't just that the phrase "not to defend others" sounded unreal in our Zone; it was that out of all of us Edita was striking for reinstatement of *her own* meeting. It would not be Galya, Tanya or I who would be embracing Edita's husband after our victory, but Edita herself. In that five-month struggle, she was defending her own rights, not anyone else's, and we pointed this out to her. But she was beyond reasoning: at that time, she maintained, she had been in a state when one's words do not reflect objective reality. We had imposed our will on her by dragging her into this strike, she continued, and she doesn't give a damn about Soviet laws, all she wants to do is get away from here. I'm sure that if any one of us had had dentures, they would have dropped out of our sagging jaws. None of us had forgotten what difficulty we had in persuading Edita not to rush into starting a strike until we knew for certain that the cancellation of her meeting had not been due to some mix-up. We could remember how she reproached us for the delay, saying that we would all be singing another tune if it was *our* meeting that had been scrapped.

Then she began talking utter nonsense: that she was not the central figure in this strike, that we could carry on perfectly well without her, and pointed out that nothing had changed when Raya dropped out of the strike. Needless to say, that suggestion found no favor. Why should we endure punishment cells and forfeit our own meetings (all of which were cancelled in those five months) while Edita sat at a sewing machine, eating the KGB's chocolates and, risking nothing, awaited the outcome of the conflict? And the comparison with Raya was not a valid one; Raya was honest, above all. If Edita had said that she could no longer stand punishment cells and could take no more, we would have been disappointed, but nobody would have said a word of censure. But the stupid and totally unnecessary lies, the attempt to depict herself as an innocent victim who had been "drawn in" against her better judgment, the whole formulation of the issue reeked of KGB interference, and Edita was undeserving of our respect. There was nothing more to discuss. We only asked one question: "Are you retracting your demand that the cancelled meeting be reinstated?"

"Yes."

And she went off to cry in the bedroom. This confrontation had been much harder for her than for us. We were defeated, through no fault of our own. Obviously, the strike must be called off; if Edita herself is not demanding a meeting with her husband, we have no authority to demand it for her. Her attempt to place the blame squarely on us also gave rise to the unpleasant thought that if we were to be tried for this strike and have our terms extended, Edita herself would be the main witness against us. Or that she would be cast in the role of a victim, into whose private life we interfered unasked.

We knew that once someone embarked on that road, not only was it practically impossible for them to go back, but even to maintain their present ethical level. And the KGB, who knew this too, must have congratulated themselves as they listened to the whole exchange over their listening devices.

It really hurt to call off the strike with victory so close! We knew that this defeat would cost the Zone dear: surrendered gains are not easily restored. It seemed that all that we had endured in the past five months had been for nothing. Well, maybe not entirely; at least the camp authorities could have no illusions now about our reaction to force. And they had broken only Edita, not the Zone. All the same, we knew that having succeeded with one, they would redouble their efforts against the others.

Tanya took the whole affair much more calmly than the rest of us; she had seen such things happen when she was in the Moscow Helsinki Monitoring Group. People would come to the Group members with genuine appeals for help, in the total conviction that they themselves were prepared to defend their rights against all odds. And later, unable to withstand pressure by the authorities, they would betray those Helsinki Monitors they had asked for support and assistance. Just to get the KGB off their own back, no matter what the cost. And who can define the fine line beyond which human weakness turns to betrayal?

There was no point in debating the issue with Edita; she was hard put to cope with our silence around the table. She knew and understood what we thought in any case, so why should we badger her any further? And to tell the truth, we all felt sorry for her. She was constantly in tears, had trouble sleeping, needed valerian drops from the hospital . . .

So we went back to our sewing and camp life as though nothing had happened. We tried not to remind Edita of what had happened in any way, but it would be futile to deny that our relationship with her remained unchanged. Sewing was resumed, but not everyone could work as before. The doctors had no choice but to release Tanya and myself from work for weeks at a time: we were both constantly running temperatures. Being unable to do anything for us, they tried to accuse us of systematic malingering, but they could do nothing about the thermometers, which stubbornly registered temperatures above normal, no matter who took the readings or how many times.

Artemyev even summoned Vladimirova for a chat about this in mid-April.

"What do Osipova and Ratushinskaya do to keep their temperatures so high?"

According to Vladimirova, she snapped at him: "It's easy with the aid of SHIZO."

So in May, they finally said to us: "You'll be getting no more releases from work. You'll have to sew even if you're running a fever."

Of course, we only sewed when we felt up to it, but that was risky. Fortunately, we felt better in the warmth of the summer months, but by the middle of autumn, everything would start again. It must have been the cold. Nor were the others in better shape: not all illnesses are accompanied by high temperatures. By that time, Pani Lida, Pani Jadvyga, Natasha, Raya and Vladimirova had been acknowledged as invalids of one category or another. In two years' time, Galya was added to the list. Lagle, Olya, Edita, Tanya and I were considered to be the strongest.

My first year in camp was over. How typical was it? How would things have been if we hadn't gone on strike and had agreed to wear identity tags? They would have been exactly the same! It's not the practice to keep politicals in camp for long stretches, even in strict regime camps; the KGB practices the "merry-go-round" system with them: camp—PKT—SHIZO—camp—SHIZO and so on. The reasons are immaterial; if an excuse can't be found, it can always be invented.

Just give them the man and they'll find a way to torment him. Valeri Senderov had to resort to striking when they refused to let him continue his work on mathematics: they would confiscate and burn all his notes. Furthermore, they confiscated his Bible, prayerbook, and the cross he wore around his neck. Anatoli Marchenko was viciously beaten when he refused to give up the books he tried to take into SHIZO.

In one way, we are better off than the male politicals, in that there were only a couple of dedicated sadists among our guards. Of all those guards and warders I encountered in our Zone and two criminal zones, I can name only four with total certainty: our Podust, and in camp Number Two in SHIZO, warders Akimkina and Ryzhova, and regime deputy camp commandant Uchaykin. Three women and one man. I am not, of course, counting the KGB personnel—they all have that strain in them—I am talking about ordinary camp personnel. But overseers for the Perm camps and the notorious Chistopol prison are chosen for sadistic tendencies uncovered in psychological tests.

When Senderov and Kovalyov were in SHIZO for months on end, they had the dubious pleasure of hearing the duty warder chatting on the phone in the corridor to one of his cronies in the infirmary, and describing his favorite hobby. He would catch a rat and chop off the very end of its tail, then apply a flame to the wound. A little later, he would chop off another bit, and burn the new wound. And so on, over and over, until the rat had no tail. Then he would let the maddened beast go, with the same valediction they utter to zeks upon release: "Off you go, and don't get caught again!"

For this, that particular warder was nicknamed "The Red Rat." I know all too many such happenings, but see no reason to sicken my readers any further. For the same reason, I will not dwell any more on all our subsequent terms in SHIZO: enough to have described the incarcerations which occurred during my first year in the camp. Endless repetitions, which violate the rules of literature, were, nevertheless, the bleak reality of our zek life. But you, who have mentally spent this first year with us, know that by now, and it's time for me to show some compassion. Enough also that we were trapped in this continuous, dull repetition. It was like the repetitive functioning of a machine, totally devoid of any element of humanity.

All those norms of human behavior which are inculcated in one from the cradle are subjected to deliberate and systematic destruction. It's normal to want to be clean? Then take your portion of salted sardelles through the hatch in your cell door with your bare hands. You will not be given plates or knives, not even a sheet of paper to put it on. And then, wipe the fish innards off your hands against your clothes, because you can't have any water! Contract scabies and skin fungus, live in filth, breathe the stench of the slop bucket—then you'll regret your misdemeanors! Women are prone to modesty? All the more reason to strip them naked during searches, and when they're taken to the bathhouse while under investigation, a whole group of leering and jeering KGB officers will enter "by chance." Once in the camp, a woman will have to convince the doctor, the camp commandant and the procurator how much water and cotton wool she requires for her intimate needs.[1] It will take about four months to convince them, and the number of lewd comments she will hear in the process is hard to calculate. A normal person is repelled by coarseness and lies? You will encounter such an amount of both that you will have to strain all your inner resources to remember that there is, there is another reality. There are decent people—in fact, they are the majority, there are whole countries where black is black and white is white, and you will not be prosecuted for saying so. But that will all seem so far away, so remote, that only by a maximum exertion of will is it possible to retain one's former, normal scale of values.

But in doing so, you must not, under any circumstances, allow yourself to hate. Not because your tormentors have not earned it. But if you allow hatred to take root, it will flourish and spread during your years in the camps, driving out everything else, and ultimately corrode and warp your soul. You will no longer be yourself, your identity will be destroyed, all that will remain will be a hysterical, maddened and bedevilled husk of the human being that once was. And this is what will come before God should such a creature die while still behind bars. And this is just what "they" want. So, when you look at any nut or bolt of that

1. Sanitary napkins are almost impossible to acquire in the USSR on the open market. Tampons are not known or produced. Cotton wool (usually in short supply) must be purchased from chemists for use during menstruation.

machine—whether he has red or blue patches on his uniform—you try to think that maybe he has children who may grow up to be quite different from him. Or you may find something amusing about him: laughter dissolves anger. Or you may feel sincerely sorry for him: no matter how grim your situation, would you swap places with him? Of course not! You see. . . ? But if you can spot no spark of humanity in him, no matter how hard you try, remind yourself that cockroaches are exterminated without hatred, rather with a feeling of revulsion. And "they"—armed, well fed and belligerent—are like vermin in our big house, and sooner or later we shall get rid of them and live in cleanliness. Is it not pathetic that they have designs on our immortal souls?

All this in sum brings about one marked change in your physical appearance; by the end of your first year, you will have what are known as "zek's eyes." The look in a zek's eyes is impossible to describe, but once encountered, it is never forgotten. When you emerge, your friends, embracing you, will exclaim: "Your eyes! Your eyes have changed!"

And not one of your tormentors will be able to bear your scrutiny. They will turn away from it, like beaten dogs.

35

We soldiered on, battling for our right to correspondence, studying every blade and leaf growing on our small patch of earth just in case it had any medicinal properties. We brewed tea with daisies, ate wild caraway plants. When goosefoot sprouted, we were able to make a salad out of it. And then, to Pani Jadvyga's delight, up came the dandelions. She had long known that there is hardly a more useful plant on earth, so she spent hours puttering around to put them to maximum use. Nothing was wasted, not roots, nor leaves, nor flowers. They're rather bitter, but we're not fussy. These plants are our lifeline. All the medicines sent by our relatives are returned stamped "forbidden." But I can't say that our medical facilities are entirely useless: we managed to get seven discarded enema tubes from there, and Natasha joined them up to make a hose for watering our plants—by using bits of sawn-up ballpoint pen cases as joints. This hose saves us the enormous amount of energy that would be needed to drag buckets of water to and fro. So doing the watering becomes one of the most pleasant chores. Admittedly, the hose doesn't reach everywhere, but that's immaterial.

The weather is becoming a little warmer, and we prepare to celebrate Easter. We'll be doing it in two stages: first the Catholic, then the Orthodox Easter.[1] Our Zone has more feasts to celebrate

1. The Russian Orthodox Church adheres to the Julian calendar, and not the "reformed" Gregorian calendar followed by Western churches.

than the average family—two Christmases, two Easters . . . Not surprising, really, when you consider that the eleven of us represent six nationalities and four Christian denominations.

The warders have whispered to us that Podust is working out her last days in the camp; in summer she will be transferred to Tambov. Still, our sky is never without a few clouds: "Barats, Abrutiene, Vladimirova, Matusevich, Rudenko! Transportation!" They claim it's not to SHIZO, but to Saransk, to the KGB prison for "re-education." We believe them, because Vladimirova is among those summoned. They wouldn't send her to SHIZO under any circumstances. Saransk is nothing to look forward to, either, but we see them off with lighter hearts than to SHIZO.

Natasha is taken into the hospital. It is ever so quiet in the Zone again. We faithfully carry out all Raya's instructions about caring for our plants, and play with Nyurka who has brought along three new kittens. They are absolute darlings. The warders have already put in their orders for boys and girls. However, Nyurka has to train them how to hunt the "grey long-tails" before they leave her. She's an amazingly good teacher. It's strange, in view of the lengths to which the authorities went to make our lives a misery, that nobody ever tried to do anything to our cat. Podust did complain a few times that we had an animal in the Zone despite regulations, but didn't actually dare to do anything about it. And, in any case, how could you keep a cat out of the Zone? Nyurka always kept her distance from the guards; she would let some of the warders stroke her occasionally, but none of the officers could ever get within reach of her. She would disappear at the first sound of boots stamping in the corridor. Unlike us, Nyurka ignores the "forbidden" strip: just try and catch her. Anyway, we would have kicked up such a row in the Zone that our smart puss would have been miles away by the time the administration could restore order. What could they do? Try to shoot her with their pistols? But in the Zone they would risk hitting one of us, and beyond the Zone there are so many fences that it wouldn't be worth the effort. In any case, Nyurka remained unmolested, and plainly enjoyed herself grooming her progeny.

One fine May morning I went outside with the hose to water our plants. The others were still inside, the loudspeaker in the neighboring zone was silent, there was total peace and quiet. Suddenly, a man dressed in black vaulted lightly over the fence into our Zone. As he came toward me, I saw by his clothes, his hair and mainly by his eyes that he was a zek.

"Hello, I'm Vasya."

"Hello, Vasya. Where did you come from?"

"The First Zone." He jerked his chin in the direction of the fence. "From the tuberculosis section. What's your name?"

"Ira."

"You see, Ira, it's this way. I gave one of the screws three hundred rubles so's he wouldn't notice my being away for an hour or so. I haven't had a woman in I don't know how long. How about it, eh?"

Vasya's offer is not surprising. The men's and women's hospital zones are adjacent, divided only by two fences and one barbed-wire barrier. The prisoners in the criminal camps have money, the guards are always willing to accept a bribe, and the women, as a rule, are only too glad to oblige; they miss men, too, and there's always the chance of becoming pregnant. This Vasya must be new, and got into our Zone instead of the hospital compound by mistake. I explain that this is the political zone.

"Go on! I've heard about it, but didn't know it was here. So you're a political?"

"I am, Vasya, I am! See that fence? There's another one behind it, then the wire, and then you're in the hospital. That's where you wanted to go. You'd better get going and not waste any more time."

"The hell with the hospital. I like you. How about it? What's that over there, a shed? Perfect!"

"Vasya, my dear, I'm married."

"So what?"

"I don't cheat on my husband."

"What? How long are you in for?"

"Seven years, plus five exile."

"I'll be damned. Religious, are you?"

"Yes."

This explanation is always accepted unquestioningly, and is understood by all. Vasya would simply not comprehend all my other reasons.

"What are you in for?"

"My poetry."

"How's that? You mean you write it yourself?"

"That's right."

"Never! Go on, read some."

"Vasya, your screw's watch won't have stopped while we're standing here talking."

"Bugger him. I've never ever seen a political before. How many of you are there here?"

"Five at the moment, but eleven all told."

"What are the others in for?"

"Some for religion, some for defending human rights, or for wanting to emigrate from the Soviet Union."

"So, what's it like here, then?"

"We're in SHIZO, mostly."

"Whew! What for? For fighting?"

"Sometimes we go on strike. And we don't wear identity tags. But mainly, it's just the KGB practicing on us."

"So you don't inform on one another?"

"You've got it."

"Yeah, that's good. Informing on your own is the pits. So come on, read some of your poems, eh?"

"Vasya, I hate to see your three hundred rubles wasted. Go to the hospital, then stop by on your way back if there's time, and we'll talk."

"Maybe one of your other girls here would agree? Or are they all religious?"

"No, not all, but you're out of luck here. Believe me."

He is convinced by my smile rather than my words; clearly, he's realized that he won't get what he's after in this place.

"Right then, Irisha, I'll be off. But I'll be back later. You don't have any informers here, do you?"

"Only one, but she's not here just now. You don't have to

worry about the others. But if the guards catch you here, you won't be able to buy your way out of that. The KGB's involved here, so you're running a big risk."

"Nobody'll catch me!"

"Then why are you in camp?"

We both laugh and he takes off over the right fence. I don't mention the encounter inside the house because of the microphones, but can't help wondering who he is. A thief? An embezzler? A murderer? Whoever he is, he's obviously starved of normal, human conversation.

I go off and start sewing. There is no new poem forming in my head today, so I work "uselessly." Pani Jadvyga is busy "darning" an old watering can which has sprung a leak. Mending dishes and pans with cotton thread is an art inherited from the *babushki:* in the absence of a soldering iron, holes must be plugged with thread. A threaded needle is pulled back and forth through the hole, leaving an overlap of thread on both sides. Eventually the hole is filled up to such an extent that the needle has to be pulled through with pliers. When it becomes impossible to force the needle through at all, you trim the "bunches" of thread on each side, and the utensil is watertight again: the thread swells from contact with liquid and forms a solid plug. We had a couple of darned saucepans in which we boiled water without losing a drop.

After about an hour of these peaceful pursuits, we were interrupted by Pani Lida, who came into the workroom and motioned me to follow her into the yard.

"Irochka, there's some young man here asking for you. He's over there behind the wood pile."

She says this with typical zek unflappability, but there are sparks of merriment in her eyes.

"You go and talk, and I'll keep a lookout for any prowling warders."

So Pani Lida goes off to stroll up and down the path, and I to talk to Vasya.

"Made it all right, did you? Everything okay?"

"Damned bitches they are, in that hospital. While I was with one of 'em, two others got jealous and went off and reported us.

Idiots! I wouldn't have refused to go with them later. As it is, I just barely got away. Don't you have nothing to do with those sluts; women'll always sell you down the river, especially the ones in the general zone. Did you say you here are different?"

I tell him about the other inmates of our Zone. Carefully, of course, no secrets. I have no way of knowing that he won't sell us down the river. Vasya listens open-mouthed: "And you'd spit on the KGB?"

"Not quite, but we ignore them."

"Look, Ira, I got only seven grades of school, keep it simple."

"Well, in that case—yes, I suppose you could say we spit on them."

We both laugh, and then he holds me to my promise to read him some poetry.

"Ira, write them down on paper, would you? One of our guys plays the guitar."

"You mean you've got a guitar?"

"Well, not here, exactly. There was a guitar here, but some of the boys used a string off it to kill the regime supervisor. Mind you, the bosses didn't find out who did it, but they confiscated the guitar all the same. But that don't matter. You see, I'm not going to be here long, I've got tuberculosis, see, so they bring me up here to the hospital for a bit twice a year. But back in my own zone, we've got two guitars, for amateur dramatics, recreation, you know the sort of thing."

"Very well, but how shall I get them to you?"

"Easy. I reckon I'd better not try coming again for a few days, but one of our boys'll be here tomorrow in the work detail that'll be tightening up your wire fences. 'Mosquito,' everyone calls him. You give the paper to him, but careful like."

"And what do they call you?"

"Shnobel."[2]

"Whatever for?"

"See the scar on my nose? Six stitches, I had, and the bridge got busted. Happened in a fight with some shyster."

2. Corruption of the German *schnabel*, beak.

Vasya is a professional thief, and started his career in the orphanage where he spent his childhood.

"It was the poverty that starts you off. It was unbearable," he explained. Predictably, Vasya found himself in a juvenile offenders' camp, then received training from the most famous pickpocket in Kiev. After that, he enjoyed four years of rich pickings and "easy living."

"Didn't get caught even once. The cops were all out to get me, but I was too good for 'em. So the bastards just pulled me in anyway, even though I wasn't doing nothing at the time. I was standing in line in a shop, minding my own business, when two of 'em pressed up beside me, and some dame started screaming that I'd picked her purse out of her pocket. 'Course, she was one of theirs, and so were the witnesses, but what could I do? So they put me away. Had everything ready. That's the way they like to work."

"Vasya, tell me: if your life had been normal, would you have stolen anyway, do you think?"

"Don't know. Wanted to be a sailor, when I was a kid, but now . . . I'm in it, you see, so I'll stay a thief till I'm dead and gone. And if I meet up with that bitch the cops planted on me, I'll kill her. Look, Irisha, don't you get no ideas about reforming me—I've had a bellyful of all that agitation about honest living. There's no such thing. Who's honest? You tell me! Just look around, and everyone steals. When I was in the orphanage, the director and the guy in charge of supplies stole what we kids were supposed to get. And it's the same here. Then the cops who set me up—d'you think they acted honest? Or the judge, or the procurator? Nah! But they got the power, haven't they? Now me—when I go out on a job, it's me against everyone. You know how good that feels?"

"You're wrong, Vasya. There is honest living. But it's harder than your way."

"You're talking about people like you in this Zone, right? Sure, I respect you all, and take my hat off to you. Only I don't see no sense in what you want. D'you really believe the whole nation can live honestly?"

"One day it will."

"Yeah, maybe, in a thousand years' time, and even then—I doubt it. Anyway, we're alive now. I bet you've never had a fur coat in your life, have you?"

"No, that's true. In fact, I've never had a proper winter coat."

"Ah, Irisha, pity we didn't meet out there. I'd have got you everything, easy. But then, I guess you wouldn't have taken it, would you?"

"No, Vasya. No stolen goods."

"God, that there's women like that about, and I never get any of 'em! Only ones that come my way stick to you like glue when you're in the money: give 'em this, give 'em that. And your guy— what's he do?"

"He was a thermal physicist, but lost his job when the KGB got to us. He's working in a factory now."

"Waiting for you, is he?"

"Yes."

"Quite right, too. I'd push his face in myself if he didn't wait. Tell you what, Irisha: if you like, you write him a letter and I've got pals outside who'll see that he gets it. You don't have to worry that they'll give you away; there's strict rules about that kind of thing among thieves. I'll pass it along, you'll see. May I never see freedom again if I don't!"

"I'll think about it. Anyway, you'd better be getting along: they'll be bringing our food any moment, and there'll be warders about."

"Irisha, can I kiss your hand before I go? I saw a film once where they kissed women's hands. God, but your fingers are thin! Well, be seeing you."

"Good luck."

For two weeks we corresponded with the TB section. The correspondence expanded to include Vasya's mentor in all matters of theft, who was known as "Vitebsky." Particularly famous thieves, whose authority is acknowledged in criminal circles, are given "aristocratic" nicknames after the cities in which they operate. This is a mark of great prestige. Vitebsky (the name derives from the Belorussian city Vitebsk) was obviously intrigued by this unusual meeting of two totally different worlds, a meeting that could occur only in the camps: our world, and the world of thieves. As time went on, our letters began to resemble mini-encyclopedias, because each side wanted to learn as much as possible about the other. We all read their letters, and Vasya was invariably referred to as "Ira's thief" in our Zone. We made no attempts to reform them, we merely tried to understand them and their world. Vitebsky wrote that he was a thief "by calling," and would have been a thief in any country and any social class, "even in America" (he thought of America as the epitome of well-being and legality). He came to respect us deeply when he found out that we refuse to carry out any demeaning orders issued by the KGB or the camp administration. He wrote that in the criminal camps, there are zeks known as "rejectors": they do not refuse to work, but despise camp officials, never try to curry favor with them, and do not allow themselves to be humiliated in any way; they prefer punishment cells rather than that. To make sure we understood, he gave an example: "If one of the screws drops his keys on purpose and orders, 'Pick them up!' I wouldn't do it even if they put me in SHIZO. But the ones who crawl to the supervisors—we call them 'goats.' "

Vasya was more inclined to the lyrical and to self-analysis. He wrote that he hated the vicious inter-zek kangaroo courts, and that he loathed taking part in beating the "guilty" one to death; but, like all the others, he had to join in, because that was their "law": no mercy for traitors. After all, he added, isn't the whole world based on cruelty? At the same time, he would ask for more poetry, and Vitebsky added a caustic postscript: "You're driving my Shnobel out of his mind. He doesn't sleep nights, but lies there muttering something."

This correspondence came to an abrupt end when there was a lightning descent on the Zone by two warders, Podust, Shalin and a couple of officers.

"Women, prepare to move to new quarters! Everything you take with you will be examined first!"

We understood now why we had been scattered here and there: to make it easier to control the move. It had long been a sore point with them that information was getting out of the camp into the free world despite all their efforts. The move provides a splendid opportunity to check all our effects, and if we leave anything behind, they can find it at their leisure later, even if they have to turn over every bit of earth and pull down the house. We know that they also suspect us of having a radio secreted away somewhere. What they conducted was more of a pogrom than a search. Into the fire went old jackets, they confiscated felt boots (*valenki*) which we had inherited from the *babushki*, seized all "excess" underclothes. Letters and any other written materials were put aside in a separate pile: "The operations section will check these, and they will be returned," we were told.

Very pedantically, we insisted on the compilation of a full list of all items being sent to the store of prisoners' personal belongings. We also insisted on standing by while the property of those out of the Zone was searched, and listed that, too: what is going where. By doing so, we managed to drag the search out until the evening, by which time the store was closed. So the administration had no choice but to place everything destined for the store, as well as all our written materials and books (the books were subject to scrutiny, too), into a small room in our new quarters for the night. Just to be sure, they sealed the door. As we were the ones who had to do all the carrying, we managed to save a few things right away, even though they watched us—zek hands are very quick hands. An exercise book full of my poems had to be left behind: it had been wrapped in plastic and buried in a place where they would not look for it in a thousand years. In August 1985, when we returned to our old Zone, we retrieved it with delight from its undiscovered hiding place.

Our saucepans, hotplate and kettle were all confiscated—in fact, they confiscated as much as they possibly could. When they had locked the gates, we took a look around our new Zone. A stone building, surrounded by a high wall, with only a narrow strip of earth between them. Nothing growing on it but tall weeds. Broken glass is scattered all over the place, no walking around barefoot here! The bedroom is half the size of our old one, and contains iron bunks in two tiers. The frames sway and squeak with the slightest movement. Sleeping on them will be a real trial. There is running water and even sewage, but if you touch the taps or put your hands under the stream of water, you get an electric shock. Apparently, everything in Barashevo is grounded to the water pipes. If anything is being welded in the camp, it's best to keep your distance from the tap. Some of the window panes in the building are smashed, and we have been robbed of what tools we had. Heaven knows how we are to make this place habitable, without even a hammer. We were not in what you'd call a sunny mood. We returned our evening meal to the kitchen.

"We are supposed to have hot water and hot food. Our urn has been confiscated, and our hotplate and kettle, too. So you provide for us as best you can."

Tired out, we settled down on the squeaky bunks. Perhaps the night will bring counsel for the morrow.

The guards, however, had to maintain an all-night vigil in the "forbidden" strip, because the administration was certain that we would try to sneak through into our old Zone for things we'd concealed. We let them cling to this delusion; moreover, the warders had whispered a warning to us about it.

36

By morning I was so depressed that at 5:00 a.m. I was already up, prowling around our unattractive new compound. Builders' rubbish, high fences, ruts and holes. The remnants of some kind of brick construction. And this is where we've got to live? I knew that we would manage, plant flowers and such with the seeds we'd sneaked through, but at that stage I still reacted to material losses, and missed our well, our poplar, rowan and birch trees, the whole way of life we had evolved for ourselves with such great effort. I really did feel like the victim of a pogrom. But relief came with Lagle's cheerful voice behind my back: "Up and about already? Look at the interesting contours here: the ground rises a good one and a half meters behind those bricks. We'll have to cut some steps into it, and make a path over here. There are plenty of stones and rubble for our needs."

And a minute later we were busily planning what we would do, and what we would sow. That hole over there can be scooped out and turned into a mini-cellar, and the remnants of the brick chimney can be made into a fireplace. We were joined by Tanya, who had discovered that the two-tiered bunks could be unfastened into ordinary camp bunks. We decided to set about that job immediately. Of course, they will not all fit into one room, but the neighboring room is empty, so we'll have two bedrooms. But we will not tolerate the existing two-tiered system for another night! We need a hammer, which we don't have, to disengage the top bunks from the bottom ones, but we find two pieces of rusty piping which will serve our purpose just as well. Natasha works alongside: not surprisingly, they discharged her from the hospital as soon as we'd been moved to the new Zone; we knew by now that her admission to hospital had been to reduce the number of people in the Zone at the time of the move. It's not easy work, though, and we forbid Pani Lida and Pani Jadvyga to take any part in it; let them put the kitchen to rights instead.

Podust descends, spluttering angrily: "Women, just what do you think you're doing? I forbid this! Put everything back as it was at once, that's an order. Ratushinskaya! You have a long meeting coming up next week. Do you want it cancelled?"

And so on, in the same vein. We neither see nor hear her, so she rounds on Pani Lida: "Doronina! Take that bunk back immediately."

It's sheer stupidity to order a fifty-nine-year-old woman to cope singlehandedly with a bunk it had taken three of us to shift, but that's Podust. Pani Lida, however, lost her customary meekness at this, and Podust had to retreat. This incident put an end to any further contact between Pani Lida and Podust . . . For the rest of that day we had a constant stream of regime supervisors, other officers and Shalin in and out of the Zone, protesting, ordering, threatening—and we kept on separating and rearranging the bunks: we put five in one room, six in the other. No more could have fitted in, but we didn't need any more. And so it remained. The administration, seeing our determination, gave up. In any case, we had the Soviet law on our side, the "most humane law in the world," which stated quite explicitly that every prisoner must have two square meters of living space, whereas the two bedrooms, used by eleven of us, made up only a total of eighteen square meters.

That night, we carefully removed the glass from the window of the little room into which our confiscated property had been placed. This was easy, because the glass was only held in place by three nails. Why fiddle about with the seals on the door when we can use a window? Lagle stayed outside to keep watch, and Tanya and I climbed inside. Lighting the occasional match and thanking our lucky stars for the moonlit night, we found the most valuable things and passed them out to Lagle: an atlas (prisoners aren't allowed to have maps, so we had to keep hiding it), all the confiscated letters and notes, our Bibles and most vital items of clothing. Naturally, we didn't forget about the possessions of those currently away from the Zone. We had to be careful not to take away too much, for that would be immediately apparent, but we removed close enough to half. Finding hiding places will be no problem, nor is it any problem to put the glass back into the window frame. Remembering the lessons of Sherlock Holmes, we put on gloves (the ones we sew) when handling the glass to leave no fingerprints. Then we relax and laugh; how's that for a spot of breaking and entering?

Tanya spends the whole of the next day walking around the new Zone picking up bits of broken glass. Lagle and I sort stones and broken bricks, keeping those which are likely to be of use in our forthcoming landscape gardening endeavors, and throwing the useless ones over the fence. Natasha is trying to construct a primitive water-boiler with a piece of wire and two bits of metal plate: the ends of the wire go into the electricity plug, and the metal plates into a container of water. So long as we don't touch the container while the power is on, we should do quite well. Both our Panis are in the kitchen, scouring and scrubbing.

And then, I am served with a notice about the cancellation of my "long" meeting, and under an unexpectedly stupid pretext at that. I had known that this meeting would be cancelled and that the official reason would be immaterial, yet a very strange thing happened to me, nonetheless. I felt that I must have this meeting at all costs, that I must be able to put my head on Igor's shoulder just once, because all his letters have been confiscated since December and my secret letters were still a one-way traffic at that time: so I sat down and wrote an explanatory letter to the camp commandant, seeking to overset their silly reason for cancelling the meeting with an equally silly distortion of facts. Then, coming to my senses (and not without help from Tanya and Lagle, neither of whom could approve such an action), I realized that, strictly speaking, I had lied in that letter to the commandant. And the shame I felt about this first lie of my entire camp life cured me once and for all from any future repetition. Forever, I hope. Even now, I cringe as I recall that incident. It's not as though I didn't know that lying to an adversary is tantamount to sanctioning his lies to you. I knew that the difference between us lay in that we had moral standards and consciences. Where had my brains been, if not my conscience, in those moments? I don't know. It was like a fit of madness. All I could think was that I needed that meeting, and nothing else seemed to matter.

Luckily, my "explanatory" note had no effect; the administration simply ignored it. They had given Igor a totally different reason for cancelling the meeting, so as far as they were concerned, the matter was closed. Actually, the second reason was just as idiotic as the first: that my jacket had been lying on my bunk. That was put forward as sufficient reason to deprive us of a meeting that is granted once a year. The fact that our jackets had been given to us only half an hour earlier, that there was not a single hanger or nail to put them on in the whole building, and that the only place we could all put them (and did!) was on our bunks—that was considered to be mere detail, having no bearing on the matter. The others showed great sympathy over the incident, and nobody ever mentioned it again; they could see how it affected me.

In protest against the cancellation of meetings becoming an established practice, I declared a ten-day hunger strike. Our administration advised me with unconcealed glee that there was a new government resolution (a secret resolution, of course) concerning administrative punishment for hunger strikes. The nub of this resolution was that hunger strikers were to be thrown into SHIZO for the maximum term allowed without a break—fifteen days. The process could be repeated indefinitely. To cut down the paperwork, they put me down for two months of PKT straight after SHIZO.

The others escorted me to the gate, as usual, and while I waited for the warder to search my things in the guardroom, I was amazed by the sudden appearance of Podust, who sailed toward me uttering totally unlooked-for sentiments: "Ratushinskaya,

I'm leaving tomorrow, so let's say goodbye. We'll never see each other again, so let's part as friends."

And—I swear this is true—she stuck out a hand toward me! It hung there in mid-air for a bit, under the gaze of maliciously smirking warders and duty officer, then descended to the table and began drumming its well-manicured nails. She heard no heartfelt outpourings from me, nor rudeness, which she may have expected with more reason. I walked past her in silence, and threw my bundle into the van. Let's go!

Two days later I was joined by Tanya. She had declared a hunger strike for the entire length of time that I was held in SHIZO on my hunger strike. They gave her the same treatment: fifteen days of SHIZO to be followed by two months of PKT. Tanya had somehow managed to smuggle in an orange-colored flower—a present for me from the others in the Zone. This flower proved to be as tough as a zek, and did not fade for an unusually long time. We kept it in an aluminum mug and talked to it from time to time, as though it were a child.

It was our good luck that this was June, and we were no more cold than one usually is during hunger strikes. We became weak, of course, but we were very cheerful. For one thing, the Zone was finally free of Podust forever: they would never find a second one like that even if they searched all of Mordovia from one end to the other. Not content with the rebuff she'd had from me, she approached Tanya with "fond farewells" when Tanya was being packed off to SHIZO, with identical results. I still can't fathom what on earth had motivated her. Some aberration of her sadistic psyche? If we had been going off to be executed, would she have tried to kiss us goodbye? I have no idea. But the best part of this story was told to us by Lagle after our return to the Zone.

The day after Tanya's departure to SHIZO, Podust came into the Zone, cornered Lagle, and after the same offer about parting as friends, demanded: "What did I ever do to you that you should call me a rat?"

Lagle made no reply, of course, but was honestly perplexed: she had never said anything like that and, in any case, quarrelling on that level was simply not Lagle's style. So she decided that

Podust must be really going mad. Later on, the warders clarified the matter. In the spring, when we had celebrated Lagle's birthday, I had written a parody of the Cinderella story, and it was among the other congratulatory messages she received from us all on that day. Lagle was the duty Cinderella that week, so I wrote about how the wicked witch *Sovdepia*[1] took Cinderella far away from her native Estonia, put her into a cocoon made of barbed wire, and so on. Every fairy tale must have a happy ending, so I had Cinderella being rescued by a handsome prince, her husband Lembit, who took her back to Estonia. The convoy "cuckoo" turned into a splendid carriage, the escort into footmen, and Podust tried as hard as she could to become a beautiful black steed, but failed: all she could manage was to turn into a rat.

We giggled over this story at the time, and then forgot all about it. There had been so many new jokes and stories since. But it so happened that Lagle rewrote this story into an exercise book, and this was confiscated when we were being moved from the old Zone into the new. All her other notes were in her native Estonian, but this piece was in Russian, so our camp officers were able to read it. Needless to say, this exercise book went around all of Barashevo before being handed over to the KGB, and was hugely enjoyed by all our guards. Some even copied it out for themselves, and as Podust was universally disliked, the joke about the rat enjoyed great popularity. Podust decided that it was Lagle who had written the story, and that was the reason for her question. Had she had the wit not to force an obviously unprofitable issue, we would never have known that our story had received such broad circulation. But the more petty-minded and silly the person, the more he is prone to seeking "explanations" and "clarifying relations": it becomes an obsession stemming, most likely, from a permanent suspicion that he has been slighted.

When Podust disappeared over the horizon, we acquired two new brigade supervisors at once: Arapov and Trimaskin. Both were perfectly inoffensive unless they had direct orders to carry out. Viktor Arapov, a young lieutenant, was simply called "Vitka"

1. Slang term for "Soviet Union."

throughout Barashevo, and the warders used the familiar "thou" in addressing him. He was the only one out of our guards who could do anything with his hands, specifically—fix television sets. He even managed to get our ancient specimen going for short bursts from time to time. He was honest and straightforward, and didn't like telling lies. When he confiscated two letters from Pani Jadvyga during a routine search and we asked him whether he had a conscience, he replied: "Orders override conscience."

Captain Trimaskin was one of those captains who never make it to major; he was dull even for a guard. He was serving out time with us until his pension, and amused us greatly on his first appearance by his brightly dyed red hair. Heaven knows where he found such a virulent shade. He lied as easily and naturally as a bird sings, and never showed the slightest sign of confusion whenever we caught him. I don't think he even realized that there was anything shameful in lying. At first he tried to conduct "re-educative" discussions with us. But it was so easy to counter his arguments and expose his ignorance that we soon gave it up as unsporting. He was such a comical figure and so harmless that we never let ourselves needle or ridicule him. We decided to adopt him as our "regimental mascot" and defend him if necessary. We always tried to avoid mentioning his name in any petitions to the Procuracy, because we did not want to get him into trouble.

Shalin was placed in charge of both the men's and the women's political zones. Although he was not a hard man by nature, he was building his career as an officer, and that meant he could not afford to be squeamish. Nor was he, although at first this obviously made him uneasy. But we saw him becoming accustomed to it as time went by. Occasionally, though, it was possible to talk to him on a normal human level, and at those times he would behave like a normal human being. For instance, he understood the seriousness of Natasha's condition, and went out of his way to avoid putting her in a punishment cell; he did not want to have that on his conscience. He held to this even at those times when Natasha's nerves would snap from illness and accumulated tension and she acted in a manner that would, officially, have been reason enough to bring down penalties. Generally speaking, he was not the worst sort of jailer, and we rarely had personal conflicts with him. All three of these officers frankly disliked intrigue and petty persecution, leaving such activity to the KGB. The only thing they did was conscientiously to halve our possessions when conducting searches: they had to have something to report to their superiors, after all! But they all lied when their orders called for it.

But in these two and a half months of our SHIZO and PKT, Tanya and I were under a different administration in camp Number Two. We immediately discovered that our cell had a means of communication with neighbors that was far superior to all the usual methods: there was a hole under the bunks, clear through into the next cell. It was a narrow hole, the width of my finger, but our neighbors started a correspondence with us while we were still doing our days of SHIZO. They were serving terms of PKT, and were thus allowed to have paper. Sheets of paper would be rolled into two thin pipes, placed one inside the other with a ballpoint pen cartridge and a note in the middle pipe, which could be pulled out in either cell. In this way, we were able to exchange notes through a half-meter-thick wall. On the day we ended our hunger strike, they filled the middle pipe with sugar for us several times. And this despite the fact that not everyone at PKT receives sugar, only those who had fulfilled the production quota (a practically impossible task) the day before. They are supposed to get 10 grams, but in practice they only get about half that amount, and it had taken the whole cell at least a week to amass the sugar for us. When we went into PKT regime and acquired the right to wear our own clothes and have paper and tobacco, we used the same method to pass tobacco to them. Neither of us smoked, but we knew that zeks are always short of tobacco, so we brought some along just for such an eventuality.

But the sugar and tobacco were of secondary importance; far more valuable for both sides was the exchange of information. Our neighbors were interested in anything they didn't know. After reading my poems, they bombarded me with questions: Who was Ulysses? What does "Cainozoic era" mean? What is this garden called "Gethsemane"? I had my work cut out writing detailed explanations of all these things, and when we got on to the poetry of Tyutchev, Pushkin, Brodsky and Samoylov—well, I would say that Tanya and I wrote a whole encyclopedic dictionary. It was quite a task, too, explaining to them about legality and human rights. Yet how eagerly they asked more and more questions!

We, too, were learning a great deal about the criminal camps. Camp Number Two had a lot of mothers with small children. By law, nursing mothers may not be put into SHIZO and PKT. So what can the administration do to get around this? The answer is simple: order the camp doctor to attest that the mother has no milk. In such cases, the doctor has the right to distance the mother from suckling her child, and she can be put into SHIZO. There were women in there with milk running down their breasts: due to the cold, they would get inflammation of the mammary glands, while their babies lay crying in the DMR[2] (House of Mother and Child). One child in eight died there, and even more during epidemics. The others grew, hardly seeing their mothers: there's nothing easier than to deprive a prisoner of the right to visit her child. Somehow these children were fed, somehow they were treated and taught something, but the mothers had no right to have any say or part in the lives of their children. Two-year-olds would know only several words, and some of them not even that. Yulia, one of our neighbors, passed a photo of her daughter through the paper pipe.

"See my little girl, isn't she lovely? You'd never say she was a prisoner's baby, would you? They're going to send her away to a children's home soon, they don't keep them here over two years old. And I've got three more months of PKT, so I don't know if they'll even let me kiss her goodbye before they take her away. Well, you finished looking at my Mashenka? Let's have the photo back, then, it's the only one I've got . . ."

2. *Dom Materi i Rebenka.*

37

It was summer, so the criminal camp was in the grip of an epidemic of dysentery. Neither Tanya and I nor the others escaped it. In SHIZO and PKT, there is no way to avoid the infection: you don't cook your own food or wash your plate, and the flies are everywhere. The shortage of water makes washing hands impossible; you get one kettleful every morning, and that's it. The administration became concerned when Tanya and I came down with dysentery: after all, we're politicals! So they let us keep our bunks down during the day, issued bedding, and even tablets every morning. We were also supposed to have injections, but that caused a lot of confusion, because the nurse who was supposed to administer them was not allowed to enter our cell unless she was accompanied by the deputy camp commandant; he, however, could hardly be expected to run around every time we were due for a jab. In the end, the warder would unlock the cell's outer door, and the nurse would give us our injections through the grating of the inner door. It would have been funny were it not so pathetic. The corridor was very dark, and she could barely see what she was doing. However, we in PKT fared better than the women in SHIZO. Nothing was done for them at all, and they just lay prone on the floor. There was a rumor that a great many children had died in the House of Mother and Child. The reported numbers of deaths in the camp varied, but were never below sixty. Then came the rumor that all mothers arrested for the second time were being dispatched to another camp, Number Fourteen, but their children were being left behind here in Number Two. To minimize noise and howling, the rumor went, they were being taken to Number Fourteen without any warning and without the opportunity to say goodbye to their babies. The mothers in SHIZO and PKT rejoiced that they were there, because they could not be transported to another zone, and this latest "campaign" might have run its course by the time they were due for release back into the camp. Some, however, were indifferent. Liza in cell Number Five even demanded to be taken to camp Number Fourteen if those were the orders. She didn't give a damn about her child, and she had friends in Number Fourteen. The warders, who showed no compunction at separating weeping women from their children, claimed to be shocked by her lack of maternal feeling, and chided her over it.

Our friend Yulia had a new problem to contend with. "Operative" Uchaykin had been showing an inordinate amount of interest in her lately, summoning her for talks over a cup of tea. He wanted Yulia to become one of his informers. As cups of tea are not much of an inducement, he found a much better form of persuasion—Article 188-3. Yulia is in PKT, and has five more months of her camp sentence to serve. So she will come out of PKT, and there will be nothing easier than to bring charges against her under this article and give her a few more years in the camps. During her time in this camp, Yulia had become close with one of the men from the LTP[1]—the Medical/Labor Unit, which is the official name for reform camps for alcoholics. That camp was adjacent to women's camp Number Two, on the other side of the fence. Yulia and her Evgeni met, fell in love, she gave birth to her Mashenka, and hoped to be out of the camp soon. Evgeni was due for release a month earlier, and he swore that he would take the baby from the children's home, wait for Yulia, and they would get married. Now all these hopes were threatened by Uchaykin. Later, he loved quoting Gorbachev's "there is no alternative!"

Yulia was no informer by nature. She wept while Uchaykin

1. *Lechebno Trudovoy Profilaktory.*

coerced her, she wept back in the cell. We did our best to comfort her, but what real comfort can there be in such a situation? Only with the feeble hope that not everyone who refuses to inform is invariably persecuted. The authorities don't lack for volunteers, alas. Uchaykin probably simply enjoyed tormenting Yulia—the sight of a young, weeping woman, ready to grovel at his feet, must have satisfied some perverted need in him. After these "chats," she would have cardiac spasms, but no medical aid was forthcoming. We used to pass Validol[2] tablets to her along the paper pipe, because at that time we were able to demand and receive medicines, so we made the most of our "privilege" while it lasted. I don't know what the outcome was, because we were taken from PKT when Yulia still had more than a month to go. How I hope that she managed to hold out, and that her life worked out as she had dreamed. But reality is rarely kind.

During our second month at PKT, the KGB began to suspect (not without reason) that the criminal prisoners were helping us to conduct secret correspondence. Their suspicions were heightened further when one of the warders spotted an exercise book with my poems in it in the neighboring cell. She saw this through the peephole in the door, so she couldn't see what was written, but just at that moment some of the girls were reading it, and someone said a few lines out loud. The warder then opened the food hatch in the door, and demanded that they give the book to her. They refused, knowing that she would never dare enter the cell alone. When she scurried off to get the duty deputy camp commandant, they quickly burned the exercise book and when officials came to search the cell about ten minutes later, maintained glibly that the poems had been all about love, and copied out by them from books from the camp library. The warder had frightened them, they said, so they burnt everything thinking that maybe having any materials about love was forbidden by regulations. Now they regret their action, and would like to apologize. Uchaykin ground his teeth audibly, but did not try to question us about the matter. Instead, he ordered an immediate thorough search of all the cells. The women in Number Four cell

2. A tranquilizer widely used in the Soviet Union.

panicked, and threw a love note received from someone in SHIZO into their slop bucket. Uchaykin happened to see this through the peephole, and ordered the immediate confiscation of the slop bucket and all its contents. The noisome receptacle was taken away for scrutiny. We almost died laughing, imagining Uchaykin fishing out scraps of paper from the stinking fluid of the slop bucket, and sending them off to be checked by the KGB. And the KGB, piecing them together into a little rectangle with the words: "Lucy, I love you more than life itself. Pass along a bit of tobacco to Number Two."

It may seem odd that we were doing such a lot of laughing under the circumstances, but this helped us to retain our sanity and, heaven knows, there was enough around to unbalance the most steady mind. There are genuinely insane people in the camps, and the atmosphere breeds psychopaths by the score. These poor souls suffer perhaps more than anyone in the camps. Over three years we got to know all the SHIZO "regulars," but the one we encountered most frequently was Kim, a Korean. We never actually saw her, but we heard her every time. Kim was really insane, and would become violent from time to time. She could not bear to be watched, but in the camps you're always under someone's eye. Kim would physically attack anyone whose eyes chanced to meet hers—and that would earn her yet another spell of SHIZO. The administration considered this easier than arranging treatment for her. Every time Kim would be taken away from the Zone to SHIZO, the other women in her brigade would breathe a sigh of relief; it's not the easiest thing in the world to live side by side with a madwoman, but they had no alternative. At the same time, the SHIZO inmates would howl with dismay: nobody wanted to be in the same cell with Kim, but then, nobody was interested in their likes and dislikes. Kim would be shoved into the first available cell, and it would not be long before you heard the first yells: "Supervisor! She's looking at me! Get me out of here before I tear her eyes out!"

The warder, waddling up to the cell, would remonstrate: "Pipe down, Kim, you're not going nowhere. And you girls, why're you watching her? You know she's a psycho."

"But nobody's looking at her, supervisor, she's imagining

things. Take her away from here, there's only six people in Number Eight, and we're already seven without her."

"Smart, aren't you?" Cell Number Eight would retort immediately. "Keep her for yourselves! Last time she was in here she knocked Manka's tooth out with a dish."

It would end with Kim attacking one of her cellmates. But she also had long periods of silence, when she would sit on the floor and stare at the wall. At those times it was impossible to make her get up and lie down on her bunk at lights out, nor did anyone care to try to force her; they were only too glad that she would be quiet for a day or two. Every time we arrived in SHIZO, the name "Kim" would be chalked on the door of one cell or another. Only on one occasion was her name missing, and we felt quite anxious.

"Hey, girls, where's Kim?" we asked our neighbors. "Is she still alive?"

"Yes, yes. They took her back to the Zone only yesterday."

Three days later, Kim was back in SHIZO. I still have occasional dreams in which I hear her frenzied, sexless and ageless voice yelling: "Supervisor! She's looking at me!"

Tanya and I, for all that we could barely stand after hunger strike, dysentery and SHIZO, were not as badly off as some of the others. There were only two of us in the cell, whereas the neighboring cells, which were supposed to hold four people, had as many as eleven crammed into them. As we were now serving PKT, we were visited by the prisoner who had been appointed librarian. Usually she would appear with a sack of books taken off the shelves at random, and shove two or three books into each cell for ten days. The books were often "about love" or "about war," without beginnings or endings, because the prisoners would rip out pages to roll cigarettes. The librarian respected politicals, and showed this by letting us make specific requests. The library had no catalogue, of course, so we just gave her lists of writers on the off-chance. The library's copies of Russian nineteenth-century classics were relatively unmutilated, and she would bring them to us ten volumes at a time. The warders made no demur: "They're intellectuals. Let 'em read. It's better than them writing complaints about this and that!"

So we passed the time reading, or by training mice. There was no way of getting rid of them, so we decided to amuse ourselves. On the one occasion during those two and a half months when they let us make purchases from the kiosk, we shared the candies and rusks we bought (there was nothing else in the kiosk) with our long-tailed friends: they needed a change from zek-issue bread, too. Fortunately, there were no rats in the SHIZO barracks, because there simply wasn't enough food for them. Their hunting ground was around the kitchens in the main zone.

Sharing a cell with Tanya was easy. In conditions where even some minor quirk of character could strain relations for both, there were never any problems with Tanya. I have lost count of the days we spent together in punishment cells. Nowadays, I often find myself looking at some new face and wondering: what would it be like to share prison skilly with you? Or carry out the slop bucket? Or conduct a hunger strike? How would you behave with the KGB? And, as a rule, the answer comes fairly quickly. This is not a deliberate exercise; it's the result of having had to assess people in extreme situations. Is this fair? Who knows . . .

That summer I completed my second collection of prison poems, and it was duly dispatched to Igor. I entitled this collection *Beyond the Limit*, the limit in question being the limit set for correspondence from PKT—one letter every two months, and even that's to be checked by the censors. So the challenge in the name of that collection was logical under the circumstances. I also amused Tanya and myself by writing a humorous "cookbook," a very relevant theme in our situation: "The author of this work has never engaged in keeping house on a regular basis. Nor has the author ever had occasion to feed any halfway decent people with halfway decent food. Indeed, the author's encounters with decent food have occurred mainly in literary works. Therefore, the author has obviously devoted a great deal of thought and feeling to tasty and healthy food, and knows everything about it that is worth knowing." This was followed by enough frivolous nonsense to fill a whole exercise book.

At the same time, we were acquiring a wealth of zek cunning:

how to pass a note from any cell to any other. The technicalities were incredible, including such aids as paper pipes, cotton thread, underwear elastic, pieces of soap, and much more. Forgive me, reader, for not describing the processes in detail. I promise to make a clean breast of it when there are no longer any punishment cells in my country.

Our neighbors, who knew everything there was to know about the alcoholics' zone and men's criminal camps, willingly answered our questions with some hair-raising details. I would not have believed some of these stories had not Igor been told the same things, quite independently, by zeks he encountered on his trips to Mordovia. One such amazing story explained how zeks manage to get strictly forbidden alcohol into the camps. The more "trustworthy" criminals are taken daily to work on sites outside the camp: doing their bit to get the agriculture of the Motherland going, chop wood for the bosses, wash dishes and so on. At night, they are marched back to their zone, and manage to bring in up to three liters of alcohol without its being found. How do they manage that? There is a special complex system to carry out this operation. A condom is hermetically attached to a long piece of thin plastic tubing. The zek then swallows it, leaving only one end of the tube in his mouth. To avoid swallowing it by accident, he wedges it in between two teeth: there are not likely to be any zeks in existence with a full set of thirty-two teeth. Then, with the help of a syringe, up to three liters of spirit are pumped into the condom via the plastic tubing—and the zek goes back to his zone. If the bonding has been badly done, or if the condom happens to burst in the zek's stomach, that means certain and painful death. Despite it, they run the risk: three liters of spirit makes seven liters of vodka! When the "hero" returns to the zone, his impatiently waiting cronies start the "emptying" process. He is hung head-down from a beam under the barracks roof and the end of the plastic tubing is held over a dish until every drop has been retrieved. Then the empty condom is hauled out; it's done its job, and the whole barracks binges.

There were times when it seemed to me that the normal human world no longer existed, and that I was living in a huge mental asylum. At such times, Tanya and I would engage in lengthy debates about the precise definition of what it is that constitutes a human being. We were never able to reach a definition that would earn an unqualified "yes," but these debates made us feel a bit better.

38

There was a wonderful surprise awaiting us when we returned to the Zone at the end of August: this previously unprepossessing patch had been transformed into a fragrant garden. The paths we had helped to start laying were now complete, and just as they should be: thirty centimeters of stone chips, covered with a layer of sand. These were probably the only paths in the entire camp that didn't turn into a quagmire every time it rained. The outdoor fireplace and the "cellar" were finished, too. The high surrounding wall proved to have advantages as well; we could go behind the house to take the sun, and nobody could see us. Every inch of ground had been raked over, fertilized and watered. Beans were trained along the fence; the warders had no idea what they were, so they didn't pull them out. Wild chives and dill were skillfully camouflaged by clumps of flowers. Some clover had already pushed up, so we were able to use it for salads. The others joked that all we needed now was a swimming pool. As for our warders—they seemed to take more pride in the achievements of the Zone than anyone else; when we arrived in the guardroom from SHIZO, they assured us that we would not recognize the Zone when we saw it. After unlocking the gate, they hopped through first and turned to see the expressions on our faces. I hope they were satisfied. The creative abilities of the politicals became legend in their midst, and I fear that our achievements were used as an instrument in denigrating the denizens of the criminal zone: "You should see what the politicals have managed to do with their zone. And all you manage to breed is dirt and rats. Useless, that's what you are!"

At first, Shalin and his satellites tried to establish good relations with the Zone: they didn't cancel anyone's kiosk rights, and Pani Lida and Pani Jadvyga were granted simultaneous long-awaited meetings with their relatives. For this occasion we had superb flowers, and prepared bouquets for each to give to her loved ones. Tanya and I found ourselves swamped with food; the others had put aside everything that would keep during our two and a half months' absence. There was bad news, too. Pani Lida's "sewing salon" had been closed down. When Vladimirova was in Saransk, she tattled to the KGB that the warders had Pani Lida sewing bits and pieces for them, and produced evidence to back her story: a few scraps of warders' uniform material, which she had sneaked when nobody was looking. I have no idea why she should have done this, for she had nothing to gain from informing on Pani Lida. But then, who can really understand an informer's mentality? The warders were officially reprimanded, ordered not to retaliate against Vladimirova in any way, and strictly forbidden to have Pani Lida make anything for them in future. They told us about this with considerable bitterness, but we'd had no illusions about our "stoolie" anyway. Furthermore, the KGB in Saransk slipped Vladimirova drugs. Olya and Raya, who shared her cell, told us about Vladimirova coming back from "talking" to the KGB and barely being able to stand on her feet: eyes unfocused, dilated pupils, muttering nonsense and unable to find her bunk . . . How on earth could we cope with her? We allotted her some space for her own vegetable patch, to keep her from underfoot, and tried to keep as much distance between her and ourselves as possible. We continued to evade her efforts to spy on us by working at night and giving her an equal share of any small packages received in the Zone. She vacillated between pestering us with conversations and enacting hysterical scenes. Shalin listened calmly to all her threats to "do us in," but made no efforts to silence her; probably this was all part of the "program" devised for us.

Our return to the Zone signalled a wave of searches. We had to contend with them practically every day. They pulled up the floorboards, poked around in the sewage pipes, went through all our papers . . . They never found what they were looking for, but the searches were carried out with a conscientiousness that would have been better applied to other spheres. While all this was going on, we continued sending information out of the Zone, copies of our declarations and my poems. It would not have been surprising if our jailers had given up their theory that we had a concealed radio and decided that we were resorting to mental telepathy. They were especially upset by the congratulatory message sent by the Zone to President Reagan on the occasion of his re-election. We had reasoned that if the Soviet government sends felicitations to a re-elected President in the name of our people (and that includes us), why shouldn't we send a personal message as well? Why leave it to Chernenko? So we wrote a very diplomatic message of good will and signed it. Reagan received this small piece of paper quite soon: I believe it was two days after his re-election. If you take into account the fact that Tanya and I—who were the top suspects of clandestine correspondence with the world outside the camp—were both in SHIZO at the time, and none of the others in the Zone had had any meetings with relatives for more than three months, what was the bewildered KGB to think? We found out that our message reached Reagan when the KGB came thundering into the Zone to berate us about it. This was very amusing, really: that we received detailed feedback by courtesy of the KGB about the success of our undertakings. It was from the KGB, too, that I first learned that my poetry was being published in the West. "You tell us a few things we'd like to know, Irina Borisovna," they suggested, "and we'll show you books of your poems . . ." Of course, that was no inducement: who knows my poetry better than I? But I was very grateful for the free information; a small thing, but pleasant.

Life went on, and we had no particular problems until autumn brought frequent strong winds. You may wonder why people living in a new building should worry about the wind. The reason is that these winds kept on bringing down the power lines, and the camp would be left without electricity. That meant no light for indefinite periods of time, but the main problem was that hot water for the heating was pumped to us from the hospital zone by an electrically driven motor. So no light also meant no heating. How we missed our solid fuel stoves in the old Zone at such times. They may have been falling apart, but at least they generated some warmth. Now, however, we were totally dependent on the housekeeping talents of our administration, and it's hard to imagine anything less efficient: they can only be described as "nil minus." Mind you, the heating was not much even when it functioned, because there was a chronic shortage of coal for such purposes. To ease the situation, Arapov brought us a "goat"—a portable electric heater which we lugged from room to room to take the chill off the air, at least. Circumstances compelled us to take up candlemaking. Galya would cadge paraffin wax from the medics to make hot poultices for her aching joints. We made wicks by rolling cotton thread, ran them through plastic tubes (made out of discarded reels from our work), then poured in heated paraffin wax. We used these candles for reading, writing letters, and for getting about the Zone when it was plunged in darkness. "Well, at least my illness is proving to be of some use," remarked Galya wryly.

When I say that there were no particular problems, I mean in the physical, day-to-day life of the Zone; the confiscation of letters for months on end, fear for our loved ones, the unceasing efforts not to sink into that colorless, bottomless pit that is called melancholy all continued as usual. Tanya received only two of the letters written by her husband from his Perm camp. Galya received more notifications of letters "confiscated due to suspect contents" than actual letters from her Vasili. She tried to dispute these confiscations, pointing out that her husband's letters would have been passed by his Perm camp censors, but to no avail. Do different censors follow different rules? No, the simple fact is that censors obey no rules—if they feel like allowing a letter through, they will, and if not, then not. Whether they want to or not is, in turn, decided by the KGB, and prisoners are not entitled to any explanations. You may write a twenty-page letter and several days later receive an official notification stating that your letter has been confiscated because its contents "may lend themselves to more than one interpretation."

"But there's nothing like that in it."

"Well, we think there is."

"Show me which lines you object to, and I'll rewrite the letter without them."

"You know perfectly well what we mean."

The real reason is that the KGB is carrying out its own plans, and they don't include Igor getting any letters from me at this stage. In the next step, when he has lived through several months of mounting anxiety, he will be summoned for a "chat," during which he'll be told that I must be saved, that he knows just how bad my condition is, and that if something isn't done soon, I'll never survive to the end of my seven-year term in the camps. Therefore, if he will only be frank with them, they just may be able to alleviate my situation . . .

Actually, Igor was very frank with them: he told them exactly what he thought of them, omitting nothing. But they don't take offense; they have plenty of time, after all. Let him kick now, they reason, and in a year's time he may sing a different tune. As for correspondence—well, it's an avenue of mutual influence, so it's better to reduce it to a minimum. Twenty-four letters a year from one's wife would be overdoing it, wouldn't it?

But occasionally letters were confiscated because the censors found them genuinely suspicious, and then they would condescend to explain. For instance, in one of my letters I poked fun at Igor and wrote something teasing about beards and whiskers. The poor censor was quite convinced that I was referring to the whiskers and beard of the father of Marxism-Leninism! She made no secret of her suspicions: "Your letter is confiscated because it mocks Karl Marx." Truly mysterious are the ways of censors' thoughts: it does not occur to her that anyone can be bearded and bewhiskered apart from their beloved ideologists! I brought her a photo of Igor, and she slapped herself on the forehead: "Goodness, now I remember giving you that photo myself. I'd clean forgotten that your husband has a beard." And my letter was allowed through.

Those who were from the Baltic states had additional problems. They were not allowed to write in their native languages,
because the Mordovian KGB could not read them, poor creatures.
So the KGB made its demands known: "Write in Russian only."

"Why should I write to my son in a foreign language?" asked
Pani Jadvyga.

"So that the censors can read it."

"I don't write letters for the censors. If you're so anxious to
read my mail, find a translator."

The KGB threatened to confiscate all letters not written in
Russian, but that got the whole Zone up in arms: we were quite
prepared to enter into a serious conflict. We would either all
refuse correspondence, or go on another strike. The KGB retreated. They sent off non-Russian letters to be translated somewhere or other, and the censors had to work with translated texts.
As a result, it took one of Pani Jadvyga's letters more than four
months to reach the addressee, and three months was the norm.

They tried the same demands with meetings: "Either you'll
speak Russian, or not at all. We have no interpreters here."

"Fine," said Pani Jadvyga, "I'll not speak at all then. But I
won't talk to my relatives in Russian. I'll simply tell them that I
can't speak to them in our own language, and spend the rest of the
meeting with my mouth shut."

The KGB realized that if something like that should happen, it
would be tantamount to a political demonstration which would
quickly become known all over Lithuania, so they had to retreat
again: "Very well, then, speak however you like."

But meetings with relatives were such a rare occurrence that
during that autumn and winter we had no occasion to think about
them. I was due for a meeting at the beginning of November, but
it was a foregone conclusion that the meeting would be cancelled;
October 30 is Political Prisoners' Day, so we would be observing
the traditional hunger strike, and that meant that on the day of
my scheduled meeting I would be in SHIZO. And that's exactly
what happened. By this time, however, I was able to take cancelled meetings calmly. I had learned a bitter lesson the last time:
just how dangerous it is, in the camps, to let something become
the focus of your desires. It makes you vulnerable, and threatens

to throw you off course. Lagle formulated the position very clearly: "You have to live in the conviction that you will be granted no meetings at all. If they let you have one—well and good; but if they don't—too bad. Our behavior has nothing to do with whether we get meetings or not, so there's no sense in breaking our necks."

She was quite right, and this became the attitude of the whole Zone. We greeted all notices about deprivations of various kinds with jokes. The relevant notifications, delivered by Shalin, we called "candies." We protested, of course, but without agonizing. We could go on strike or hunger strike—but we did it with a smile. And we smiled when they marched us off to punishment cells.

39

On the eve of October 30, Tanya and I were suddenly told to prepare for transportation. They did not say where they intended taking us, but assured us that it was not to SHIZO. None of us knew what to think. Pani Jadvyga, in a burst of optimism, suggested that we might be sent to the West in exchange for Soviet spies or some latter-day Luis Corvalán.[1] But that seemed too far-fetched, nor did either of us wish to be currency for the Soviet regime to purchase its captured spies. At least by sitting in camp we were being of some use, if only be proving that one can bear anything and not recant one's convictions. Even women. And if women can do so, then the more shame to those men who are too cowardly to try. And if the men in our country can overcome their fear, then our situation is bound to change for the better beyond all imagining.

Still, we knew that in such exchanges nobody asks the people involved whether they want to be the pawns or not. We assumed that we were being taken off for another session of "re-education." It was rather a bleak prospect: twenty-four hours on hunger strike during transportation would tax our physical resources greatly. The others stuffed broth cubes into

1. Luis Corvalan was First Secretary of the Communist Party of Chile, and imprisoned for his convictions and activities. The Chilean government let him go to the USSR in 1976 in exchange for the release to the West of Russian political prisoner Vladimir Bukovsky.

our bags, made the sign of the cross over us—Catholic and Orthodox style—in both directions.

The search in the guardroom was quite cursory: strange. We had no inkling of where we were being taken until we arrived in the Potma transit prison. We were put into a cell for "state criminals due for release" (that's what it said on the sign on the door) and left there. The cell was tiny. It contained two bunks, one above the other, a slop bucket and a bedside table, everything so crammed in that there was barely room to move. The beds, however, had blankets. Luxury! But why the devil did they bring us here? And where will we be going? Potma prison is only for transit, after all. Well, whatever lies ahead, we seize the opportunity to lie down and rest. Only now do we realize how exhausted we are.

In the morning we write an official notification about our hunger strike, with a brief explanation of the significance of Political Prisoners' Day. We return our breakfast untouched. An hour later, a young local officer comes to our cell: "What's the matter with you women? Hunger strike, indeed! Are you having such a hard time here?"

We explain the situation, about the traditions of prisoners of conscience and about our Zone's position.

"And you think that will change anything? Yes, I can see everything that goes on just as well as you can, and it makes me sick. Everyone knows the situation, but what can anyone do about it?"

We talk some more in this vein. The young officer demonstrates understanding: "All right, if you must write an official declaration about your hunger strike, go ahead. But why actually do it? Nobody will ever know. I've got some sugar here for you, some corned beef and some white bread . . . "

We refuse his offerings, and explain everything once again . . . Oh, how many times we had to give similar explanations over the years! The officer leaves, but returns a couple of hours later with a young male prisoner. "Here, women, I've brought this fine young lad for you. If you like, I'll leave him here for a couple of hours and you can have a bit of fun. And here's some food as well."

The offer was more than a *double entendre*. I know it sounds incredible, and would probably not have written about it, certain that nobody would believe me, but there is a living witness to back up my words—Tanya Osipova, who now lives in New York, and who sat there beside me, open-mouthed with amazement, on the lower bunk. We refuse as tactfully as we can.

"What, you don't fancy him? I can bring you another one if you want."

Striving to be as polite as possible, we say that the young man is wonderful (why hurt the poor fellow's feelings?) but that it would be against our moral principles . . . And hear again the expected question: "Religious believers, are you?"

"Yes, yes!" we chorus.

Tanya did not consider herself a believer, but this was no time for theological discussion. As soon as the cell door closed behind our guests, we collapsed on the bunk in fits of laughter. Who on earth thought this whole thing up? How did they visualize the practical enactment of their scenario? Having laughed our fill, we noticed a considerable drop in the temperature in the cell. I cannot say whether this was a mere coincidence, but the heating pipes remained stone cold that day. Even now, when Tanya and I discuss this episode, we are unable to decide whether that officer had simply wanted to tempt us with all those things which are usually unattainable for zeks in order to sink our hunger strike, or whether he was acting out of the goodness of his heart on a genuine, if misguided, impulse to do us a good turn, as he saw it. Who can say? A mystery it was, and a mystery it remains.

For some reason, I found this one-day hunger strike more difficult than any other. I kept feeling as though my heart would stop beating at any moment. I lay on the bunk as quietly as I could and concentrated on breathing. Tanya's condition was a little better, but she was terribly worried about me: we had conducted so many hunger strikes, often lasting much longer than a day, but none of them had ever affected me like this. However, we survived until morning, even though we froze to the marrow of our bones. We dissolved a broth cube in a mug of hot water, ate a crust of bread each . . . Then they came and took us to a cell for criminal prisoners awaiting release, to wash before resuming our travels. Naturally, we were not told our destination. The cell to which we were brought was empty of people and contained some twenty to twenty-five bunks. It didn't resemble a cell all that much. Of course, the door was locked and the window was barred, but there was a mirror on one wall, and an ironing board and an iron as well as a toilet and a wash basin . . . It was also unusually clean. Yet for some reason, that room struck me as one of the most frightening places I have ever been in.

Maybe it was because so many thousands of women must have stayed in it upon completing their sentences. They are brought here to Potma from all the camps, held until the legal expiry of their term—and at 6:00 a.m. on the designated day, released with an attesting document and a directive to their place of residence. What did they think about on their last night in prison? Did many of them really have somewhere to return, was anyone waiting for them? I had already heard how on release days lots of local women gather at the prison gates and sell moonshine vodka for triple the usual cost, so the newly released can celebrate their liberty on the spot. Many of them get drunk and find themselves in the hands of the militia again, without even having left Potma. Others reach the railway station and try to steal the first thing that catches their eye, out of reflex rather than need. And earn a new term of imprisonment. The ones who have no homes to return to are directed to the factories and building sites of our vast country, where they have to live in so-called workers' hostels where ten to fifteen people are crammed into one room. No chance to be alone to gather oneself together, no privacy, and certainly no chance to acquire a family. This drives them to look for "something better," and their efforts bring them back to Potma, heading for a new camp to serve a new sentence . . . As for those who have families to go back to—the luckiest and happiest of the lot—how will they settle back into their old life? Tired, embittered, psychologically disturbed and branded "jailbirds"— how will they be able to stand on their own feet again?

How many faces were reflected in this mirror before ours? How many dresses, which had lain in store for years, has this iron smoothed? How many dreams have been absorbed by these

shabby pillows? And, maybe, how many tears? Who has not com-
forted a weeping woman with the words: "Come, now, don't cry!
The worst is over." But that's why she weeps, because it's over.
The tears are the release of earlier horror and earlier exhaustion.
Leave her alone, let her weep. She'll feel better for it.

No, there was no joy in the air of that room, and we made
haste to move away from the mirror.

They loaded us into a *stolypin* railway carriage, and off we
went again. Where? We couldn't even begin to guess. But how we
burst out laughing when, several hours later, we alighted again in
our very own Barashevo! So the whole farce had been concocted
merely to get us out of the Zone for the day of the hunger strike.
The KGB probably decided that we were the ringleaders, and
hoped that the hunger strike would fall through if we were not
there. It didn't, of course, and the others greeted us happily as we
swapped notes. The administration had tried to convince them
yesterday that Tanya and I had called off our hunger strike, and
pointed to us as a good model for the others to emulate. How
cheap can you get? That evening there was hot water, so I took
advantage of it to wash my hair. I had just worked up a lather
when a warder came stamping in: "Ratushinskaya! Where the
hell are you? Fifteen days in SHIZO for hunger-striking! You've
got fifteen minutes to get ready."

I managed to rinse the soap out of my hair, but it was still wet
when I climbed into the frost-covered van. Tanya was also given
fifteen days, but they left the others alone for the time being. That
is, they didn't send them to SHIZO, just cancelled meetings with
family and their rights to use the camp kiosk. They were also
warned that any hunger-striking on December 10 (Human Rights
Day) would result in SHIZO for everyone.

Meanwhile, Tanya and I were back in the by-now familiar
SHIZO cell, with Mashka the mouse poking her sharp little nose
out of her hole in the skirting board, and neighbors banging on the
pipe and calling out greetings. They stripped us very thoroughly:
all we were allowed were the SHIZO smocks on our otherwise
naked bodies. I was feeling extremely ill—probably I'd caught a
chill. I lay flush up against the heating pipes, but to no avail,

because they were cold. I fell into a delirious fever; in that delirium, I kept feeling that I was being drawn into the shapeless stain on one of the walls, and clutched at the pipe to avoid being sucked into that dark patch. A day or two later—I can't remember for sure—Tanya's shouts and demands eventually brought a doctor, who took my temperature, gasped, and ordered that I be given a jacket. Out of the first ten days of that spell in SHIZO, all I can recall is seeing Tanya blocking the holes in the window frames with the soggy prison bread. At that stage, cold posed a greater danger to us than hunger. It took Tanya two days, and all the bread issued in that time, to block the holes. How she found the strength—I don't know. More than a year later, sitting in PKT, I was to do the same (only on that occasion we managed to get the prison staff to issue us some putty) and realized just how much effort that job entails: you have to hang from one hand, poking the other through the mesh in front of the window to reach the blasted gaps between the glass and the frame. Occasionally, your hand would get stuck in the mesh, and you would spend many painful minutes trying to free it. It took a week for the bruises and lacerations to fade from my wrist. I don't know how that stretch of SHIZO would have ended for me had Tanya not been there. A week later, the heating came on; the trouble turned out to be nothing more than an air bubble. It could have been fixed in a trice: all it took was for a workman to come to the cell for fifteen minutes, unscrew a bolt, let the trapped air out and drain off a bucket of dirty water. However, it was a week before the KGB agreed to assume the heavy responsibility of letting a workman enter a cell occupied by two dangerous state criminals. We spent the remaining days against the relatively warm pipes, I dutifully swallowed the tablets prescribed by the doctor, and my condition began to improve. Of course, they immediately took away the jacket issued earlier, and I must have looked a very sorry sight when—I think it was the last day of my SHIZO—they took me along for a talk with Tyurin, one of the KGB officers. Not only did my SHIZO smock have a plunging ballgown neckline, but it had a big tear down the front. The result was than any movement made it slide off one shoulder or the other. Pins and needles are not allowed in SHIZO, so there was no way of fastening the garment to make it a bit more decent.

The warder who escorted me from the cell shook her head wonderingly: "Just like Zoya Kosmodemyanskaya,"[2] she pronounced.

It was a matter of total indifference to me whether Tyurin would be shamed by my appearance or not. If he thought I would be discomposed, he was due for a disappointment. I was prepared for much worse things than that, thanks to having read Solzhenitsyn's *Gulag Archipelago*. I maintained my usual silence while he told me how the KGB has my best interests at heart, that any problems are due solely to my recalcitrance, and returned to my cell. For some reason, Tanya was spared a session with the KGB this time. Very likely they thought they could bend me when I had been weakened by the fever.

My meeting with Igor was cancelled on the pretext that on such-and-such a day and at such-and-such an hour I had been "talking on the pipe" to the neighbors, but on the day in question I had been unconscious and was in no state to say a word, even to Tanya, let alone to anyone in the neighboring cell. But that, naturally, is a petty detail, unworthy of the Procuracy's valuable time. The reason for the cancellation of the meeting is unimportant; what is important is to have the official cancellation order.

During this spell of SHIZO, our neighbors from the criminal zone amused us by telling us about a favorite activity—almost a sport—among those due for release. Their entire Zone detested regime supervisor Ryzhova, and not without cause. Apart from her greed for bribes and similar pleasant characteristics, Ryzhova had a fixation about women's underpants. In SHIZO and in the camp zone alike, she was obsessed with lifting up the women's skirts and checking that they had not put on a second pair of pants against the cold. If someone had, then Ryzhova would yank them off with her own hands. The girls would grit their teeth and wait, but on the eve of release, they would stop holding back and

2. Zoya Kosmodemyanskaya was one of the heroines of World War II. She took part in guerrilla actions against the Germans after the German invasion of the USSR, and was captured, tortured and then hanged by the Nazis.

hurl as many obscenities as they could think of at Ryzhova during line-up for inspection. There was nothing anyone could do to stop them, not even put them into SHIZO, because they had to be transported to Potma. The administration thought they had found a way to avert such scandals by putting them into SHIZO ten days prior to release, but the women simply poured out their abuse at Ryzhova two weeks earlier. If they were going to be put in punishment cell anyway, they reasoned, there was no need to forgo the pleasure of foul-mouthing Ryzhova. We heard about this "tradition" from Lyuba and Katya, who were in the opposite cell, Number Eight, for that very reason. They repeated, word for word, what they had said to Ryzhova, and all the other cells joined in the fun of devising what they would say to Ryzhova when their turn came.

We returned to the Zone and took up the reins of our usual camp life. All of us had, by this time, developed our own fields of expertise: Pani Jadvyga became a specialist on the medicinal properties of plants and medical advice; Raya—on gardening; Natasha—on repairs of all kinds, irons, the heater and so forth; Pani Lida—on sewing; Galya—on laundering (that winter we managed to get the administration to give us an ancient washing machine, and grappling with it was not an easy task); my specialties were embroidery and hairdressing; Lagle was our expert on design and building work. We had little sewing to do at that time because of constant power failures. Vasili Petrovich, unlike the monsters in Number Two, did not demand that we turn the wheels of the sewing machines by hand. I think he would have been honestly offended by such methods of operating an electric sewing machine.

Having no expectation of being able to conduct a regular correspondence with Igor, I tried an experiment with the text of the last letter written by the French poet Robert Desnos, which I found in one issue of the journal *Foreign Literature (Inostrannaya Literatura)*. Desnos wrote this letter to his wife from Flossenburg concentration camp, where he died several months before the end of World War II. The Nazi censors had allowed this letter through. I thought it would be interesting to find out how our camp censors would react to it. To allow the KGB some odds, I did not reproduce the whole letter, only the very beginning, and the closing sentence: "I send you as many kisses as will be allowed by the censors who will read this letter." Then I addressed it to Igor. The letter was confiscated, of course, all three lines of it! The Zone laughed about this for a long time.

On December 10 they really did send everyone to SHIZO, including our two Panis. Everyone except Olya, that is. She was merely deprived of kiosk rights. This was a tactical move on the part of the KGB, calculated to make us suspect Olya of having "earned" leniency. Edita and Vladimirova took no part in the hunger strike, Raya was on hunger strike unofficially, so their situation was quite clear. But our "reformers" could not resist the temptation to try to drive a wedge between Olya and the rest of us. Because of personal traits of character, relations occasionally became strained, and those KGB idiots thought they could exploit this and provoke a serious conflict. We could see through their unsavory schemes, and did our best to reassure Olya before they took us away. We knew that under the circumstances she would suffer more than anyone else. Olya, however, had no intention of accepting the situation meekly, and declared a hunger strike that very day, demanding that either they send her to SHIZO with us, or at least release our two pensioners. The following day she was informed that her next meeting was cancelled, and four days later she joined us in SHIZO. Theoretically, she came off worse than anyone; we received no notification of cancelled meetings and kiosk rights. But as we all shared any purchases from the kiosk as a matter of course, and there was nobody to come to visit Olya (her husband was imprisoned and her parents too old and frail to make the journey), Olya merely chuckled about it. Her hunger strike discouraged the KGB from any further efforts at intrigues of this nature.

The "highlight" of this particular SHIZO spell was the administration's effort to stamp out religious singing. Galya and Pani Lida had already become a very accomplished duet at singing psalms and hymns, and what better occupation can there be in a SHIZO cell than to praise the Lord? The regime supervisors, who never objected to the most lewd ditties sung by the criminal prisoners, were terribly incensed: "Stop that at once!" They stormed and threatened, but they had chosen the wrong targets for their wrath: Pani Lida and Galya were both perfectly prepared to accept punishment for singing psalms.

Those of us not endowed with musical talent entered the fray: "What is it you object to? The fact that they're singing, or that they're singing religious songs?"

It must have been the latter; had our friends started singing some popular rubbish, nobody would have said a word. But our administration could hardly admit to political prisoners that the objection was to songs about God, and risk this fact being publicized by Western media a week later. So they tried to wriggle out by claiming that prisoners are not supposed to sing at all, unless they do so as part of approved "independent amateur group activities."

"Fine!" we responded. "We hereby form an independent amateur group for the study and performance of spiritual songs."

"Such groups can only be organized by the camp management."

"Why are they called 'independent,' then?"

"Women—you talk too much."

An unbeatable argument, that. And, indeed, why bother trading words with them? It's better to sing. But just let them try to do anything to our singers! I swear that if they had done so, we would all have started singing, voices or no voices. The administration, however, did not go beyond threats. So the words of hymns and psalms sounded sweetly in the echoing corridors of the SHIZO block, and the criminal prisoners joined in once they managed to pick up the unfamiliar words.

Lagle, Tanya and I returned to the Zone on Christmas Eve. Galya, both Panis and Natasha were already back, as they had been given fewer days in SHIZO. Olya remained behind. Before parting from her we slipped her as much clothing as we could from our own things—tights, undershirts, and when she put them on, we wound our towels around her. She could barely move by the time we were through, but the extra clothes were not outwardly noticeable: she was so dreadfully thin that all her ribs protruded. "The heat won't do them any harm!" we joked. We kissed her goodbye and the van rolled away over a powdering of Christmas snow. It broke down halfway and it took our cursing escort an hour to get it moving again. Meanwhile, teeth chattering, we froze in this metal box of a vehicle. Still, we got there eventually, to find dinner awaiting us.

We gather around the table, and the words of the Lord's Prayer ring out in Lithuanian, Latvian, Russian and Ukrainian, although Orthodox Christmas[3] is still to come. Pani Jadvyga divides up a Communion wafer from Lithuania, so that there is a bit for everyone. This wafer, no thicker than a sheet of paper, was sent to her by relatives in an envelope. The censor let it through; either she had no idea what it was, or refrained from confiscating it without a direct order to do so. "Silent night, holy night," sing Galya and Pani Lida in two languages. And we, despite our various creeds, never doubted for a moment that God was looking down on us all at that moment. Then we pray for Olya, that she, too, might be eased in her solitude: that she would not be too cold, that she would not succumb to sadness.

We could only marvel at the dinner prepared by our friends; we knew how little they'd had to work with.

On New Year's Eve we sang traditional carols called *Kolyadki* at which Olya (who had returned by that time) excelled. We also observed the ancient Slav ritual of "sowing," as we chanted: "Sow, grow, rye and wheat, for happiness and health, for the New Year . . ." We had no wheat, of course, so we used crumbs of bread . . . We even had a small but real Christmas tree: Vasili Petrovich brought it for us when he delivered that last batch of gloves. We decorated this tree as best we could.

3. In accordance with the Julian calendar, the Russian Orthodox Church celebrates Christmas on January 7.

40

It was January, and the frosts which are always linked with the Feast of the Epiphany were severe. Tanya, Olya and I decided to observe all the national traditions which accompany this feast. From time immemorial, both in Russia and Ukraine, the custom was to pour water over oneself while standing in the snow, or to dip into a river through a hole cut in the ice. Folk tradition maintains that this will bring good health, and none need fear that it will cause so much as a cold. Our elders, hearing about our scheme, only shook their heads despairingly. Still, they made no serious efforts to dissuade us: if that's what we want, what's the point of arguing? There are times when one moment of pleasure is more beneficial than any medical precautions. Moreover Tatyana Mikhailovna Velikanova, who was old enough to be our mother, always doused herself from the Zone well on Epiphany, and it did her no harm . . . We have enough other causes to catch cold: Olya's been in a punishment cell, and Tanya and I are in and out of SHIZO all the time . . .

We were undeterred by the lack of a well in our new Zone. After lights out, when all the others had gone to bed, we dragged buckets of water and a tub into the snow outside, and set them down among the drifts. The frost fairly crackled, but the stars were unbelievably bright, and we felt so excited on this special night. We checked the outside temperature with a small thermometer Igor had managed to get smuggled through to me. Not bad. Twenty-five degrees below zero! But our heads are full of intoxicating, youthful daring: nothing can happen to us on a night like this. Our scheme is to strip naked, run through the snow to the buckets and tub, pour a couple of buckets of water over ourselves, then back into the house to dry off and get warm. Tanya goes first. She runs back, soaking wet and laughing happily. Heavens, even her hair is wet!

I'm next. The snow burns my bare feet, the stars laugh at my protruding ribs, and joy bursts inside me like a small firecracker. Here are the buckets. The water feels quite warm. To avoid spilling water on the path (it's my turn to clear it tomorrow) I jump into a snowdrift, and empty the bucket over myself there. After a searing moment, I no longer feel cold. Turning, I run back to the house. Halfway there I am unable to stop myself from waltzing instead of running. Tanya throws a towel over my shoulders. We do not need to look for reasons to laugh this night.

Olya sprints off, and is gone for quite a while. Suddenly, something white and thin raps on the window. It's Olya: she can't find the buckets of water (they had been set out by Tanya and me), and she had run in the wrong direction! Where are they? she asks from outside. Tanya gives her precise instructions, and in a few minutes Olya is back in the house, soaking wet and (we don't believe our eyes) with roses in her cheeks! After drying ourselves, we brew tea. The compassionate duty Cinderella had given us some tea leaves for the night with the words: "So that you lunatics can at least get warm when you've finished dousing yourselves." What we talked and laughed about—I don't remember. Then we recalled that another Epiphany folk custom is fortune telling: putting mirrors face to face "to see the future" in them, pouring wax, burning paper and looking at the silhouettes it casts on the wall to see what they resemble.

> Once upon Epiphany eve
> Young girls guessed their futures
> Taking off their little shoes,
> Cast them o'er the fence . . .

We are all staid married women, of course, and instead of "little shoes" we have only soldiers' tarpaulin boots. Yet I must confess that three such boots were sailing out of the door a minute after we remembered this custom. We know the points of the compass by the sunrises and sunsets. We pull out our old atlas to see where the toes of our "little shoes" are pointing. Olya's boot points toward Ukraine, Tanya's points to some place east (exile, maybe? Her term expires in the spring) and mine, quite plainly, in the direction of Yavas, where camp Number Two is located with its SHIZO and PKT cells. But this does not diminish our fun. Next, we put two fly-blown mirrors facing each other in a dark room, set out a candle on both sides (all strictly according to the rules!) and peer into the murky corridor of reflected flames:

> My destined groom,
> Come dine with me!

It seems to me that I saw a movement of something light at the other end. But maybe I'm imagining things?

No, we were not out of our minds that Epiphany eve. We were just—young . . . And as tradition maintains, we came to no harm, not one of us developed so much as a sniffle. Our "little shoes," however, foretold the future more precisely than we could have wished. Olya really did go to the Ukraine next autumn, and then returned under special KGB escort. Her father died, and she was allowed to visit his grave and have a meeting with her grief-stricken mother. Tanya was given an additional sentence of two years when her term expired—for her hunger strikes—under the nefarious Article 188-3. She was taken east, to the criminal camp at Ishimbay. As for me—I had three more "tours" in SHIZO that year, and I greeted the following year, 1986, in solitary confinement in PKT. In the meantime, my "destined groom" was reproducing my poetry in *samizdat*, passing the *Chronicle of the Small Zone* to the West, appealing to Western parliamentarians. He had to defend himself physically against the KGB, who, in the Ukraine, are particularly fond of "re-educating" dissidents by physical assault. He left three of them lying on the ground, wondering what had hit them—karate is a useful thing to know! On that occasion, he had a collection of my poems hidden inside his jacket, a collection he had just received and of which only that one copy existed. Had they managed to overpower and search him, these poems would surely have been confiscated. He had good reason to fight.

Years later, we were asked in one house in England: "To what do you feel allegiance?"

And we answered: "To human rights."

41

The snow still swept across our Zone, and there were still no letters from home. But we knew that we were not forgotten, either at home or abroad. The only difference was that it was more dangerous for Soviet citizens to remember us, and even more perilous to try to do anything to help us.

A week after my arrest, the poet Elena Sannikova arrived in Kiev, and read my poetry for the first time. We are of the same generation, and have a similar understanding of Russian literary traditions. These traditions bind one to a certain code of behavior—to our grief and to our joy. Even though she was sentenced to a year in the camps to be followed by five years' internal exile, Elena had no regrets that she had signed petitions in my defense, talked about my poetry to foreign journalists, and retyped my poems and my biography for the *samizdat* collection which figured in the indictment at her trial.

Her period under investigation and trial lasted more than ten months, and the sentence was such that the only place where they could send her would be our Small Zone. In other words, she would spend several months with us (the period under investigation is deducted from the sentence) and would then go into exile, armed with the latest information about our Zone. For obvious reasons, the KGB was very reluctant to let this happen. It was vital for them to find some other way of holding her for the time remaining before her exile term came into effect. Elena insisted that she be sent to join us: the law is the law, she pointed out, and that's where she should be. But let Elena tell her own story. The following is extracted from a letter written by her:

> After the trial, I was anxiously awaiting transportation, fearing that time would run out before I could reach your Zone. They lied to me from day to day, saying that transportation was imminent. Subsequent events showed these lies to be deliberate. First of all, they kept putting off the date when my sentence was to come into effect. The official notification of the sentence being in force was brought to me more than a month after the trial. Then followed a seemingly endless period of waiting, and for the first time I began to feel that I was not free, it was as though the feeling of inner liberty was slipping away. Only after I started lodging two official complaints a day did they finally make any move to transport me to the camp. They kept me in Potma transit prison for ten days. When I finally arrived in the guardroom of Barashevo camp, I could hardly believe that I'd made it. So you can imagine how shocked I was when they took me through into the hospital compound and locked me up in one of the so-called wards. I had forgotten completely about the "quarantine" regulations!

Not surprisingly, this quarantine was implemented especially for Elena's benefit. None of us had had to go through a period of quarantine when we were brought to Barashevo, even though this formality does exist on paper. But enough of my interruptions!

> On the ninth or tenth day, when they finally unlocked the "box" in which I was being held, and (for the first time in eleven months) I had more space than a cell in which to move around, I spent many hours walking along the length of the hospital block or standing on the steps at dusk, staring at the Small Zone and at the two fences and wire separating us . . . I could see the lights coming on in your house, and I could not tear my eyes away from your windows . . . If only you knew how my soul cried out to be there, with all of you. How much I would have given for that . . .
> The worst feature of that year of confinement was the total lack of contact with live and normal people, being surrounded instead by those with whom I had absolutely nothing in common,

and who were sad parodies of human beings. Such as the hideous bribe-extortionists in Lefortovo, and in the camps—the criminals masquerading as human beings. Admittedly, the latter were a vast improvement on the creatures in Lefortovo, but still . . . The situation was aggravated by the difficulty of adjusting to such surroundings, by taking everything too close to heart. And in moments of tiredness I could not help thinking: when will I finally come across someone whose psyche has not been distorted, whose views and values have not been turned upside down, who thinks and acts like a normal human being?

From my first day in Barashevo, Shalin lied fluently that I would be transferred to the Small Zone "any day now." As this was what I wanted above all else, like a fool I believed him. It was only in my third week in Barashevo that I realized, in horror, that I would be sent away from here without the chance to get any first-hand information about your Zone.

The situation was so tense that it's a wonder every hair on my head didn't turn grey. First, there was the not knowing whether I would get to spend any time in the Small Zone at all, and the interminable waiting. Then there were Shalin's lies in response to each and every question I put to him. When I asked him about correspondence and a meeting, he answered smoothly that both would be possible after my transfer to the Zone in a few days. Some ten days later he said breezily that transfer to the Zone was not a prerequisite, that I could write a letter where I was, and the censor would come round for it that very evening. Needless to say, the censor did not come that day, nor the next, nor the one after that. Losing patience, I took up station one morning by the mailbox in the dining area and, ignoring everyone, waited for the arrival of the censor. She came an hour or so later, and was very surprised to learn of my existence. Nobody had said a word to her about me. I gave her my letter, which my mother never received, despite Shalin's promise that it would be sent. And that was typical of everything.

It was also very trying to deal with the people surrounding me. A week after my arrival, a young woman whose surname is Tikhomirova (nicknamed "Tishka") was brought into my ward-cell from camp Number Two. She was a sick, pathetic and broken figure, highly nervous and with a certain pathological tendency. I don't know what the administration's purposes were in putting her in with me. Her constant presence was an added burden. She spoke a great deal about her admiration for "politicals," professed her keenness (in words only) to help me in some way (again, without specifying how and why), claimed to know you and Tanya from having sat in neighboring cells in SHIZO and even recounted a number of incidents—how Tanya was force-fed, how she refused to wear the SHIZO-issued smock, and so on. It all sounded quite plausible. Others assured me that she had been put in with me as an informer. Whether this was so, I can't say, but she was not in the hospital compound for treatment and I learned later, in SHIZO, that she went back to Zone Number Two the day after I left Barashevo. She professed herself ready to help me get some food across to the Small Zone, swearing to do so, come what may. Therefore, I left her everything I had, although I was not without doubts that she would actually carry out her promise.

I also found it psychologically difficult to cope with the fact that every time you exchanged a few words with someone, others would make it their business to whisper to you that that person was an informer. I witnessed a hysterical scene between Tishka and one Kostenetskaya, each accusing the other of informing on me to the camp bosses. Both were agreed, however, that Vashchenko was definitely a stool pigeon. This was really intolerable!

How vividly her words make me recall Shalin, who had stopped blushing by that time, and Tishka, whom we really did know from SHIZO (and who was not placed into Elena's quarters by chance!), with her aggressive lesbianism, delicately described by Elena as "a certain pathological tendency," and the whole atmosphere of the criminal camp hospital. It takes time for one to overcome a natural feeling of revulsion and to begin to feel compassion and understanding instead. Elena had insufficient time for that, but the beginnings of compassion are evident in her letter, and I am glad for her sake that she had already begun to feel it. I can also understand that our little house seemed an unattainable dream to her, for I remember my own joy upon arrival there after investigation and trial. Hunger and all difficulties are gladly accepted if it means being among one's own. They never did transfer Elena to the Small Zone, but she made a heroic attempt to reach the window of the bath hut when she saw us being taken there. All she needed was a moment to arrange to come to our fence at an agreed time. We would come to our side, and be able to talk.

One such meeting actually took place, and Tanya brought her up to date on our latest news. This had to be done very briefly. A follow-up meeting was agreed to, and we compiled a comprehensive account on a tiny slip of paper. But Elena was unable to get as far as the fence. She was intercepted and locked up, and it is not hard to guess where she spent the rest of her stay. It was in SHIZO, of course, "for an attempt at communicating with the Small Zone," in which she herself should have been placed a month earlier. In SHIZO, she came down with pleurisy, and had not recovered from it when they came to transport her to her place of exile in Siberia.

After my release, I spoke to Elena on the phone. It was heartbreaking to know that there I was, at home, solely due to the efforts of so many people the world over, and Elena was in exile for being one of them. Of course, that was not the only reason for her sentence, there was also her participation in compiling the clandestine *Chronicle of Current Events,* and other human rights activity. But her efforts on my behalf were a factor, too: if Russian poets are allowed to get away with defending each other, who knows to what it might lead?

The Americans, meanwhile, were innocently asking members of the Soviet Writers' Union: "Why are you silent when your colleagues are imprisoned?"

They were silent because they knew that they only had to open their mouths to follow in Elena's footsteps. They did not share her courage; officially acknowledged writers lead an easy life, they have a great deal to lose. In any case, we're not their colleagues—we have never participated in any of the Soviet propaganda activities which are mandatory for Writers' Union members, so we were not members ourselves. For it is impossible to serve both God and Mammon. One must choose. And the choice was made: we chose one, they chose the other. We have never regretted our choice, and I don't think they regret theirs. Different people have different destinies . . .

Yet Elena still managed to get some information about our Zone: about the incarceration of invalids in SHIZO, about the reprisals for hunger strikes, and how we conducted those hunger strikes. I have never met Elena face to face—I know only her voice at the other end of the telephone wire, her photos, and her poetry:

> Blue cornflowers pattern the edge of a path
> And fields roll away like an ocean
> Reveal to me, cuckoo,[1] reveal to me true,
> How much of my freedom is left me?
> And what of the combat with forces of dark,
> And shall there be joy in my lifetime?—
> I'm asking you, cuckoo, to tell me, please tell . . .
> But why are you suddenly silent?

Another friend made in this world. My dear ones, my dear ones! How numerous you are. And how fortunate for us that this is so.

---

1. There is a Russian superstition that when you hear a cuckoo calling, you ask it "How many years do I have to live?" and then count the number of its calls.

42

Spring. I am busy embroidering a "graduation" blouse for Tanya. Making things like cases for spectacles, purses, and embroidering bookmarks is something I do all the time, to bring a little pleasure to myself and the others. But the end of a sentence calls for something really special, so Pani Lida and I cook up a plot: she'll do the sewing, and I'll do the embroidery, so Tanya will knock everyone out with her elegance in her place of exile. Of course, Tanya is not supposed to lay eyes on the blouse until her birthday, but how can we be sure of the measurements without an actual fitting? We resolve the problem by blindfolding her, and Lagle and Natasha stand by to make sure she doesn't try to peek. As usual, Tanya is irrepressible.

"I can see, I can see," she teases, "it's something blue and green."

The others sit around laughing, because the embroidery is red and yellow. Pani Lida, imperturbable as ever, sets pins marking where to take the blouse in and where to let it out. Soon, soon we shall wave goodbye to Tanya, she will go into exile, and a year and a half later her Ivan will be out of camp, too. They may find themselves in the permafrost zone, but at least they'll be together. Actually, that is not one hundred percent certain: it's up to the authorities to decide places of exile. Can they send husbands and wives to different places? That would mean another five years of separation![1] Tanya sends a query to Moscow, to the

Central Administration of the camps. She receives a reply which states that there is no legal obligation to send spouses to the same place of exile. That is up to the local authorities in the area where the prisoner is serving his or her camp sentence. Not a particularly encouraging prospect, to say the least. Those swine are quite capable of sending Tanya and her Ivan as far away from each other as possible. We do our best to reassure Tanya that this is unlikely, that our administration would not risk the ensuing uproar. We did not know then that our administration and the KGB were busily putting together a case against Tanya under Article 188-3. Their plan was to spring it on her at the last moment. Psychologically, a second sentence is much harder to accept than the first, and these great psychologists were obviously expecting Tanya to break at that point. Idiots! They should have known her better by then.

Knowing nothing of their intentions, we saw Tanya off with high hopes and a host of good wishes: Tanya would get medical treatment, then she and Ivan would have a quiverful of kiddies during their exile, little poppets just like their mother! Friends would travel up to see them, just as Igor had gone to see Tatyana Mikhailovna and sent photos of the two of them amidst the stones of Kazakhstan. We had entertained ourselves by wondering whether Tanya's place of exile would be one where she would have to use camels for transport or, on the contrary, reindeer.

It turned out to be neither. She went to the strict regime criminal camp in Ishimbay instead. Apart from our Zone, there were only three other "strict" women's zones in the camps: Orel, Bereznyaki and Ishimbay. Ishimbay was considered to be the most terrible; women being sent there howl in terror. When Tanya was in Ryzhayev prison, she heard someone comforting a woman who was en route to the Bereznyaki camp: "Why are you crying? It's not as though you're being sent to Ishimbay." But the indomitable Tanya set off for Ishimbay with the keen curiosity of

1. Persons serving terms of internal exile may not leave their designated places of residence without specific permission from the authorities.

a scientist: there had been no politicals in these camps before, and very little was known about the conditions in them. The inmates of these camps are habitual criminals who have already served a number of sentences. There is a three-week period of quarantine upon arrival, and it is spent in SHIZO, no less. No other facilities are available, and from the point of view of the authorities, there is no need for such. Because Tanya knew the law, she was able to get bedding, but as a general practice, this was considered to be an unnecessary luxury. If you're in SHIZO, you may as well live in SHIZO conditions. There is a shortage of mattresses even for PKT.

The Ishimbay camp, built to house three hundred prisoners, contained eight hundred, making it impossible to observe the legal provision of two square meters of living space per zek. Here, there was less than one meter. How so? Easy: each bunk is shared by two prisoners. It can be used on a rotation basis, because the prisoners work in three shifts. So, while one works, the other can sleep. In fact, the bunks can be used by three people, in view of the three work shifts—why have equipment standing around unused? In any case, some of them can sleep on the floor; this is not a holiday resort. And so it goes, year in, year out . . .

Maintaining personal hygiene is not without its interesting aspects, too. Take the bathhouse, for instance. There is no hot water there, of course, but nobody will object if you heat up a bucket of water and bring it along for a wash. The problem is that one bucket has to be shared by fifty people, and the camp regulations allow prisoners only one hour a day to themselves. The bathhouse closes at 7:00 p.m. Dinner is between six and seven, and that is preceded by an hour of compulsory "political education." Each day, for an hour, you are compelled to hear all about the enormous strides with which we are heading toward communism, and you just try getting out of it. So securing a bucket and having a wash after work is up to you. The camp administration does not demand that you wash. This is not an ideological issue. Some old women, who were incapable of working and had been banded into a special brigade, were unable to wash for months on end because they did not have the physical strength to carry a bucket to the bathhouse, even when two of them tried. Occasionally (but rarely) someone would take pity on them and bring them a bucket of hot water. Sometimes they "bought" hot water in exchange for a month's ration of tea. But mostly they just became steeped in filth. Everyone held their breath when the old women's brigade passed by.

There is a laundry in the camp, and it contains seven washtubs for eight hundred inmates. You can wash to your heart's content. In your one hour of free time, naturally. And your clothes must be dry by the end of that hour, too. There are no clothesdryers, only a couple of clotheslines. These clotheslines are used according to strict rotation, because there is not enough space for everyone. Even when you've hung up your pathetic bits and pieces, you must not move away, or they'll be stolen.

Although Tanya enjoyed universal respect as a political, her uniform was stolen. She had only just hung it up to dry when she was summoned to the "operative" section. Free time does not mean that you cannot be bothered for any reason. When she got back, her dress had disappeared. The administration replaced it—at Tanya's expense. When it's raining or snowing, washing clothes becomes impossible, because there's no chance of drying them. And you have to be careful with washing clothes generally: prisoners are issued one summer and one winter dress each. You may not wear your winter dress during the months you are supposed to be wearing the summer one without "breaching camp regulations." And that means punishment. Once you have taken off your dress to wash it, you are technically in breach of camp regulations until you put it on again. If you're lucky, none of the camp personnel will spot you until you're dressed again. If not, you'll just have to put your clothes on even though they're still wet. The administration does not object to that. And so on.

Tanya was assigned to a privileged brigade: the pattern cutters. The authorities provided better conditions for them because they had to use knives in their work. And what guarantees did the camp bosses have that the prisoners wouldn't use these knives on the staff if they were pushed too far? The cutters were considered "rich": they had a whole two buckets for fifty people. Tanya had a bunk to herself. The administration decided to take no chances—you never know with politicals, they know the laws, and she could possibly make trouble by lodging all sorts of complaints with various government bodies.

Just to show Tanya where the power lay, though, they gave her forty-five days of official SHIZO after her "quarantine." The situation became so bad that some of the criminal prisoners went to the camp commandant to intercede on Tanya's behalf. This step of theirs required immense courage, for voicing any objections at all to the commandant was considered to be the most grievous and heavily punished offense in the camp. The penalties for this were even more severe than the penalties for non-fulfillment of work quotas. Tanya enjoyed excellent relations with these "unspeakable criminals." She was respected and called upon to arbitrate in conflicts. On top of that, Tanya was well versed in the law, and one would be hard put to find a more receptive audience than the one in Ishimbay. But Tanya has an even more valuable gift—the ability to listen and commiserate, so she was the constant recipient of the uncomplicated histories with which the women came to her for a little attention and human sympathy. According to Tanya's statistics, 97 percent of the prisoners were in the camp for theft. Many of them started stealing in childhood and, after passing through the camps for juvenile offenders, became professional thieves. Put an ordinary child into such a camp, and you can be sure that in a few years' time he will become an accomplished thief and a positive virtuoso at swearing, fighting and lying. If he has some potential psychological aberration, you can be equally sure that it will come to the fore. The camps don't exist to form character, they exist to destroy the persona. The only psychology acceptable in the camps is the psychology of a slave and all its revolting attributes. If you try to preserve your sense of human dignity, you will find yourself under the wheels of the formidable administrative-punitive machine. We, of all people, knew that from personal experience.

Many of the Ishimbay inmates had started stealing during childhoods spent in orphanages. Poverty, identical ugly clothing, envy toward those who had parents to dress and care for them,

working for a pittance when they were old enough to get jobs . . .
How else could all this affect a girl whose only idea of "real life"
came from films? Just look at the clothes and hairdos on those
actresses. Look at the sheepskin jacket on the woman who has
passed by in the street. There are imported boots in the shops—
fantastic!—selling for three hundred rubles, but her monthly salary is only eighty, and she has to pay for her accommodation in
the hostel out of that, damn it!

Some turned to theft "for love." There was one woman in
Tanya's brigade who was nicknamed "Ducky" because she devoted every possible moment to washing or laundering. In view of
how difficult it was to carry out either activity in Ishimbay, her
obsessive cleanliness was treated as a standing joke. She was a
semi-literate, very kindly soul, who had started stealing to fi-
nance her husband's drinking. "Get the money somehow, or I'll
leave you," he used to threaten. So in desperation Ducky climbed
through someone's window and stole three hundred rubles. This
was only the beginning.

Once begun, stealing is hard to give up. The excitement and
the easy pickings are as intoxicating as alcohol. Stealing becomes
a reflex rather than something done out of need. Galya Khramova
was brought back to Ishimbay within half an hour of being released. She had served her sentence and by dint of working like a
slave had managed to save two thousand rubles out of the miserly
salaries paid to zeks. With this enormous sum in her pocket, she
left the camp for the railway station to go home. Then on the
platform she saw a drunk, sleeping on one of the benches. He was
wearing a gold signet ring. And despite her current wealth, she
could not overcome the temptation to try to steal it. Unfortunately for her, the drunk was no drunk, and there were militiamen lurking behind some bushes, ready to spring. The trap was
set because the local militia was obeying a government instruction to step up the fight against petty theft. How else could they
show results except by an increase in the number of arrests? So
Galya Khramova got another five years.

Some returned to theft after their first camp terms out of sheer
desperation: those who have spent time in Soviet prisons con-

tinue to pay the price for the rest of their lives. The stamp in their document is an eternal stigma, and negates any chances of getting a decent job or a place to live. They may live to be a hundred years old, but the stain will remain: "She's a criminal. She's been to prison." But in the company of thieves this doesn't matter, and makes life a lot easier.

This is how former kindergarten supervisor Lyuda became a "second offender." She took over the job as head of a kindergarten as a young woman, and signed the inventory shown to her by her predecessor without checking it first. The retiring head assured her that this was a mere formality. Seven months later, an auditing commission uncovered embezzlement to the tune of many thousands of rubles. In vain, Lyuda tried to convince the auditors that she physically could not have stolen equipment to that amount during her short tenure of the post, and all testimonies by kindergarten staff about Lyuda's honesty fell on deaf ears. The deficit is there, so there must be a culprit. Lyuda was sentenced, all her belongings were confiscated, and she was ordered to pay the remaining enormous sum in any way she could. That meant paying even after her term in the camps. So she turned to theft for this reason, and then couldn't break away.

The majority of the inmates admitted their crimes and did not dispute the justice of their arrest. What they did consider unjust was the length of their sentences and the inhuman conditions in the camp. But for those who were imprisoned unjustly through some quirk of fate, the injustice was a constant worm gnawing at their soul, giving them no respite. Sveta Grivnina told Tanya how she had decided to go straight after serving two sentences for theft. She was lucky enough to get a job as a nurse, marry a good man and have a baby. One day, when she was on duty in Casualty, a woman came in to have a cut on her hand bandaged. When the woman left, Sveta saw a bundle of banknotes on the floor— four hundred rubles. As all visitors to the clinic had to register their names and addresses, getting the careless patient's telephone number was no problem. Sveta phoned the woman, told her that her money had been found, and agreed to drop it around to the woman's flat on her way home: the woman specifically asked Sveta to do this, claiming she did not feel well enough to return to the clinic. When Sveta knocked at the door and handed the woman her money, two militiamen burst into the room. The "patient" began screaming that Sveta had tried to rob her and had been threatening to kill her. During the investigation it emerged that the woman was a psychiatric case; she had been discharged from psychiatric hospital a month earlier, and was committed there again even before Sveta was brought to trial. By the looks of it, the case could be closed, as the accusations of someone whose mind is disturbed could hardly be deemed reliable. At first Sveta was treated politely, because it was patently obvious that the whole incident was unwarranted. Then they discovered that Sveta had served two terms for theft, just what she had been accused of by that mentally unbalanced plaintiff. The attitude to Sveta changed at once, and despite all her tears and the evidence that she had built an honest life for herself since her release, she was brought to trial as a habitual criminal. In desperation, she even tried to commit suicide. Being pregnant, she induced a miscarriage by tried and tested zek methods—she'd simply lost the ability to think rationally, and said in Ishimbay that she now could not understand what drove her to such an extreme. She was able to speak quite calmly and objectively about her first two terms—she'd committed crimes and paid the penalty—but she could not mention this third term without tears: "If I'd really stolen the money, it wouldn't be so hard!" she maintained.

While Tanya sat in Ishimbay, having already sacrificed her health in SHIZOs and hunger strikes in our Zone, and surrounded now by the filth and foul-mouthed clamor of a criminal zone, we were visited by KGB officers. "Osipova has received an additional sentence," they informed us, grinning from ear to ear. "The same will happen to all of you if you don't mend your ways." Shalin tried spinning us stories that Tanya had finally seen the light and was now on the best of terms with the KGB. Nobody gave any credence to these lies, and we warned Shalin that if we heard them again, we would instigate court proceedings against him for slander. He took us at our word and never raised the matter again; he knew as well as we did that no court would take up such a case, but he knew equally well that we would ensure that the story would become known outside, and that would not be to his advantage.

Tanya was released from Ishimbay six months before the end of her sentence. She had not retreated a step from her ethical positions, recanted nothing, and lodged no appeals for clemency. Her release was due to external circumstances: Gorbachev had ordered the release of a number of well-known political prisoners, and Tanya and I were among those chosen. Others are still inside, and are probably hearing the same lies as the ones we were told.

43

Lagle and I were taken to Saransk for another dose of KGB "re-education," to endure another round of their dreary monologues in the course of which they tried somehow—anyhow—to provoke me into responding. The underlying theme was: would you like to go home? Back to your husband? All you have to do is write a statement or recantation. As a model, they pointed to a similar statement made by former Ukrainian Helsinki Group Monitor Oles Berdnyk. In his statement, which was published in the Soviet press, Berdnyk said everything the KGB could have wished: he denounced his former views, saying that he had let personal vanity lead him astray, but now he realizes that it's much wiser to leave such matters to the government; he touched upon the threat of nuclear war, and that this is no time for internal conflicts in the USSR; he asked the authorities for forgiveness and thanked them for their leniency; he libelled his former friends, and simultaneously expressed the hope that they too, would "reform." Just reading all this was enough to make me feel physically sick. There are clemency pleas and clemency pleas. There are times when a person can take no more, denounces himself, and wins release. But why slander others? Only because they have proved to be morally stronger? Some reason to join the ranks of the "re-educators," I must say! I later learned that Berdnyk entered into his new role with great zest. No wonder the KGB was so insistent, in the summer of 1986, that I should have a meeting with Berdnyk. They would not let me see my husband, but I could have met Berdnyk any time I liked. The KGB would only need to whistle for him to come running to the prison, to persuade me to follow his example. I had plenty to talk about with the KGB in those last months: I was demanding the unconditional and irrevocable release of our entire Zone. They already knew that they would have to release me. I had no such certain knowledge, but I did not exclude the possibility. And just so the KGB would not foster any illusions, I made it quite clear that I wouldn't rest until all my fellow prisoners in the Zone were at liberty.

But I refused to see Berdnyk. I told them that I had seen enough scum in that building already without having to look at one more. This was impolite of me, but that's what I said, and it would be dishonest to dress up my reply differently. Yet that spring in Saransk, the KGB could think of nothing better than to stick Berdnyk's intricate lies under our noses. Even if anyone had been tempted to purchase freedom for a sheet of writing, Berdnyk's nauseating confession would have put an end to any such thoughts. Having wasted the requisite amount of time on us, they sent us back to Barashevo. The trip to Saransk was not entirely useless from our point of view, because in the KGB prison you can buy food up to the value of ten rubles a month, and we were not denied this opportunity. The warders and ordinary prison personnel were quite pleasant, and it seemed odd to see the blue KGB patches on their uniforms. They delivered all our purchases without demur: milk, eggs, vegetables, all of which were untold luxuries. So we were able to bring back supplies for the others in the Zone, and to celebrate Orthodox Easter in style— while still in Saransk. The prison staff celebrated Easter, too, and when our bewhiskered warders led us out into the exercise yard, they gave us dyed Easter eggs. We, in turn, gave them the ones we had colored the day before with green paint.

We celebrated Lagle's birthday in Potma transit prison. We spread an embroidered cloth on one of the bunks, and celebrated as gaily as we would have anywhere else. I recalled how I had spent the night in this same cell on my way to camp two years before. I seemed to have acquired a great deal more *joie de vivre* since then. The carefree zek "nothing is too much" attitude helps you to take the daily tribulations of prison life in your stride. When the regiments of the famed Potma bedbugs began to advance on us that night, we turned it into a comedy. Because of the enemy's superior numbers, the battle raged until dawn, with the advantage passing back and forth. Our foes were not intimidated by the light in the cell; they were accustomed to it, and attacked without waiting for the cover of darkness. So we decided to bring the situation to the attention of the medical administration. Of course, ridding the prison of bedbugs would be an impossible task, but why should the zeks be the only ones to have to worry about them? Our interest lay in seeing how various government bodies would go about denying the undeniable existence of these insect pests. In the best traditions of Marxist-Leninist materialism, we resolved to supply them with concrete evidence of our allegations.

Our first victim was the prison governor. We waited until he had made the expected pronouncement that the prison is free of vermin of any kind, that we're imagining things, and then produced a medicine phial containing a number of specially selected and very mobile specimens. We were interested to see whether he would maintain that the little bottle was empty, or whether he would say that he had never seen a bedbug in his life and was therefore unable to identify our specimens. He chose neither option: thinking on his feet, he claimed that we must have brought the bedbugs with us. We even took offense at such a suggestion on behalf of the KGB; no need to slander the service, the truth about it is bad enough! The Saransk KGB prison happens to be exceptionally clean, and we were able to take baths whenever we asked for them, instead of once a week. Rendered speechless by this sudden defense, the prison governor took the bottle and went away, muttering that we must have been badly searched upon arrival in Potma, otherwise we would not have had any glass objects in the cell. Poor, naïve man! He thought he'd removed the evidence . . . But the evidence was there for the catching in its thousands. The bedbugs were easy prey: victory or captivity, they didn't care, so long as they could enjoy human society. We did our best to satisfy their lust for recognition—we sent one of them, in a carefully sealed plastic envelope, to the Central Medical Administration of the regional camps, with an accompanying letter. Another one was sent to represent the bed-bug population of Potma prison to the Procuracy of the USSR. Naturally, we did not send these envelopes from Potma (they would have been confiscated) but from our own Zone upon return. As the documents accompanying the specimens contained no complaints about our camp administration, they were duly dispatched, and a grinning Shalin gave us the mailing slips to prove it.

Several months later we received replies which stated that there are absolutely no bedbugs in Potma prison, and there is no basis for our complaints. Tricky, these materialists: how can you hope to understand them after something like that?

But long before the arrival of these replies, Lagle and Olya were sent to SHIZO " for the brewing of *chifir* in transit prison." So it said in the SHIZO order, and any person who has had occasion to stand on either side of prison bars would know what that means. "*Chifir*" is a special zek invention. A 50-gram pack of tea is emptied into a mug, covered with water, and boiled. There is very little fluid left, and the saturated tea leaves take up more than half the mug. But what little liquid there is is so strong that it induces a state equivalent to narcotic intoxication. In the criminal camps, the prisoners seize any chance they can to make *chifir*, and tea is commodity number one on the camp black market. Drinking *chifir* is severely punished in every camp—and in every camp they go on making it. This would be impossible without illegal supplies of tea for the simple reason that a zek may not purchase more than 50 grams of tea a month, and none at all if he's forfeited kiosk rights for some time. Zeks are supposed to be given 1 gram of tea daily as part of their rations, but as a rule the inmates of the criminal zones never see it; they are given a yellowish fluid which goes under the name of tea in their mess hall. The bulk of the tea is stolen and used by the camp personnel. Not being involved in the black marketeering of tea, the Small Zone made no *chifir*, and would not have been able to even if there was a desire for it. We didn't have enough tea just for ordinary use. Our warders were well aware of that, and so was the camp administration. But one excuse for SHIZO is as good as any other, and who can disprove it? And who will listen to you even if you try?

Olya and Lagle were taken away on a beautiful day in May, and we hoped the warm weather would hold, so they would not have to freeze too much in SHIZO. Alas, there was snow and frosts several days later. Such are the vagaries of the Mordovian climate. In May, the heating does not function. After Lagle returned, there were periods when she would lose all sensation in her left arm; she had a weak heart, and this spell in SHIZO placed an extra burden on it. Ten days later it was Galya's and my turn to go to SHIZO—for going on strike in defense of Olya and Lagle. This time they took us to SHIZO in another camp, Number Six. It was here that we realized that in the SHIZO of camp Number Two they were positively liberal with rations. After a week at Number Six we were faint from hunger. One would think that "reduced rations" could hardly be reduced any further. But we had obviously forgotten what we had been taught in school—that nothing is impossible for the Soviet people!

There were other differences from the conditions in our customary Number Two: a lavatory bowl and a tap in the cell. At first we were delighted—wash as much as you like, no slop bucket to haul back and forth, no stench in the cell. But the water pipes leaked, and water slurped under the floorboards. It is not hard to imagine how that affected Galya's already painful joints. Added to that, she came down with tonsillitis on the third day of the fifteen we were to spend in this place. Hordes of mosquitoes, squealing with joy, battered against the windows, attracted by the light and the damp. We killed as many as we could with our slippers, but it was a lost battle from the start. One day we had a competition, to see how many mosquitoes each one of us could kill before dinner. We got as far as three hundred, but then lost count and gave up. The mosquitoes giggled in shrill triumph as they circled around the lamp above our heads. At times we felt that all the biting power of Mordovian prison convoy dogs had been inherited by these mosquitoes. This theory would also explain why the dogs accompanying our escort when we were taken from place to place were invariably lazy, apathetic, and sometimes downright friendly; nothing at all like the frenzied monster I'd heard when I was climbing into a *Stolypin* carriage for the first time on my way to camp.

The camp regime supervisors were as ubiquitous as the mosquitoes: just about everything was on the forbidden list in camp Number Six. A girl in the neighboring cell got fifteen days' SHIZO for singing the song "Harlequin" in the workroom. The popular Soviet singer Alla Pugacheva, who has been singing this song all over the place for years, would probably never suspect that there are places where that song can land you in punishment cell for fifteen days. When our poor neighbor finished her fifteen days, they gave her another fifteen on the basis of the same report. We heard it being read out to her, with our own ears. Apparently there had been some mix-up with the paperwork, and the order to send her to SHIZO went on a second round. Of course, she tried to convince them that she had already served this punishment, but inevitably to no avail.

Another thing to which the administration of camp Number Six took exception was the cross I wore around my neck. It was doubly precious to me because Igor had made it. In our Zone and in Number Two, they preferred not to notice it, in the absence of a direct order from the KGB. But here they were onto it in a flash: "What's that cord around your neck?"

"She's wearing a cross."

"Take it off at once."

"Not on your life."

"We'll call up a guard detail, and they'll take it off by force."

"Will you now? I'd advise you not to assume such a responsibility, though. Have a word with your superiors first."

This suggestion found instant favor: who wants to get involved in a conflict with one of the politicals, and then bear responsibility for the consequences? Along came senior regime supervisor Zuykov. He, at least, was a brave soldier, and not afraid of making independent decisions.

"Prisoners are not permitted to have amulets, crosses or talismans," he told me firmly.

"There is no law forbidding the wearing of crosses," I retorted.

"There's an instruction."

"So how are we supposed to act: in accordance with the law, or in accordance with instructions?"

"Look here, Ratushinskaya, you needn't think you're the first political I've had to deal with. We've broken tougher ones than you. Do you know how many years I worked in the Administration?"[1]

"In which years?"

"Before your time. Since '79. I remember your *babushki*, and Velikanova, too."

"So you took away their crosses?"

"I don't think the problem ever arose."

"Well, I daresay you'd have remembered it had you made such an attempt. Do you remember Tanya Osipova, too?"

He's thinking fast, you can tell by his face. Of course, he remembers Tanya and her famous "dry" hunger strike for the return of the Bible they'd confiscated. Four days without a drop of water—that had them all running around in panic! He remembers that they'd had to give in, too. It's a marvellous thing, the human memory.

"So you . . . "

"Look, there's no point in debating the matter: Let's just see what happens when you try to take away my cross."

He looks at me searchingly, straight in the eyes, and manages to hold my glance longer than any of the others. Finally, however, he turns away. "If only you'd cover the cord so it won't be visible."

But I can do nothing to satisfy his wish: it was not I who designed the SHIZO costumes with their plunging necklines. Tanya's hunger strike saved me from the necessity of conducting a "dry" hunger strike of my own, then or at any other time. I don't know how I would have managed, had the need arisen. On the

1. KGB

other hand, I would not have had much choice. But Tanya, tied as if for crucifixion to prison trestles, with intravenous drips attached to her legs, had won us not only our Bibles, but my cross and the psalms sung by Galya and Pani Lida, for all our SHIZOs. Tanya, who considered herself a non-believer.

But everything comes to an end eventually, and we returned to the Zone where the others were waiting for us. All except for Tanya, who was on her way to Ishimbay. Nyurka, who met me at the gate, miaowed questioningly, wanting to know where her favorite mistress had disappeared. She was used to seeing Tanya and myself returning together. I picked her up and went to sit with her near the fence, where the clumps of goosefoot were highest, and cuddled her whiskered head against my face. We sat there for a while in shared sadness, and then went to the house. Nyurka could smile as well as any Cheshire Cat.

44

Lagle's mother died. The telegram came with considerable delay, reaching Lagle after the funeral. On the day following the receipt of this telegram, Lagle's meeting with her husband and sister was cancelled. The one annual meeting which can last from one to three days ... How could we do anything to alleviate Lagle's grief? As always, she bore herself with strength and courage. Yet however much we wanted to help, it is hardly likely that anything could have lessened her pain. To hell with the "legal reason" (refusal to wear an identity tag), we thought, and immediately went on a one-day hunger strike of protest. Lagle also declared a work strike for fifteen days. This time, nobody was punished: the administration obviously decided that we'd been pushed far enough. This was a very wise decision on their part, for we were furious enough for anything. There are times when it's best not to tangle with someone. In this instance, it was definitely better for them not to tangle with the Small Zone—a complex body, but invariably united in moments of joy or sorrow.

Searches of the Zone became increasingly frequent and thorough, more and more was confiscated, and on one occasion I was almost caught red-handed. In their presence, I quickly had to stuff a bit of paper into my mouth and swallow it. The paper had Zone information on it, and my latest poems. As was to be expected, I was sent to SHIZO for a week; the only surprising thing was that it was for such a short time. But why were Olya, Galya and

Natasha sent to SHIZO for a week at the same time? The explanation proved to be quite simple: half an hour after they took the four of us away, a veritable crowd streamed into the Zone: "Women, prepare to return to your old Zone!"

So we had simply been removed so that there would be fewer people in the Zone. They launched into a second pogrom, which made the first one seem trivial by comparison. All letters and any documents were taken away for yet another scrutiny. Out of our personal possessions, they simply confiscated or stole as much as they could—starting with Raya's underpants and ending with bits of my embroidery. For some reason, they confiscated Galya's Bible, but left two others. They threw Pani Jadvyga's Communion wafers on the floor, and ground them into dust with their boots, they stole her rosary with a cross. Even postcards with reproductions of icons by Dionysos and Andrei Rublev, which had been officially ordered through the "book post" system, were confiscated as "religious material." They burnt all of Natasha's drawings, and all the poetry copied out and sent to me by Igor and Mama. It made no difference that it had been copied out of Soviet publications, and that the source of each poem was clearly indicated: publisher, year, volume, page number . . .

The immortal words of Pushkin, Tyutchev and Fet were consigned to the flames yet again . . . A familiar process for them by now. They also burnt all the journals we had bought over the years out of our miserable zek pittances. All our books and clothes were locked away in the camp store; from now on if we wanted anything out of them, we could get it only in the presence of Shalin and Arapov. The windows of the store were tightly sealed off with iron sheets, and there was no light inside. When we returned from SHIZO a week later we discovered that all our bedclothes and underwear were in the store, and nobody knew when Shalin was likely to come round again. So we had nothing to change into: "welcome news" for me in particular, as I'd picked up scabies from the SHIZO smock, which had not been washed before it was issued to me.

Before that we'd had quite a jaunt, because when we arrived at camp Number Two, they refused to take us in for some reason, and sent us straight back to Barashevo. You could see the reasoning of the Number Two administration: we weren't "theirs," and only caused them a lot of bother. They couldn't allow themselves the liberty of beating us, or swearing at us, and then there was our constant stream of written complaints about the cold and filth. They swore every time that they'd never have us in their SHIZO again, but there was nothing they could do against a direct order from the KGB. This time, however, they rebelled. Back in Barashevo they kept us in the van. Then along came Shalin, red-faced and with a murderous look in his eyes (we'd never seen him like that before), and commanded in the voice of someone who's lost the ability of coherent thought: "Hand in all the things you've got with you!"

A number of junior officers climbed into the van, and seized all our bags and bundles. They didn't leave us so much as a comb or a toothbrush, and off we went again to Number Two, which had been brought to heel by a phone call from the appropriate quarter. The final blow on that mad day was that the van hit a deep rut, so that everyone's teeth closed with a snap, and I lost consciousness. It was that jolt on top of my earlier concussion that did it.

I don't remember being dragged out of the van and being half-led, half-carried to the SHIZO by Olya and Natasha. I have a vague recollection of a room where we changed into SHIZO smocks. I was sitting on the floor and Olya was demanding that a doctor be called, and begging everyone not to touch me in the meantime. Warder Akimkina, whom I had already had occasion to "laud," decided that the first thing to be done was to drag my clothes off me. Then I don't remember anything until I regained consciousness on the floor of a familiar cell.

Olya and Natasha told me that they had been taken to the cell, and some time later I was dragged in by my arms, unconscious, and left on the floor. Then the local doctor came, diagnosed concussion, prescribed Dimedrol and left. So many events, and I missed them all! Still, I'm now wearing the regulation smock (I didn't know it would give me scabies) with nothing underneath, barefooted ... Everything in accordance with the regime. My head is splitting, and I feel nauseated. Very gently, Olya gives me water from a battered mug and urges me to lie still. I'm only too glad to obey: moving is the last thing I feel up to.

For some reason, I spent the first twenty-four hours frantically worrying that I had lost part of my memory, and lay there remembering, remembering, as if attempting to fix the most important things in my brain. First I went through the whole chronology of the Zone: who had been in punishment cell and for how long, all the hunger strikes and work strikes, who had had what illnesses, whose meetings had been cancelled and for what reason. All those memories seemed to be intact. Forward! "The right to receive and disseminate information irrespective of state frontiers"—what article of the International Covenant[1] is that? And what about the one concerning everyone's right "to leave any country, and to return to one's own country"? Yes, I remember all that, too. This makes me calm down somewhat. Then for some reason I have a vivid recollection, with colors and smells, of how we celebrated Janis' Day this summer. Janis' Day (known in Latvia as *Lígo Svétki)* is the Baltic equivalent of the Slavic Day of Ivan Kupala.[2] We lit a fire in our homemade fireplace behind the house and wove coronets out of flowers. Pani Lida made *kvas*[3] out of black bread and we toasted bits of bread in our fireplace. There was a heavy dew, so we sat on the ground on our jackets while Pani Lida sang old Latvian *daini*[4] and Olya Ukrainian songs. Fire has a tendency to draw and focus one's gaze, and it was somehow particularly magnetic this time. Warder Tonya came on her night round, but didn't interfere. She sat with us for a while, had a sip of *kvas*, then left. When the flames died down, we just sat there, looking at the stars.

Then I am jolted by a new fear: my poems! Maybe I've forgotten my poems! I haven't risked writing them down for some time,

1. The International Covenant on Civil and Political Rights.
2. Ancient agricultural festivities which, with the coming of Christianity, became linked with the feast of St. John the Baptist. The rituals during these festivities return to pagan times, and there is a whole plethora of superstitions connected with them. It is on June 24 according to the Julian calendar.
3. A mild, yeast-based drink, somewhat similar to root beer.
4. Folk songs.

all I have are a few well-secreted tiny slips of paper with an index. I use this index daily to revise the poems in my head. Not all of them, of course, about twenty to thirty at a time. I work my way through to the end, then go back to the beginning. What if I've forgotten them now? And where's the index? I always have one copy with me. Thank God they haven't found it; but I can't pull it out and start looking at it now, it's too risky. There's an eye at the peephole in the door every few minutes. A political with concussion is not a particularly welcome addition to their responsibilities. So I'll have to go by memory. What was the last one on the list?

> When you comb your hair, the forgotten lock
> Means a journey.
> So let us go—God be with us—nothing to lose
> From dungeon to dungeon.
>
> Through the iron chink the same refrain
> Of birches and fences.
> Write to us and forgive us for delaying:
> You'll have no speedy answers.
>
> Rocks pounding, van shaking:
> We're going along the railway.
> No time for sightseeing—bones aching,
> Even the chink's gone away.
>
> Which dusty road are we measuring?
> Which centuries?
> On our bodies we shall go on treasuring
> The hard Earth's unevenness.
>
> But we'll get out in the year dot.
> Perhaps we'll return.
> Send us your letters, whether they reach us or not,
> One day we'll read them in turn.

That seems right. Was it worthwhile swallowing these poems during a search, learning them off by heart and, in the end, getting them to the outside world, risking not just myself but another person I cannot name, but whom I shall remember before God? I don't know, and it's not for me to judge. It was for me to do what I did then.

We return to Barashevo in the same van, dirty as never before, because for a whole week we had nothing to wash with, not even a comb for our hair. My head rests in Olya's lap and she tries to cushion me against all the jolts and bumps. They prop me up as we walk through the camp, because my legs are too unsteady for me to walk unaided, either as a result of the concussion, or a week of taking Dimedrol. The first person I see is Lagle: she looks at me, and her face changes. It's all right, my dears! Everything is all right!

45

Pani Jadvyga feels that she has committed a great sin—weak and ill though she is—by being unable to save her Communion wafers, which had been blessed in Lithuania, from desecration. All our attempts to convince her otherwise prove useless; only a priest can absolve her, and priests aren't allowed into the camps. There is a Catholic priest imprisoned in the men's zone, but our communications with them aren't functioning at present. So Pani Jadvyga decides to do penance: she makes a vow of silence for a year. We could see that nothing would dissuade her. The only concession we were able to win from our inflexible Pani was a promise that she would write when necessary, instead of speaking. This would keep her relatives from worrying unduly, and make it possible for us to know exactly what was wrong if she should fall ill. This form of communication is essentially brief—after all, we write down anything we don't want the administration to hear over their concealed microphones, and formulating succinct messages on paper is much harder than speaking. Furthermore, Pani Jadvyga is even more limited than most of us, because she finds writing in Russian difficult at the best of times. Still, it has taken us several days of sustained persuasion to talk her into even this concession, and that probably worked only because we found an irrefutable argument: "Your family are in no way to blame for this situation. If they don't hear from you for a whole year, they will be out of their minds with worry!" So finally Pani Jadvyga agreed to write, but not to speak under any circumstances. True to her vow, she even remained silent throughout a meeting she was granted with her son. She did not utter a single word from August 19, 1985, until August 19, 1986. When she moaned in her sleep—even then, without words—we could hear how her voice changed through disuse: it became dull and hoarse.

We were astounded, though, by the degree of fury which Pani Jadvyga's vow provoked among the KGB and our camp administration. For that year of silence, Pani Jadvyga would abstain from any hunger strikes, she would only maintain silence and fast; nothing in that, one would have thought, to upset the KGB and the camp bosses. Yet the vow infuriated them more than all the hunger strikes put together. Was it because it was "a religious action," as they described it? Or because in refraining from strikes and hunger strikes Pani Jadvyga qualified her stance by stressing that she supported those on strike wholeheartedly and prayed for them, refraining from participation only because she had insufficient strength for everything at once? Or maybe because this was such an unusual step, and they did not know how to cope with it? Whatever the reason, they tried everything they could think of to force her to speak. For instance, they brought along clothes from the store, clothes which we may buy only once a year: vests, boots, cloth for dresses and shirts. The amount one may buy is strictly limited, but without that you would be practically reduced to walking around undressed. We all wrote out our orders, Pani Jadvyga included. And what do you think? "Bieliauskiene, Shalin has directed that we can only accept a verbal order from you. Nothing on paper! If you don't say what you want, you'll get nothing. So, what would you like?"

Pani Jadvyga only smiled, left her order on the table and walked out. Of course, we immediately divided up her order among ourselves, and the bookkeeper had no choice but to authorize the issue of the items ordered by Pani Jadvyga to us, as part of our purchases. Our support provoked even greater anger, for we systematically checkmated any moves to bring our recalcitrant Pani Jadvyga to heel. When they tried the same tactics in the kiosk and failed just as dismally, they gave up and let her have the items written down on her list. They could not accuse her of violating camp regulations, because there is no regulation that makes it compulsory for a zek to talk. The warders refused to harry her in any way over her silence, because they found it awe-inspiring. "Women," they asked us unbelievingly, "is she really not going to say a single word for the whole year? We couldn't hold out a day. The hunger strikes must be easier!" Nice feminine logic! How can one pass up a chance to comment in any situation?

We also had another pressing concern arising out of the pogrom: to get back Galya's Bible. We sent off a written demand for its return, and sat back to await events. We had agreed among ourselves that if the authorities refused to comply, Galya, Pani Lida and I would declare a hunger strike. Pani Jadvyga also decided to waive her abstention from hunger strikes in this instance, because the matter concerned a Bible.

Returning a week later after a spell in SHIZO, we were sent back for further punishment; Olya and I were consigned to PKT for five months each, Natasha for two. In other words, back we went to the same cell, the only difference being that this time we would be issued bedding and could wear our own clothes (nothing warm, though). We were hardly delighted by this prospect, but we were not unduly depressed, either. The three of us could stand up to them easily enough. Furthermore, when you're in PKT you don't have to wash bending over the slop bucket, but are taken to a tap every day. The day on which the hunger strike would start had been agreed, and I would keep it in the punishment cell. We had also agreed on a secret signal: if the authorities returned Galya's Bible, Lagle would send me a pair of blue socks; these are allowed in PKT, and I "forgot" to pack them.

In due course, these socks arrived—brought to me by an unsuspecting Shalin, who assured me with great fervor that Galya had her Bible back, that he had personally put it into her hands. Clearly, the administration knew of our intention to go on hunger strike. And I was able to smile as I took my much-darned blue socks, knowing that this time, at least, Shalin was not lying.

The PKT stretched drearily before us. Olya and Natasha were due for release in the spring, so it was clear why they had been put here: their sentences could be extended under Article 188-3, the KGB could try blackmailing them, and stand to lose nothing. It was not quite so clear why they had put me into PKT, because I still had more than four years of my sentence to serve. On the other hand, why should they put off my "re-education" until the end of my term? They had warned me that I would face constant punishment, and were keeping their word. I had not even had time to get rid of the SHIZO-acquired scabies before I was back in punishment cell on PKT regime. Still, the authorities were not mean with supplies of sulfur cream, as half the inmates were afflicted.

Yet looking at the situation from all angles, Olya and I were still somewhat puzzled: the KGB would decide whether to release her and Natasha at the last moment, depending on the international situation. At present, the KGB were being quite circumspect, just in case they had to release both—and in that case, the less Olya and Natasha had to tell to the outside world, the better. By the same token, they would have to be fairly easy on me, too, in the presence of such witnesses. True, Natasha would be leaving earlier, but Olya's PKT term was due to finish at the same time as mine. We did not know, then, that Olya would be taken away to Kiev in two months' time, leaving me alone for the KGB to do with as they liked.

Certain things they began to practice almost immediately, though. On the very first evening back in the cell, when we unrolled the flimsy mattresses that are issued for the night and taken away in the morning, we found a strange note, written in an unfamiliar hand, and claiming to be from a cell at the far end of the block. This note asked us to give a written exposition of our political views and the essence of our disagreements with the authorities, all in the line of "enlightening" the alleged authors of the note. They suggested that we leave our reply in the mattress slot next to ours when we surrendered our bedding in the morning.

We were on our guard immediately: firstly, because the wording of the request bore little resemblance to the usual phraseology of the criminal prisoners, and secondly because the hiding place suggested was such a stupid choice. The warders check all bedding when it is issued and surrendered. We also found it odd that a note tucked into our bedding had escaped detection. The whole set-up reeked of a trap: the KGB must be short of material against Olya and Natasha. When our would-be correspondents started shouting their questions to us down the corridor, the inmates of our neighboring cells hastened to join in with a warning: "Don't answer them, girls! They're working for the 'operative'!" Naturally, we left no notes in any mattresses, but a week later found another missive—written in the same hand—in our bedding. The tone of this note was distinctly offended: how could we refuse a request from someone seeking enlightenment? What price our vaunted dedication to human rights? And so on. The next note, we were informed, would be hidden behind the fire extinguisher in the washroom, and on the morning of such-and-such a day we should leave our reply in the same place when we were taken there for our morning wash. We were also asked to supply addresses of people "outside" who could be consulted on dissident matters.

On that morning, Natasha "accidentally" left her toothbrush behind in the washroom, and went back for it when we were already halfway back to our cell. Two warders were busily poking around behind the fire extinguisher, and began yelling at Natasha as soon as they saw her; who had allowed her to come back? The negligent warder received a reprimand, but our doubts were resolved: the KGB were out to get Olya and Natasha. Well, they were out of luck.

By the beginning of September Natasha had caught a severe cold, and we tried to put as much clothing on her as we could sneak out of our own bags. Autumn and spring are the worst times, because it's very cold and the heating is not functioning at all. The cell becomes riddled with damp, and your clothes are permanently clammy. Luckily, they let you have newspapers in PKT, and we spread them under ourselves during the day. They make really excellent insulation. And to think we had been underestimating the value of the Soviet press all our lives . . .

The mice in our cell became quite frisky, because they could pick up crumbs from our bread ration. Even though you're on reduced rations in PKT, there is still bread and skilly every day. We had a whole family of mice sharing our cell: father, mother and babies. Chasing them away was useless; they'd scuttle away into their hole, only to re-emerge a few minutes later. We had to shake them out of our bedding every day, and on one occasion, a baby mouse landed right on Olya's face when she was doing exercises, with the obvious intention of diving into her open mouth! Irresponsible little creatures, all of them. Fortunately, they caused us more amusement than irritation.

Natasha was having a very difficult time of it this PKT. Physically the weakest of the three of us, she took the daily annoyances caused by the warders closer to heart, and had to cope with the rising anxiety as to whether she would be released in the spring or have her term extended. Olya paid no heed at all to day-to-day aggravations, but she had by then received a letter about the serious condition of her father. If relatives write something like that to the camps, then the situation must be really critical. Olya started to demand transportation to Kiev to see her parents, and finish her term of PKT after that. Then came the telegram saying that her father had died, and all Olya's grief was bottled up in the four walls of the cell. The first night we sat up with her, talking until morning. We talked about anything and everything, because she would not have slept anyway.

That was around the end of the second month of PKT. Then we were showered with new demands: why do we not wear identity tags in PKT? Why do we not report to the authorities? "Reporting" means that on the two occasions when the cell is searched every day, the duty prisoner in the cell (there is such a designation) must say: "Citizen supervisor, there are so many prisoners in the cell, no violations of the regime have occurred" (or report violations, if there are any). We had no intention of calling them "supervisors" or helping them to count to three; they must have all had at least a year of schooling. They can count their wages without any problems, and the numbers involved in this exercise are considerably higher than three. Therefore, we refused to give reports, and when they asked us who was the duty prisoner, we replied that we all took equal share in cleaning the cell. As for identity tags, we considered any discussion superfluous.

Predictably, we were threatened with SHIZO. But on the eve of Natasha's departure, Artemyev came to camp Number Two for a "talk" with Olya: he promised that she would be taken to Kiev, and gave assurances that the threats of SHIZO were a misunderstanding, that it would not be inflicted on anyone. All this sweetness and light perturbed rather than comforted us. Yet Natasha really did leave, she waved as she passed our window so that we would know that everything was all right. So we allowed ourselves a cautious hope that Olya might be taken to see her mother after all. Her main worry was, however, over what would happen to me when I was left here alone. I tried to calm her down as best I could, pointing out that this would not be my first solitary confinement. They would probably not dare to beat me, it was by no means certain that I would be put into SHIZO, the worst effects of concussion were behind me, and I was almost clear of scabies. Certainly, they would badger me and try to pressure me into recanting, but that was nothing new. Truth to tell, I felt almost guilty. I was much more fortunate that Olya—my parents were alive, Igor was waiting for me, I'd received a whole lot of letters (we got more mail in PKT than in the Zone, for some reason). What more could I ask? As for Olya—the only thing left of her face in those days were her eyes, and it was painful to look into them. They took her away toward the end of October, and on the 30th I staged the traditional one-day hunger strike to mark Political Prisoners' Day.

After lights out on the night of October 31, they stripped off my clothes and transferred me to SHIZO regime. Smock on my bare body, snow on the window sill, and KGB officer Yershov standing by and gloating: "Well, Irina Borisovna, you've really done it this time, haven't you? Don't you realize that your imprisonment can be for life?" Then he repeated all the stock threats about extending my sentence, that the SHIZO could become my permanent place of residence, that I really ought to write a clemency plea. I had no reason to disbelieve him: they had obviously decided to finish me off—gradually, without haste, by cold and hunger. They have no need to resort to physical assault; they will simply continue to strip me naked every day and run their slimy paws over my body to ensure that I am wearing nothing but the smock and briefs. They'll check those, too, just in case I've sneaked on a second pair. I will have to endure their filthy innuendo and eat their rotten skilly every second day. I shall become progressively weaker, less capable of resisting the humiliations they will heap on me, and they will go on inventing more and more of them . . .

No, I decided, I won't let that happen. I have had enough of your punishment cells and your intrusive hands. You want to finish me off? Then the sooner, the better. I am leaving your walls—I'm free of you! Do you really think that I shall try to hang on to a life which you have turned into torture? So I sent back their skilly untouched, and they came on the run: "Are you on hunger strike? Where's your notification?"

"You've had hundreds of notifications from me, including those about hunger strikes. I have nothing more to say to you."

"But you must eat."

"I don't have to do anything."

"But you'll die."

"That's just what the KGB promised. Do you want to extend the pleasure? Torture me for a while longer? You see how every breath condenses into vapor in this cell? How long do you think I'll last even if I do eat your swill?"

"So you intend to die, and we'll have to answer for it?"

"You should have thought of that sooner. That's all. The audience is over."

Artemyev came to the cell like a shot: "Irina Borisovna, what on earth are you up to? The doctor will examine you and give you a jacket if you're cold. Yershov is a young hothead, he couldn't have said something like that to you really . . . "

Then how do you know what Yershov said or didn't say? I haven't told you. And why do you suddenly look so frightened? Have you realized now what it means to turn fiction into fact? This is much harder than trampling over nameless zeks, isn't it? You're afraid of a scandal? Quite rightly: there will be a scandal, an absolutely splendid one. The KGB will think twice before putting anyone in punishment cell after this. You think you can pacify me with a jacket? As if I don't know that it will be stripped off me the moment I start eating. You're not quite through with me yet? Be satisfied with what you've had, you Fascists!

I said no word to him, of course, but these were my thoughts. The warder escorting me sighs solicitously: "Oh, Irina! Do you really intend to die?"

"That depends on the will of God. But this is the last time they'll torture anyone. Haven't you seen how they keep dragging us to SHIZO all the time, even the old ladies? Enough of that. This time they've overreached themselves. I'll be their last victim."

"I've heard that they talked about you on the radio, from England or America, I'm not sure. They must be trying to do something for you over there, mustn't they?"

"Well, this is certainly the right time for it, and not just for me. You've seen how they're pressing us all to recant. It's worse than in Andropov's time."

"But they say that Gorbachev wants there to be more freedom."

"Ah, so that's why they're pushing us so hard. He's claimed that there are no political prisoners in the Soviet Union, so now they'll either have to kill us or release us."

"Well, good luck to you, anyway. I'm just about to finish my shift. Hang on a moment, I'll just check that there's nothing in your pockets."

Five days, six. A week. With a feeling of gladness, I sense how everything in me that can feel pain becomes more and more remote. I feel light and untroubled. I am not hungry, and I've stopped feeling the cold. Pale, watery daylight seeps weakly through the window bars. How different is it from the light I shall see in another week or two? My soul is calm and peaceful, and I don't mind the greyness around me: not the fences, not the Mordovian autumn, not my tattered smock, not even the warder's greatcoats.

On the other side of the wall, life continues with its attendant tragedies: "Women, assemble for work! Who's that lying over there on the floor? What's her name?"

"She's sick, she can't get up."

"She'll get up soon enough when we give her another fifteen days."

"Supervisor, I really can't get up. Can the doctor be called?"

"Right, that's it! Consider that you've just got yourself another fifteen days for refusal to work. Doctor, indeed! Damned malingerer. Yes, you just go on lying there and look forward to SHIZO!"

The locks rattle, feet scuff past to the workroom. She's in that cell all alone. I don't know her, and have never seen her. Her name is Galya, and they brought her here recently. After some hours, which I spend in a state of semi-being, keys rattle again.

"Dinner, you lazy good-for-nothings!"

The work shift is returning to the cell for skilly.

"Supervisor, supervisor! Blood!"

"What blood? What the hell are you going on about? Here, get away from the door!"

"She's cut her veins!"

"No she hasn't. She's bitten clean through them with her teeth! Oh my God, how awful! Supervisor, she's not breathing!"

"Back! Back, the lot of you! We don't need you here. And keep your mouths shut—I don't want to hear a word!"

With difficulty, I pull myself up to the window and see several medical orderlies running across with a stretcher. Then they return. A shapeless form lies on the stretcher, covered with rags. Right until the evening I hear the cell next door being swabbed out. There must have been a lot of blood. Nobody will be held responsible for this death, and it will not be reported by the world press; it will pass unnoticed, nobody will know. She'll be written off with a convincing diagnosis, the records will be clean, and another nameless, numbered grave will be dug in Mordovian soil, to be powdered with grey snow from a grey sky. A few years later it will be bulldozed, to make room for more.

46

On the eleventh day, the family of mice moves out of my cell. They trot in single file across the floor, and squeeze out into the corridor through the space under the door. Without any particular emotion, I watch the last grey tail flick and disappear as I lie on the floor. The hand under my head has been numb for a long time, and I do not feel either the knotty floorboards or the draft from the window. I have no more debts to anyone or anything: they have been paid, and the books balanced. A strange warmth steals over what is left of my body, and I rock to the crooning of a lullaby:

> The comfort that you bring reminds me
> Of distant childhood's gentle crib . . .

Where have I heard that song before? Oh yes, Tatyana Mikhailovna, her hand stroking my head . . . Igor, his eyes haunted by sleepless nights . . . Tanya Osipova, jauntily toting her zek bundle, chin in the air . . . Mama—how she tried not to cry at that first and last meeting . . . The taxi driver, whom I asked to "lose that tail" (there was a car following us quite obviously) and he did . . . The young escort guard, surreptitiously taking my hastily sealed envelope . . . An unknown American chemist called David, who sent me his regards in a letter to Igor. . .

I did not know, then, that on that very day a service of intercession was being held for me in a far-off English city, that Soviet diplomats everywhere were being pressured about my case, that a new camp commandant would arrive tomorrow (the old one was quickly pensioned off) and that this new commandant would turn out to be Zuykov, the same Zuykov who drew back from tearing off my cross in camp Number Six. And that Zuykov would give a human cry: "I didn't put you into this SHIZO. Why should I answer for someone else's stupidity if you should die?"

"Because you, too, would have signed that order without batting an eyelid."

"No! I swear to you—no. No SHIZO. I wouldn't have signed it, and that's that. I'm the camp commandant. Call me anything you like if I should deceive you."

And I believed him: the truth was in his eyes, he wouldn't sign. So why should the blow fall on him? All I need to do is wait until anyone at all from our Number Three Zone is sent to SHIZO, and then I will embark on a final hunger strike, with a sign reading "Stop Torturing Political Prisoners!" They would tear it away from me immediately, of course, but the others would know my last demand. Zuykov and I look at each other steadily . . . Very well, you stubborn old warhorse, in your own way, you are right. But if only you knew how reluctant I am to return from my present beatific condition, knowing that I will have to repeat everything again from scratch should there be cause. And starting to eat again after a hunger strike is such a painful process. The roof of your mouth smarts, as if it has been burned.

"Very well. Transfer me onto PKT regime. I'll eat."

"Start today! Or at least let them rig up an intravenous drip. The doctors are worried . . . "

"Your doctors can wait. Let them treat me in PKT."

Zuykov kept his word. This was indeed my last SHIZO, and while I was in PKT he did everything he could to make my time there as "pleasant" as is possible in such a place. And this was really the end. Nobody from our Zone was sent to SHIZO again, and the slogan I had prepared with green paint for a last hunger strike lay under a pile of jackets until my departure for Kiev. We found the jackets all jumbled up one morning, but the sign with the slogan had not been removed during what must have been a furtive search in the night. I was quite pleased, actually: let the KGB know that I was ready for anything.

Toward the spring of 1986 they started feeding us properly, and the KGB seemed anxious to please, even talking about release without any "confessions" or recantations. Yet for some strange reason it was at this time that Edita, who had lost all control over herself, not only allied herself firmly with Vladimirova, but went even further by trying to attack us physically. I heard about this when I returned from PKT, but could hardly believe my ears. I believed it quickly enough, though, when in May the KGB instituted criminal proceedings against Pani Jadvyga and me "for assaulting prisoner Abrutiene." Even though everyone knew this to be nothing but make-believe, for which Edita richly deserved a clout or two, I refrained. The accusation against Pani Jadvyga was too laughable to contemplate: she was almost twice Edita's age, and didn't have a quarter of her physical strength. These proceedings were halted just as easily as they had been started; the attempt to blackmail us by the threat of criminal charges left us unmoved, and the whole exercise was obviously a last-ditch attempt to scare us into a recantation. When the KGB saw that the desired result would not be achieved, they dropped the matter. And indeed, it was greatly more to their advantage to get rid of us as quickly as possible rather than to prolong our sentences. Edita and Vladimirova were curtly told to shut up, an order which worked like a charm.

The following day I was sent off to Kiev "to be released." They held me there, however, for another three months, demanding, threatening, attempting blackmail, but at the same time assuring me that there was no longer anyone in the Small Zone, even though at that time it was a lie. When they could not extract either a clemency plea or a recantation from me, a secret order for my release was signed by Gromyko two days before the Reagan-Gorbachev summit in Reykjavik. I was not allowed to keep this document, but they did explain why it was secret: "As you did not lodge a plea for clemency, the Presidium of the Supreme Soviet of the USSR cannot pardon you officially."

"I don't want a pardon, I want exoneration."

"Come now, Irina Borisovna, you can't have everything at once. Exoneration may be possible later. But in the face of this order, we can no longer hold you here. Get your things, and we'll take you home." I go to gather my possessions, still not knowing whether they are telling the truth or lying.

And here I am, riding along in a black Volga . . .

EPILOGUE

As I write now, in September 1987, there really is nobody left in the Small Zone. It has been closed down. Lagle is in Estonia, Pani Lida in Latvia, Pani Jadvyga in Lithuania, Natasha and Galya in Russia, Raya and Olya in the Ukraine, and Tanya is in the United States. But Tatyana Mikhailovna Velikanova and Elena Sannikova are still serving their terms of exile, and there are still hundreds of political prisoners in other Soviet camps, prisons and psychiatric hospitals. As for zek slaves, who were arrested on criminal charges, though not invariably for crimes actually committed—their numbers run into millions. Human rights champion Anatoli Marchenko died in camp without being released, and others die every day, today and tomorrow . . .

Yet I am alive, and that is probably unjust. I treasure my old zek uniform, made by Pani Lida, even though it means nothing to anyone here. And at times I pull out this camp "skin," which has seen so much, and press it to my cheek: grey, my very own grey color! The color of hope! How much longer will those camps stand upon the soil of my country? How can I sleep while they exist?

But it was our Zone that had a grey uniform. The majority of zeks wear black. What hope do they have? Perhaps only that which we can offer.

A NOTE ABOUT THE AUTHOR

Irina Ratushinskaya was born in Odessa, Ukrainian SSR, on March 4, 1954. After receiving a degree in physics in 1976, she taught at the Odessa Pedagogical Institute. On September 17, 1982, she was arrested by the Soviet government for dissident activities, and on March 5, 1983, she was sentenced to seven years' hard labor and five years' internal exile. She was released on October 9, 1986. Her many collections of poetry include *Poems; No, I'm Not Afraid;* and *Beyond the Limit.* Currently she is a poet-in-residence at Northwestern University. She is married to human rights activist Igor Gerashchenko.

A NOTE ABOUT THE TYPE

The text of this book was set in a film version of Trump Mediaeval. Designed by Professor Georg Trump in the mid-1950s, Trump Mediaeval was cut and cast by the C. E. Weber Typefoundry of Stuttgart, West Germany. The roman letterforms are based on classical prototypes, but Professor Trump has imbued them with his own unmistakable style. The italic letterforms, unlike those of so many other typefaces, are closely related to their roman counterparts. The result is a truly contemporary type, notable for both its legibility and its versatility.

Composed by American-Stratford Graphic Services, Inc.,
Brattleboro, Vermont

Printed and bound by Fairfield Graphics,
Fairfield, Pennsylvania

Typography and binding design by
Dorothy Schmiderer Baker

ократ — ...
гда не льстилась чужой дорогой,
се проводы собирала силы:
ять, на последнем взмахе не дрогнуть!
этих всё-таки не хватило.
олитва твоя не уберегла:
з все сметённые берега —
дением, ветром издалека
жённая — хлещет из жил тоска!
айте, прощаться невыносимо!
— иное небо с другим законом.
а вас обрушит снега Россия,
вам в них стынуть крылом калёным.
ь вам облаком —
че лёгкого!
а доброго —
елётного!
тайте — долой с глаз!
овожаю — в какой раз? 1984

ень избранья президента
ли мы без документов,
овеческой одёжки,
ешительной кормёжки,
ижки, кошки,
ки — ложки,
зато нам дул в окошко
шительный озон,
положено в ШИЗО.
ка голосовали,
овали,
ли — вали,
сидели и гадали:
ько нам добавки дали,
или ШИЗО,
кой тому резон.
режимник прибежал,
о врал и угрожал,
о нашим по расчётам
о время штат Дакота,

иссури, и Канзас
ь радовали нас.
тбою, вероятно,
всё уже понятно.
гли мы к батарее,
она совсем не греет,
у дунуло по рёбрам,
здохнули...
доброй

Господину Президенту,
Вашингтону,
Континенту,
На котором он стоит,
Всем, кто там ещё не спит...
Знайте: мы не спим здесь тоже!
Мы — в сплошной гусиной коже —
Бьём зубами дробь не зря:
Завтра — праздник Октября!

6 нб 1984,
ШИЗО

нились, наверно, закатывать время в консервы,
щённую ночь подмешали во все времена.
т век всё темней,
скоро придёт двадцать первый,
стереть со вчерашней тюремной стены
имена
го нагружали
ших друзей голосами,
ждённых детей именами — для новой
стены,
такою любовью его снаряжали, но сами
му не гребцы,
на борт его не званы.
тмеренный груз укрывая рогожею грубой,
ещё успеваем горстями просеять зерно,
изранить ладони,
выбрать драконовы зубы
посева, которому встать после нас суждено.
1984, ШИЗО

а кутать бессмысленной рванью озябшие
плечи,
сквожённое дырами платье сводя на груди
полезным движением, зная — закалывать
нечем,
горячкой свободы вмерзая в сегодняшний
вечер
е ведая, сколько таких вечеров впереди.
имя чего,
кого прозрения ради?
жель для края, где прячут в ладони лицо?
гробницы следят за всеобщим участием в па-
раде,
итежные дети ведут голубые тетради,
еют их прятать от слепорождённых отцов.
астав из наследства,
книжек и песен вчерашних,
робей опериться, назначенный к жизни птенец!
летейской воде окрещённый кораблик бумаж-
ный
ерни и прочти:
мирать — это тоже не страшно, 1984,
ь немного тошнит,
да входишь в пятно на стене. ШИЗО

но только бы не думать о дороге —
ретой, пыльной — чтоб идти, идти...
ни меня, храни, рассудок строгий,
отпускай узды на полпути!
нам долго вместе отбиваться
каторжных удушливых ночей,
рожных снов — почти галлюцинаций,
смысленных издёвок палачей,
дательства уставших, и отравы
поцелуев... Сдохни, но скости —
знал срока, не имея права

...чамом,
О том, как вам были изитом
Затворённые ставни
И строгая воля народа:
Не позволить глумленья!
(Ну как не любить англичан?!)
Обезлюдевший город,
Закрытые глухо ворота —
ни единой души,
разве только считать палача.
Впрочем, был ли палач?
Может быть, я его сочинила!
Но в подобных делах
как же можно его обойти?
Как лукавит судья,
как могильщик копает могилу —
так палач ожидает
на каждом бессмертном пути.
Но глаза палача не видны
Сквозь разрез капюшона,
как во все времена
(может, им не положено глаз?)
В целом мире лишь двое:
Граф Ковентри, глядя с балкона,
Да безглазый палач
провожают в изгнание вас.
Только топот коня
в переулках пустынных немеет.
Как забытое слово,
что в шорох веков сорвалось.
Здесь заклинило время стоп-кадром,
и ветер не смеет
шевельнуть небывалым плащом
из тяжёлых волос.

Ах, отважная леди,
Пришпорим коня без боязни —
Да проедем насквозь,
Не считая годов и минут,
Как слоёный пирог,
Прорезая эпохи и казни,
И другие эпохи,
Которые следом придут.
Продразним историю —
Нас она, что ли, жалела?! —
Сквозь ратуши угол,
Пугая судейских крючков,
И в чужое столетие прорвёмся
С конём ошалелым,
Отразившим расколотым
Удивлённым зрачком!

А не пора ли обратно,
Мы так задержались тут.
Пересохнут наши каналы,
И ветры наши уснут.
Наши кони забудут руку,
А планеты забудут бег.
Не пора ли, Отец,
От чужих берегов — к себе?
Всё, что Ты велишь, мы оставим в этом краю!
И своё дыханье, и труд,
И печаль свою.
Но, пройдя из конца в конец эту землю —
Ты видишь сам —
Мы на каждой тропе опознаны —
по слезам!
Мы у каждой стены расстреляны —
Без суда!
Сколько раз умирать,
пока Ты не скажешь „да"?
Не пора ли обратно,
Мы выплатили долги —
За себя,
А потом ещё за других.
Мы стократно преданы, всё исполнено — что ещё!
Под какую лавину ещё
Подставлять плечо?
Между двух врагов кидаться —
В какой борьбе?
И какое небо ещё держать на себе?
Наши кони ждут, Отец,
Наши травы медлят расти.
Посмотри —
Мы прошли назначенные пути,
В здешний камень врезали
Все слова, что стоит сказать —
Ради права уйти,
не оглядываясь назад. 1985

Перед боем
Кони щиплют клевер на завтрашнем поле боя
Полководцы
Мерят циркулями поля — выбирай любое!
Не политы
Муравьиные тропы ещё ни свинцом, ни кровью.
Только утром —
Грянет, и бледный всадник лицо откроет.
Перед боем
Молодые солдаты слушают байки старых.
Офицеры
Пишут письма, а после кто-то берёт гитару.
Затихают
К ночи травы на поле боя, и пахнет мёдом.
Только утром —
Грянет, и ~~[illegible]~~ будут уже от мёртвых. 1984
ШИЗО

А когда тебя скосит в битвах,
Ты увидишь: люди пришли 1984
На тебя, ещё незарытого, ШИЗО
Они бросят комья земли.
И друзья, и просто знакомые —
Вон их сколько! И странно разве,
Если брошенные комья
Обернутся комьями грязи.
Кто-то робко, а кто-то смело:
— Эка невидаль — за свободу!
Ты погоди для них не сделал.
... от плохой погоды.

Закр...ит поль...
и ...ький ме...
Суме... в о...
Мы ... ведём
Чтоб з... век...
Если д... ути —
посреди января
1985

Наш свод достит...
Как холод стекл...
Наш мир достан...
Мы ракеты пси...
Но все же мы пи...
Пустынными кол...
Ты разве не зна...
Гомункулюсы уп...
И будут плодить...
Стыдящихся чер...
Умеющих с Бож...
Скрестить глаза...
Мы будем угл к...
(Ох, береги приб...
На все Твои люби...
Вдумываясь — пер...
На смертную на...
Слагай слова не...
Ни боль — закусыв...
Без стона: в Ко...
Не Твой ли закон...
...нь крепче посл...
Что если сунны у...
Трубки нерастор...
В мерцающую ко...
Оглядясь — и мах...
Ну что тебе в цел...
Ведь снова стел...

Что колышется в...
Только то и в...
В небе — черне...
А в столетиях...
Что сменяем...
Погоди, февраль, д...
Но ...ят вер...
Не с мороз... в...
Скинем шкуры...
На весенние к...
Оставляя — ни...
Ни прошедшего...
Не возьмём в в...
Но ещё не прос...
По раскинутым...
Улёгся нежуж...
А придётся — ...
А когда претр...

Приз...
Сегодня Господу...
Вылепил Микел...
Ты видишь. Эт...
Над временным...
Над морем и гор...
И над шкурой з...
И — слышишь — у...
Торжественная...
Сегодня строгу...
И подставь бибе...
Смотри, какой...
Первый от сотв...
Исполнится вс...
Тебе — и резец...
Ликует тяжёл...
И рвётся дика...
И вечность...
Без мерка твоя...
Сегодня ты —
Назначишь ли...
Из всех чудес...
Труднейшее...
Не какие ты...
Таким и взгл...
Так встань п...

Престу... ...
Устроим же...
О да, я знаю:
Такие же че...
Восточней...